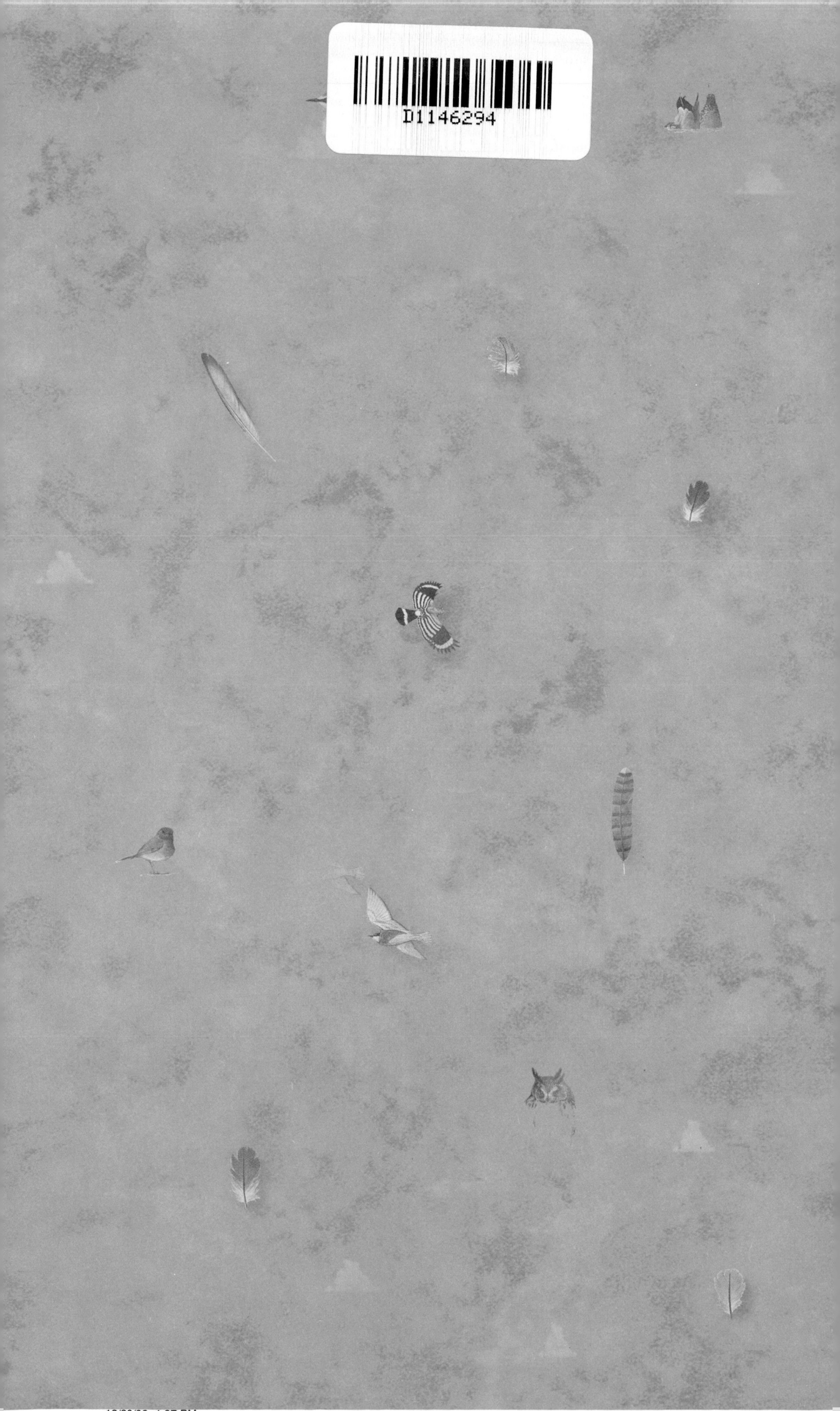

BIRDWATCHING

BIRDWATCHING

ARNOUD B. VAN DEN BERG,
TOM VAN DER HAVE, GUIDO KEIJL

CONSULTANT EDITOR
DOMINIC MITCHELL

ILLUSTRATIONS
GERALD DRIESSENS, FRITS-JAN MAAS,
KAREL MAUER, ERIK VAN OMMEN

Published by HarperCollins *Publishers*
77-85 Fulham Palace Road, London W6 8JB

Conceived and produced by Weldon Owen Pty Limited
43 Victoria Street, McMahons Point, NSW, 2060, Australia
A member of the Weldon Owen Group of Companies
Sydney • San Francisco

First published in the UK 1997

The European edition of this title has been created by
UNIEPERS B.V. ABCOUDE, THE NETHERLANDS

WELDON OWEN PTY LIMITED
PUBLISHER: Sheena Coupe
MANAGING EDITOR: Lynn Humphries
PROJECT EDITOR: Scott Forbes
ART DIRECTOR: Hilda Mendham
JACKET DESIGN: John Bull
PRODUCTION MANAGER: Caroline Webber
VICE PRESIDENT INTERNATIONAL SALES: Stuart Laurence
COEDITIONS DIRECTOR: Derek Barton
CONSULTANT US EDITION: Terence Lindsey
CONTRIBUTORS US EDITION: Joseph Forshaw, Steve Howell,
Terence Lindsey, Rich Stallcup

UNIEPERS B.V.
EDITORIAL CONSULTANT: Dominic Mitchell, Birdwatch, London
COPY EDITOR: Arnoud B. van den Berg, Dutch Birding, Amsterdam
CONTRIBUTORS: Arnoud B. van den Berg, Tom van der Have, Guido Keijl
COORDINATING EDITOR: Annelies Bouma
EDITORIAL ASSISTANT: Marielle Hovemann
PICTURE RESEARCH: Arnoud B. van den Berg; Maartje Snel;
Foto Natura, Wormerveer
ILLUSTRATIONS: Gerald Driessens, Erik van Ommen,
Frits-Jan Maas, Karel Mauer
PAGE MAKE-UP: Erik Sok, Kjeld de Ruyter
PRODUCTION DIRECTOR: Marinus H. van Raalte

ISBN 0 00 220093 7

Manufactured by Kyodo Printing Co. (Singapore) Pte Ltd.
Printed in Singapore

A Weldon Owen Production

Do you ne'er think what wondrous beings these?
Do you ne'er think who made them, and who taught
The dialect they speak, where melodies
Alone are the interpreters of thought?
Whose household words are songs in many keys,
Sweeter than instrument of man e'er caught!

The Birds of Killingworth,
HENRY WADSWORTH LONGFELLOW (1807–82), American poet

Contents

FOREWORD

Birds are not only the most conspicuous of nature's wonders, they are surely also the most fascinating. From the centres of vast cities to remote mountain tops and the open ocean, birds are constantly around us and continue to intrigue us; and the more they do so, the more we attempt to delve deeper into their remarkable lives.

We have learnt much about them. No longer are they creatures of myth and legend: they share our gardens, they nest in our countryside, and we watch them depart in autumn, when their places are taken by others, only to return again in spring. They live singly or in communities, and have helpers and hierarchies; they can be perfectly camouflaged or dressed in the gaudiest breeding attire (they can even alternate between the two!); they build nests in underground burrows, on pack-ice in sub-zero temperatures, and even in boxes we give them; and they can fly like nothing on earth, for many thousands of miles or for many months on end without even stopping to rest.

Perhaps it's because they can accomplish such remarkable feats that we have taken to them so much. In Britain, more than one million people now belong to the Royal Society for the Protection of Birds, and every year we spend a small fortune on feeding, watching, studying, protecting—and reading—about birds.

Whether your appreciation of them is new-found or you've enjoyed watching birds for years, this book will help you discover more about their lives and behaviour, and what makes them such fascinating creatures to observe and study. *Birdwatching* is your guide to the world of birds and everything that it offers the enquiring mind. It has been specially designed to provide you with the knowledge and skills you need to understand more about birds. In the following pages, you'll find an insight into every aspect of their lives, from courtship, plumages, songs and anatomy to migration, habitats and much more—including, just as important, the art of watching and identifying them successfully.

Read it for an excellent introduction to this absorbing pastime and to the birds you will encounter, and keep it handy as a reference which you will be able to use time and time again to get more from your hobby.

I hope you will enjoy *Birdwatching* as much as you will enjoy the birds!

DOMINIC MITCHELL,
Publisher and Editor
Birdwatch magazine

In a world that seems so very puzzling is it any wonder birds have such appeal? Birds are, perhaps, the most eloquent expression of reality.

ROGER TORY PETERSON (b. 1908),
American ornithologist

Chapter One
Understanding Birds

THE WORLD *of* BIRDS

Dark-eyed Junco

Step out of your door, almost anywhere in the world, and, within minutes, you will see birds of one kind or another.

Birds are among the most mobile of all animals. There are other animals that roam widely, but birds alone can, at least in principle, go anywhere they please on the Earth's surface.

Although most numerous in marshes, woodlands and rainforests, birds inhabit the most inhospitable of deserts, and have been seen within a few miles of both poles. Some never stray from home in their entire lives, but others can, and frequently do, span entire oceans or continents, sometimes in a single flight.

There are about 9,300 species of bird in the world, and they range from the tiny Bee Hummingbird, which weighs little more than a penny, to the imposing Ostrich, which stands taller than a man and weighs over 300 pounds (136 kg). Among these species can be found almost any colour under the sun. These colours may be arranged in the dazzling patterns found in breeding Peacocks or in the astonishingly effective camouflage of birds such as the Tawny Frogmouth, which evades predators by imitating a dead tree stump.

Some birds hover on the brink of extinction; on the other hand, there are far more domestic chickens on Earth than humans.

Pacific Golden Plovers, taking off with a load of fuel almost equal to their own weight, fly non-stop from Alaska to Hawaii and back each year, while Peregrine Falcons reach speeds approaching 200 miles (320 km) per hour as they dive upon their winged prey. In contrast to these masters of the air, there are a few birds—the Ostrich, for example—that cannot fly at all.

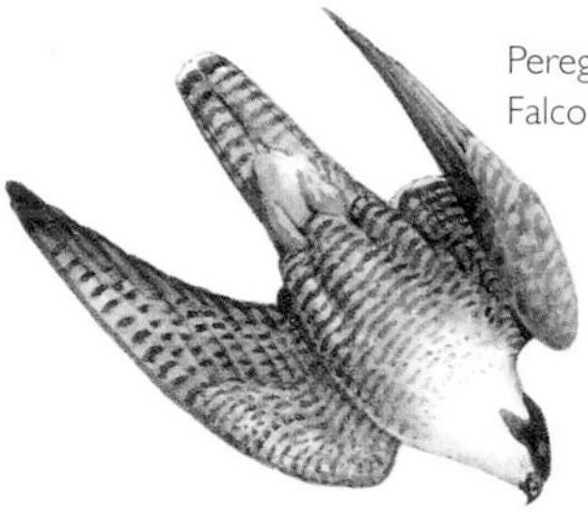
Peregrine Falcon

Ostrich

Tawny Frogmouth

The maps on these pages show how species density varies around the world. Tropical rainforests have most species, polar icecaps fewest. Note that most mainly temperate areas, such as North America, Europe, and Australia, have roughly similar numbers of species.

- 50 or fewer species
- 50–250 species
- 250–500 species
- 500–1,000 species
- 1,000–1,500 species
- over 1,500 species

BIRDS, REAL *and* IMAGINARY

From the Phoenix rising from the ashes to the sacred Garuda, king of the birds, from the dove of peace to the robin of happiness, birds real and imaginary have featured prominently in the human imagination.

THE ROC *One of the oldest and most widespread bird myths concerns this giant bird that feeds on elephants. In this scene from* The Arabian Nights *(left), merchants pull a Roc chick from its egg.*

It is, perhaps, not surprising that birds, being among the most easily observed of all animals, have captured the human imagination. Their attributes and habits have proved a rich source of inspiration to us since prehistoric times.

Birdsong, for example, has inspired some of the finest poetry in the English language, and for centuries the power of flight was the envy of humankind.

BIRD-MAN *One of the earliest images of a bird—dating from over 15,000 years ago—is to be found in the Lascaux caves in France. It depicts a bison, a bird and what seems to be a bird-headed human.*

Throughout history, birds have been used to symbolise particular qualities and states: the wise owl, the dove of peace, the robin of happiness, and so on. And deep in our past lurk myths and legends about birds, some of uncertain origin.

CLASSICAL MYTHS

One of the most enduring of bird myths is that of the Phoenix. This legendary bird was well known to Greek and Roman scholars more than 2,000 years ago, and elements of its story can be traced to the ancient Egyptians, several thousand years earlier.

In most legends, the Phoenix is a bird of great beauty that lives for 500 or 600 years in the Arabian desert. It then burns itself to ashes on a funeral pyre, from which it emerges with renewed youth.

Through the Dark Ages, this story was commonly used as a metaphor for the resurrection of Christ, and there are many references to the Phoenix in literature. The Phoenix is still referred to today, to symbolise a new structure or idea arising from the ruins or ashes of its predecessor.

Another story of uncertain origin is the Greek myth of the Halcyon. This bird, often associated with the kingfisher, floated its nest on the open sea. Aeolus, god of the winds, decreed that all storms must cease while the Halcyon's young were reared. This fable gave rise to the expression "halcyon days", which is used to describe any interlude of peace and serenity.

Now I will believe …
that in Arabia,
There is one tree, the
phoenix' throne,
one phoenix, At this
time reigning there.

The Tempest,
WILLIAM SHAKESPEARE (1564–1616),
English playwright

SYMBOL OF POWER

Few birds have impressed humankind as much as the eagle. Its powerful flight was noted in The Song of Solomon, and an eagle was the emblem of the Babylonian god Ashur. An eagle adorned the sceptre of Zeus, supreme god of the ancient Greeks.

In Hindu mythology, it was an eagle that brought to humankind the sacred drink soma, and in the old Norse sagas, Odin, king of the Gods, often took the form of an eagle. The warbonnets of American Plains Indians were dressed only with eagle feathers. The double-headed eagle was a common Byzantine motif, and eagles were adopted as imperial symbols by a number of nations, including Austria, Germany, Poland and Russia.

Today an eagle appears on the Mexican coat of arms and is the national symbol of the United States of America.

EASTERN LEGENDS

Myths involving birds of supernatural proportions are common around the world. One of the most monstrous of all birds, real or imaginary, is Garuda, sacred to the Hindu god Vishnu, preserver of the world. King of birds and herald of storms, Garuda is a huge winged monster that feeds on snakes. Its image can be seen wherever the Hindu religion has spread, and has been adopted as the symbol of Indonesia's national airline.

The Roc, or Rukh, entered Western folklore from a fifteenth-century collection of Arabian tales called *The Arabian Nights*. The central character, Sinbad the Sailor, is wrecked on an island in the Indian Ocean, where he encounters a bird so enormous that it feeds its young on elephants.

An almost identical story is found in ancient Chinese literature, and the bird was even mentioned by Marco Polo, who recorded that a Roc's feather was presented to the Mongul ruler Genghis Khan.

AMERICAN MYTHS

Most of the native peoples of North and South America have myths of monstrous birds. The Thunderbird, for example, is an eagle-like bird so huge that lightning flashes when it blinks and thunder rolls at the slightest movement of its wings. This fabulous bird is known to the Athapascans, Inuit and Hopi among others. According to the Tlingit tribe, of the Pacific Northwest, it carries a lake of water in the hollow of its back that, spilling out as it flies, produces torrents of rain.

MYTHICAL BIRDS *The Hindu god Garuda (top); and the Thunderbird of Native American legend (right), depicted as part of a totem pole.*

SELF-SACRIFICE *A pelican feeding its young on its own blood, in a woodcut from Ulisse Aldrovandi's* Ornithologiae *(1559–1603).*

MYTHICAL QUALITIES

Alongside stories of imaginary birds, legends relating to real birds have been common, too.

In ancient China, the pheasant was regarded as a symbol of harmony and heaven's favour. The "love-pheasant" was, in fact, one of the four chief supernatural creatures of Chinese mythology, ranking equally with the tortoise, the unicorn and the dragon.

In medieval Europe, it was widely believed that the pelican fed its young on its own blood, and the bird became a common symbol of Christian piety.

Today, among Aboriginal people in Australia, the Willie-wagtail, a small song-bird, is widely regarded as a tattler. It is said to hang around the mens' councils picking up secrets that it then carries to the women.

In many countries in Europe, the wood-pecker is believed to call up rain.

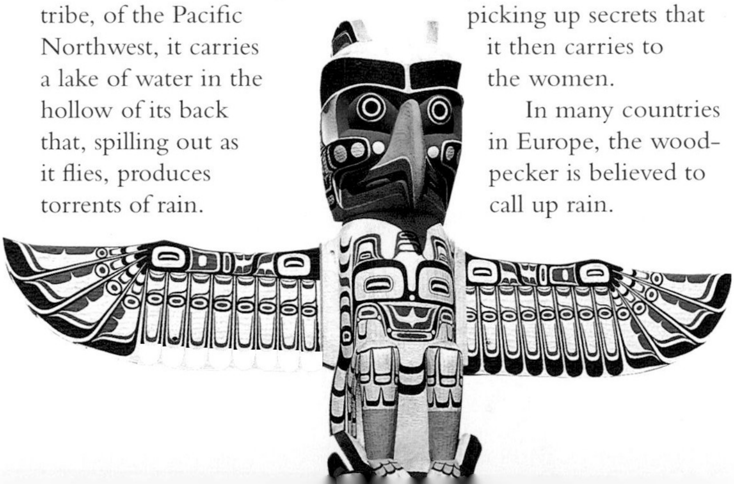

THE ORIGINS *of* BIRDS

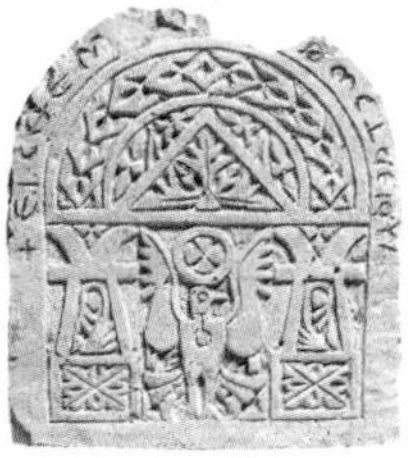

Contrasting markedly with our comprehensive knowledge of living birds is our tentative, piecemeal understanding of their origins.

Birds are poorly represented in fossil deposits for a variety of reasons. Bird bones are fragile and many are hollow, so they are easily broken and fragmented. In addition, few land birds die where their remains can be buried in waterlaid sediments, the richest source of fossils. It also seems likely that many ancient birds, like birds today, were preyed upon by carnivorous animals.

IMAGES IN STONE *Both nature and humankind have created images of birds in stone. This Egyptian carving (left) dates from the eighth century.*

It has been estimated that between the time of *Archaeopteryx*, the earliest known bird, and the present, between 1.5 million and 2 million species of bird have existed. Of these, we have specimen evidence for the existence of fewer than 12,000 species!

"FEATHERED DINOSAURS"

The exact origins of birds are still uncertain, but it has long been thought that they evolved from reptiles. One popular theory links birds to a specific sub-group of dinosaurs called theropods, which were common approximately 200 million years ago.

THE EARLIEST KNOWN BIRD

In the Jurassic cycad forests of Europe, about 150 million years ago, a group of dinosaurs was browsing on plants along the shoreline of a Bavarian lake, while in the taller vegetation strange bird-like creatures were clambering among the branches and fluttering from tree to tree. Perhaps in a frantic effort to escape capture by an arboreal predator, one of these creatures lost its balance and fell into shallow waters at the lake's edge, where it drowned and sank into sedimentary silt.

Some time in the first part of the nineteenth century, a worker in a quarry near Solnhofen, in Bavaria, Germany, found a fossilised feather. Then, in 1861, in the same quarry, the incomplete fossilised skeleton of the bird-like creature was found. German paleontologist Hermann von Meyer examined these remains and made a formal description of them, naming this earliest known fossil bird *Archaeopteryx lithographica*.

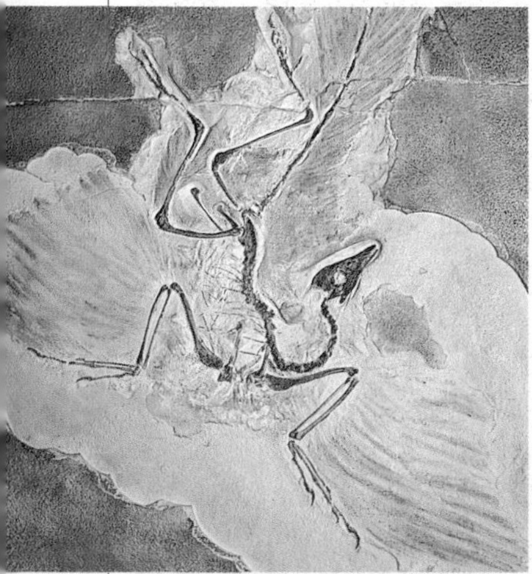

FOSSILS *(above) have provided us with a fairly clear idea of what* Archaeopteryx *must have looked like (above right).*

Archaeopteryx provided what is still the most important evidence of the link between birds and dinosaurs. *Archaeopteryx* was certainly a bird, as it clearly possessed feathers and a U-shaped "wishbone", but it also had prominent reptilian characteristics, including teeth and clawed digits on the forewing.

About the size of a crow, *Archaeopteryx* was a predator, and probably caught insects or small vertebrates, such as lizards. Recently, there has been much debate about its flight capabilities, and whether it was terrestrial or arboreal in its habits. Some authors claim that it would have been a weak flier, while others argue that it would have been capable of sustained flight.

HESPERORNIS, *a flightless fish-eating bird, first appeared over 100 million years ago during the Cretaceous period. Many present-day waterbirds, including the pelican (below right), have their origins in this era of prehistory.*

An important piece of evidence for this link is a U-shaped furcula or "wishbone" found both in birds and in some theropods. In birds, this feature plays an important role in flight. In the dinosaurs it probably evolved as a support for the short forelimbs that they used for catching prey.

Cretaceous Birds

Though only slightly younger than *Archaeopteryx*, birds of the early Cretaceous period (about 130 million years ago) were much more like modern birds. Most were undoubtedly strong fliers.

Probably the most famous of the many Cretaceous fossil birds are *Hesperornis* and *Ichthyornis* from North America. Both are notable in that they possessed teeth, a primitive condition prominent in *Archaeopteryx* and its theropod ancestors. *Hesperornis* was a flightless, fish-eating, diving bird, whereas *Ichthyornis* was a powerful flier.

The Pleistocene Epoch

Fossils of the Pleistocene epoch (2 million to 10,000 years ago) include many species that are alive today, as well as numerous species that are now extinct.

A rich source of these fossils are the Rancho La Brea tar pits in California. These have yielded specimens of birds like the *Teratornis*, which used its 12½-foot (3.8-m) wingspan to soar across the skies of North America.

Modern Birds

Present-day birds really are not so "modern", since most of the species we know today have been around for thousands of years. Indeed, about 11,500 species probably occurred during the Pleistocene—approximately 1,500 more species than exist today. Bird species probably reached a peak from 250,000 to 500,000 years ago, and have been in gradual decline ever since.

In times prehistoric, 'tis easily proved ... That birds and not gods were the rulers of men.

The Birds,
ARISTOPHANES (c. 448–380 BC),
Greek dramatist

TERATORNIS *Many fossils of this large, vulture-like predator that lived in western North America in the Pleistocene epoch have been found in the Rancho La Brea tar pits in California.*

Naming Birds

The spectacular diversity of birds is a delight, but it presents us with the challenge of establishing which birds are related and how best to classify them.

The science of classifying living things is called taxonomy. Early taxonomists based their classifications of birds almost entirely on external appearances, in the way that a child might organise building blocks according to size, shape and colour. These methods frequently resulted in birds that were not related being linked and some that were related being kept apart.

Advances in scientific procedures have led to new techniques being applied to determining alliances between kinds of bird, and the systems of classification have become increasingly sophisticated. Taxonomy now draws on a synthesis of data from many fields of biology, including paleontology, ecology, physiology, behaviour and DNA and protein analysis.

SYMBOLS AS NAMES *The ancient Egyptians used several birds in their system of hieroglyphics. The falcon (left), for example, represented the god Horus, personal god of the ruling pharaoh.*

The Species Concept

The keystone of modern taxonomy (and the focus of bird identification) is the species. A species is defined as a population whose members do not freely interbreed with members of other neighbouring populations (although this is sometimes difficult to establish one way or the other).

Within a species, there are often groups or populations which differ in minor ways, such as in size or plumage coloration. These interbreeding groups are recognised as subspecies or races. Populations separated by geographical barriers (such as mountain ranges and oceans) are known as isolates.

Higher Categories

All birds are related to some extent and the practice and procedures of taxonomy operate to establish different levels of relationship. Above species level, related species are grouped into genera, related genera are grouped into families, and related families into orders. Some intermediate categories are used by taxonomists to express fine distinctions, but these need not concern the beginner birdwatcher.

Together, birds form a class, Aves, and, along with other classes of backboned animals, this class is part of the Subphylum Vertebrata (the vertebrates) and the Animal Kingdom.

What's in a Name?

Most animal species have a common name—the English name in English-speaking countries—and a scientific name. The latter consists of two main elements: the genus and the specific name. Where there are subspecies, the subspecies name is sometimes included as a third element.

The scientific name is latinised and highlighted in a different type (normally italic). Only the generic name is capitalised.

FAMILY TIES *The close relationship between the three American bluebird species—Mountain Bluebird (left), Eastern Bluebird (above right) and Western Bluebird (far left) is described taxonomically by their inclusion in the genus* Sialia. *The Blackbird (opposite), on the other hand, is obviously related, yet not closely enough to share the same genus. It belongs to the genus* Turdus. *Both genera are members of the family* Turdidae.

CAROLUS LINNAEUS

The system of biological nomenclature used today was devised by the Swedish botanist, Carolus Linnaeus (1707–78).

Linnaeus was born in South Rashult in Sweden. From an early age, he loved plants, and this led him to a career in botany. In the course of his studies, he became aware that every organism needed to have a unique scientific name that could be used and understood by people of all nationalities. He therefore developed a system using Latin names, Latin being the language used by scholars throughout Europe at the time. This system, still referred to today as the Linnaean system, was presented to the scientific community in the *Systema Naturae*, published in 1735.

In 1741, Linnaeus was appointed to the chair of medicine at Uppsala University, but in the following year he exchanged this for the chair of botany. In 1761, he was granted a patent of nobility, becoming Carl von Linné. During his lifetime, Linnaeus published more than 180 works. It was in editions of the *Systema Naturae* that many species of bird were first formally named.

The purpose of scientific names is to provide an internationally recognisable system of classification. A single species' common name may vary between languages and countries, but its scientific name will always be the same. Conversely, one or more birds may have the same common name in different countries but not be related at all. For example, Americans often talk about "robins", but the "robins" of the UK and Australia are quite different birds. Use of the scientific name eliminates any confusion.

THE CODE OF LIVING THINGS

A computer simulation of the structure of DNA (below), showing its intricate double-spiral structure.

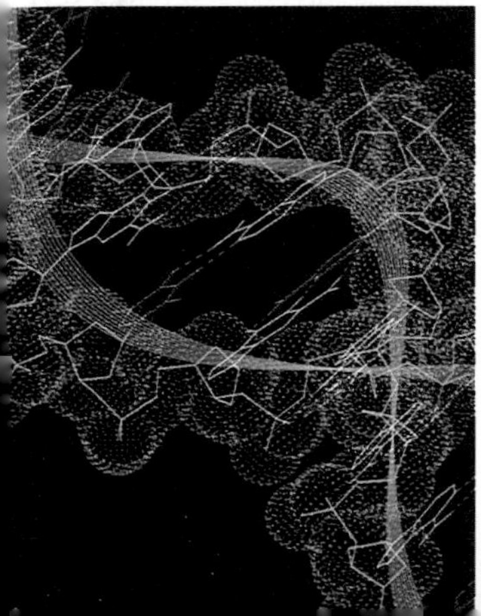

DNA Classification

Recent work in the field of biochemical research, especially analyses of DNA (deoxyribonucleic acid)—the essential genetic material—has proved a powerful tool in clarifying the relationships of birds.

Pioneered by Charles Sibley and Jon Ahlquist at Yale University, this research started out using protein material from blood and egg-white for analysis. It has now reached the point where the scientists are able to examine the DNA itself and measure relatedness in an extraordinarily precise manner.

Some fascinating results have emerged from these studies, and Sibley and Ahlquist's findings have allowed researchers to resolve a number of long-standing uncertainties in the field of taxonomy.

CLASSIFYING THE BLACKBIRD

The purposes of taxonomy are twofold: to assign a unique name to each species and to place it within a structure of relationships. The Blackbird, for example, is classified in the following way:

- Class Aves
- Order Passeriformes
- Family Turdidae
- Genus *Turdus*
- Species *merula*

Subspecies may also be named. Blackbirds breeding on Madeira, for example, are identified as *Turdus merula cabrerae*.

Bird Anatomy

Despite their external diversity, birds are remarkably uniform in basic structure. This similarity results chiefly from adaptations associated with flight.

Birds are the only living things with feathers. Also, they are vertebrates, which means that, just like reptiles, amphibians, fish and mammals (including ourselves), they have a jointed internal skeleton with two forelimbs and two hindlimbs; the brain is encased in a strong bony container (the skull); and the main nerve route in the body is carried down the centre of the back inside a flexible column of bones (the spine).

If you compare the skeleton, muscle and organ systems of a bird with those of a human, you will find many points of similarity. Broadly speaking, the same basic elements—eyes, ears, skull, ribs, lungs, heart, and so on—are found in corresponding places in both and serve comparable functions.

Skeletal System

Almost all of the differences between human and bird skeletons are the result of profound modifications in birds to enable sustained flight. The sternum, or breastbone, for example, lies in the same relative position and serves the same basic function as the sternum in our own bodies. However, in birds it is much bigger in relative terms and bears,

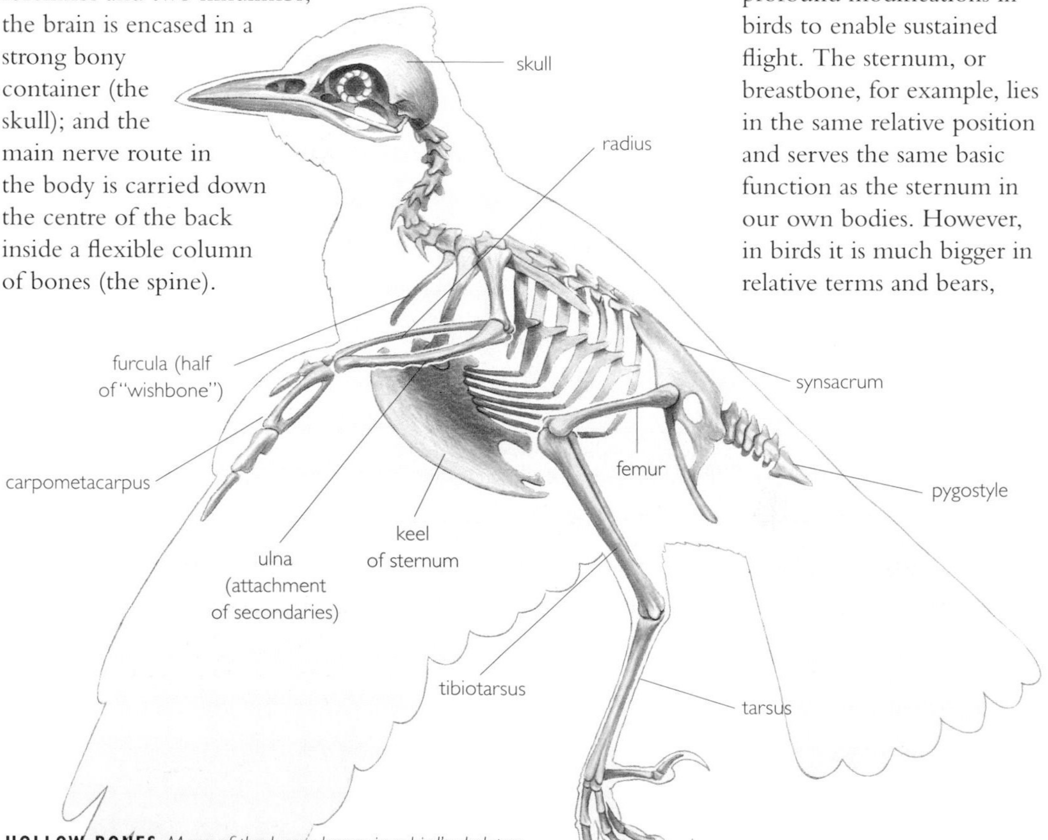

FORMED FOR FLIGHT *A Hen Harrier (top left) soars through the open skies. The skeleton of a bird (above) could be described as a typical vertebrate skeleton that has undergone significant modification to support powered flight.*

HOLLOW BONES *Many of the larger bones in a bird's skeleton are thin-walled and hollow, to minimise weight, but intricately braced and strutted inside, to maximise strength.*

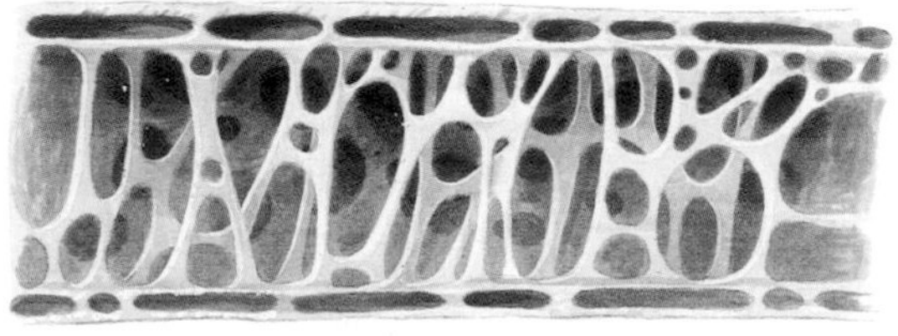

projecting at right angles, the most obvious and distinctive of avian skeletal structures: a large flat keel (called the carina). This serves as a point of attachment for the huge pectoral muscles used to flap the wings.

Another unique feature of the avian skeleton is that in many birds the collarbones have fused to form a rigid brace for the wings: the furcula or "wishbone".

Organ Systems

The organ systems, too, are comparable to those of other vertebrates but are heavily modified to service the needs of powered flight. In particular, they support a far higher metabolism than that of most other animals. The large size of a bird's heart is an indication of this.

Birds have a highly specialised and remarkably efficient respiratory system. A multitude of empty spaces (called pulmonary sacs or air sacs) extend throughout the body, in many birds extending even into the hollow bones. Air flows through this system of interconnected sacs almost like blood in the circulatory system. The lungs are located so that air flows through them, not in-and-out as in other vertebrates. Oxygen transfer to the blood is therefore a continuous process, taking place during both inhalation and exhalation. This system is so efficient that, paradoxically, birds get by with much smaller lungs than other vertebrates.

NEVER OUT OF BREATH *The net result of a bird's sophisticated respiratory system (below) is that air flows through the bird's lungs, rather than in-and-out as in humans and other animals.*

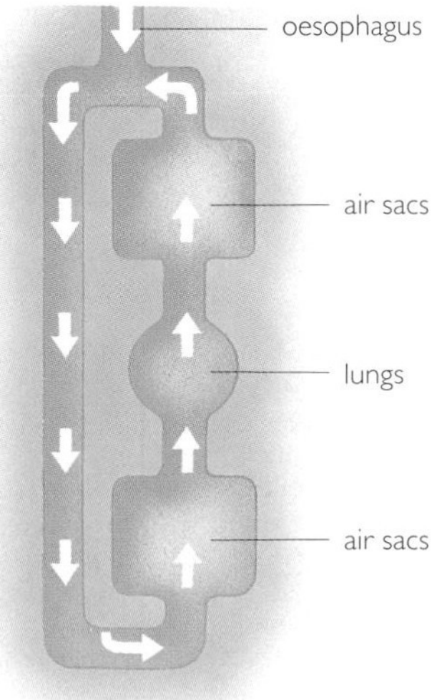

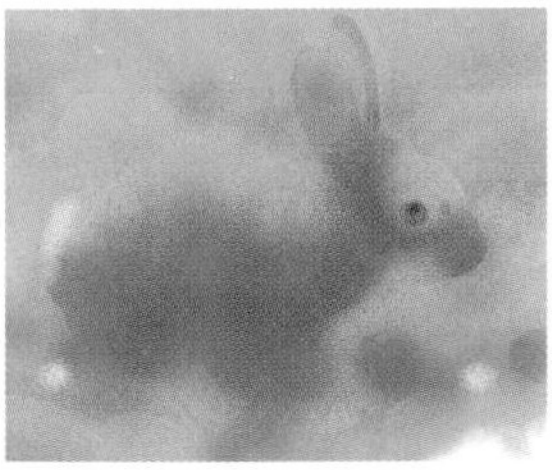

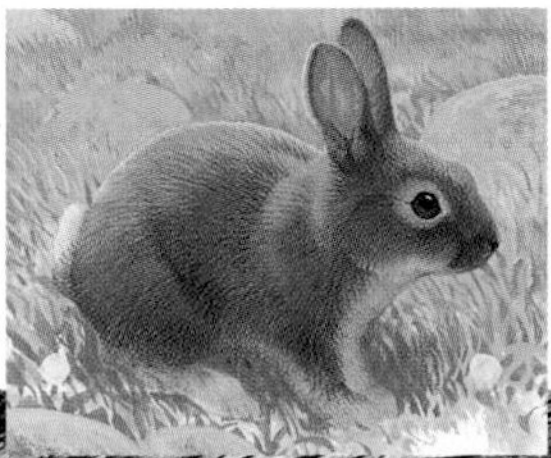

KEEN EYESIGHT *An image of a rabbit (left), as it might be seen by most animals, compared to the same rabbit as it might be seen by an eagle (below left). The much higher definition results largely from a far higher concentration of receptors in the retina of the eagle's eye (below). Owls (bottom) combine sensitive night vision with forward-facing eyes for accurate depth perception. This second-century coin is from Greece.*

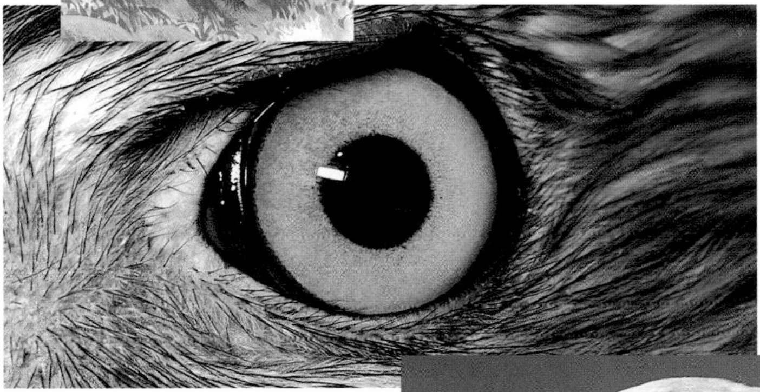

Sensory Systems

Birds have poor powers of smell but acute hearing, and their eyes are among the most sophisticated sensory organs in the animal kingdom.

The eye of a large eagle, for example, is approximately the same size as a human eye, but has a far greater density of sensory elements (rods and cones) in the retina (the rear inner surface of the eye on which the image is formed).

A unique feature of birds' eyes is the pecten, a highly vascularised structure that emerges from the retina. Despite numerous studies, its function is still unclear, but it is believed to play a role in improving the supply of oxygen and nutrients to the light-sensitive cells of the retina.

My heart in hiding

Stirred for a bird,—the

achieve of, the

mastery of

the thing!

Gerard Manley Hopkins (1844–1889), English poet

FEATHERS *and* PLUMAGE

Feathers define birds and are unique to them—no other animal has feathers. The feather itself is a complex product of a bird's skin, and its structure is one of nature's great wonders.

One of the marvels of animal engineering, the feather is light, flexible and strong. Feathers play a critical part in controlling a bird's internal temperature, and an obviously crucial role in flight.

MATERIAL AND DESIGN

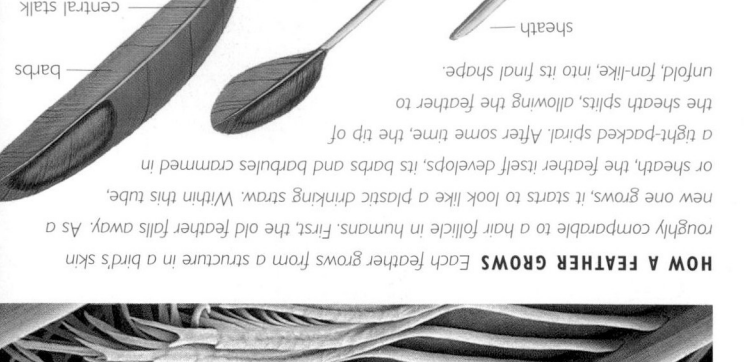

The material from which the feather is built is keratin, the same substance that makes up our hair and fingernails. Along the length of the central stalk (rachis) of a feather, structures called barbs emerge in parallel and on one plane, in an arrangement reminiscent of a plastic comb. Each barb in turn carries even smaller structures called barbules, arranged in the same manner along its length. The whole assembly is held together by myriad tiny hooks on the barbules which lock onto the barbules of the neighbouring barb.

A bird spends part of each day making minor repairs to tears in its feathers (preening). Most repairs involve reattaching the hooks, rather like reclosing Velcro strips. The bird does this by nibbling along the barbs of each feather to bring the "Velcro" in contact again.

COLOUR *Feathers come in all colours, from the sober shades of sparrows to the vibrant hues of the Caribbean Flamingo (above) and the male Golden Oriole (below).*

BARBS AND BARBULES *This electron microscope photograph (below) shows a barb and the barbules arranged along its sides. Each barbule bears tiny hooks (left) that lock the whole structure together.*

HOW A FEATHER GROWS *Each feather grows from a structure in a bird's skin roughly comparable to a hair follicle in humans. First, the old feather falls away. As a new one grows, it starts to look like a plastic drinking straw. Within this tube, or sheath, the feather itself develops, its barbs and barbules crammed in a tight-packed spiral. After some time, the tip of the sheath splits, allowing the feather to unfold, fan-like, into its final shape.*

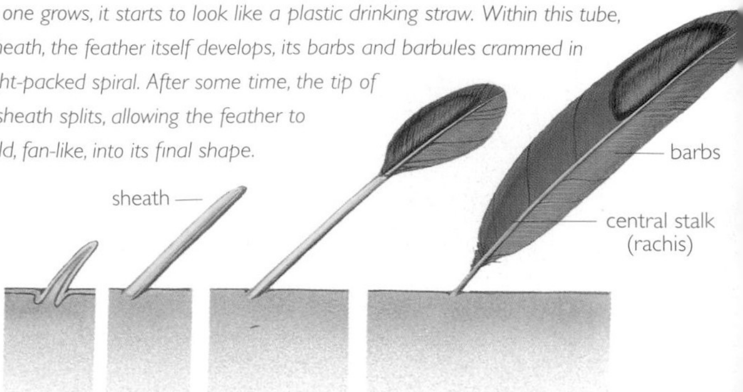

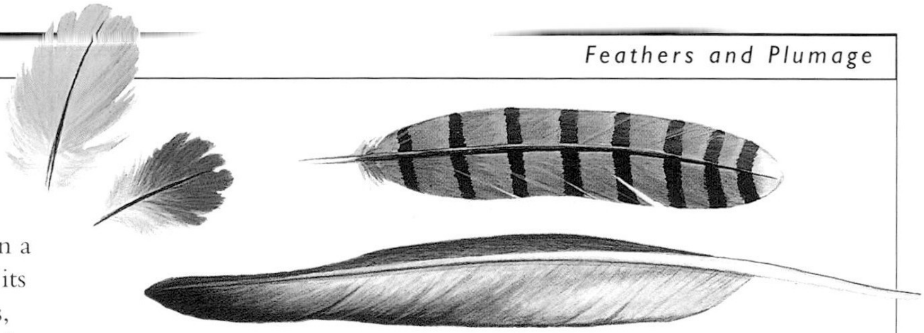

Plumage

The mass of feathers on a bird's body constitutes its plumage. In most birds, feathers tend to clump in distinct tracts, known as pterylae (the spaces between the tracts are apterylae). As a general rule, birds' colour patterns are built of these units—which is why it is valuable to know the details of a bird's surface "geography". Bird identification is simpler and more reliable if you can express pattern in terms of feather tracts.

Birds have many different kinds of feather, but most of them are either contour feathers or flight feathers. Contour feathers are those that cover the body itself and are basically there to keep the bird warm. The flight feathers are those directly involved in the business of flying. These are considerably longer, stiffer and less curved than contour feathers, and are aerodynamically shaped.

Other types of feathers include down feathers, which form a soft underlayer that further insulates the bird. Some birds also have specialised feathers called powder-down. These break down into a waxy powder that the bird spreads throughout its plumage during preening.

TYPES OF FEATHER *Most contour or body feathers (above left) are small, blunt and fluffy, whereas flight feathers (top and above) are larger, longer, stiffer and more smoothly shaped.*

The total number of feathers on a bird varies widely, though it correlates, roughly, with body size. A typical hummingbird has about 1,000 feathers, whereas a swan has more than 20 times as many. Plumage represents a substantial proportion of a bird's total body weight. A frigatebird, for example, is outweighed by its own feathers. The feathers of a typical songbird are about one-third its body weight.

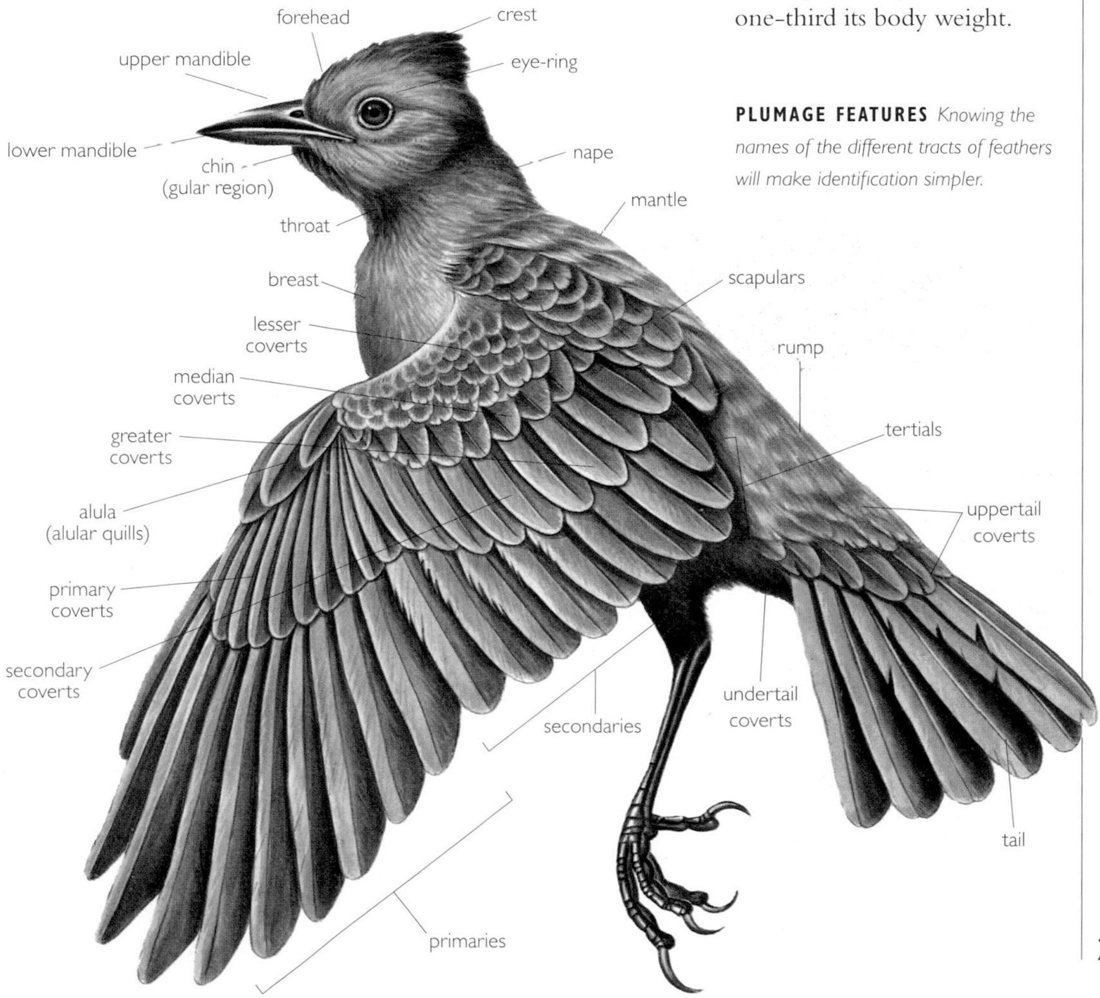

PLUMAGE FEATURES *Knowing the names of the different tracts of feathers will make identification simpler.*

Plumage Cycles

As a bird matures, so its plumage changes. In addition, plumage varies from season to season in many species and will, at least once a year, be completely replaced in a process known as moult.

Despite preening and constant care, the marvellously intricate structure of the feather inevitably wears out. All adult birds moult their feathers at least once a year, and if you carefully study the birds you see around you, you will learn to recognise the frayed, ragged appearance of feathers that are nearing the end of their useful life.

Moulting is one of the most intricate things a bird does in its annual life cycle. Two distinct processes are involved. The first step is when the old, worn feather is dropped, or shed. The second is when a new feather grows in its place. When each feather has been shed and replaced, then the moult can be said to be complete. This, however, is an abstraction that often does not happen: incomplete, overlapping, and arrested moults are quite common.

THERMAL UNDERWEAR *A Pine Grosbeak fluffs up its contour plumage to keep out winter cold.*

Timing

Moult requires that a bird find and process enough protein to rebuild around one-third of its body weight, so it is not surprising that a bird in heavy moult often seems listless and unwell. But far from being random and ad hoc, moult is controlled by strong evolutionary forces that have established an optimum time and duration.

Generally, moult occurs at the time of least stress on the bird. Many songbirds, for instance, moult in late summer, when the hard work of breeding is done but the weather is still warm and food still plentiful. This is why the woods in late summer often seem so quiet, when compared with the exuberant choruses of spring.

Intricacies of Moult

Moult of the flight feathers is the most highly organised part of the process. Some species, for example, begin by dropping the outermost primary on each side (to retain balance in the air) and wait

A MATURE LOOK *A first-year Northern Gannet is grey-brown, flecked with white. Over the next three years it acquires more white until it finally reach its adult plumage (above left). The feathers on the back of this young Ring-billed Gull (below) are fresh, but its wing feathers are badly worn and frayed, yet to be moulted.*

until the replacement feathers are about one-third grown before shedding the next outermost, and so on. Others always start with the innermost primary and work outward. Yet other species begin in the middle and work outward on both sides. Most ducks shed all their wing feathers at once, and remain flightless for two or three weeks while the replacement feathers grow.

Duration

Moult may be overlapped, extended, incomplete or interrupted, so it is almost impossible to generalise about the time it takes. Furthermore, the process is strongly influenced by the season, and the age and general health of

YEAR-ROUND CAMOUFLAGE *In the Willow Grouse, moult changes the bird's appearance so that its camouflage is effective in winter (below) and throughout the rest of the year (left).*

the bird. On the whole, a songbird takes around three weeks to complete its moult.

Identification and Moult

A basic understanding of the moulting process can be very useful in birdwatching. As colour and pattern are very strongly influenced by feather wear, and of course completely changed by moult, you may often find that the bird you are looking at through your binoculars looks quite different from its picture in your field guide.

This is often the case, for example, with migratory waders. In a process known as arrested moult, they replace their flight feathers quickly after nesting, then put the rest of the moult on hold until they have completed their migration. As a result, they spend much of the year in a plumage that is neither "summer" nor "winter", but somewhere in between.

Plumage Sequences

When a bird first hatches from the egg, it may be nearly naked, as in a typical songbird, or covered in down, like a baby chicken or a duckling. In either case, development of the ability to fly is generally the point at which the young bird reaches independence.

The juvenile plumage of a bird is the first plumage state in which true contour feathers are present—effectively the first set of feathers with which flight is possible. Any subsequent plumages between the juvenile plumage and full sexual maturity are collectively referred to as immature plumages, though in some species, for example gulls, they are often described in more detail (such as "first-winter" for a bird around six months old, "first-summer" for one a year old, and so on).

In most birds, first breeding marks the point at which an adult cycle of plumages is attained, which will then continue throughout life. In many birds, this involves a continuous cycle of two alternating plumages: summer and winter, or breeding and non-breeding.

Not all birds breed in summer, however, and some birds court and form pair bonds in their "breeding" plumage but moult out of it before they actually breed. These terms are therefore not always precise, so some specialists refer to winter or non-breeding plumage as the "basic" plumage, and any other plumage states (such as summer) as "first alternate" and "second alternate".

DRESSED TO IMPRESS *In birds such as the drake Mandarin Duck, moult alternates a dull "eclipse" (winter) plumage with a bold breeding (summer) plumage (right).*

FLIGHT

The size and shape of a bird's wing can tell you a great deal about its lifestyle and feeding requirements.

In the same way that aircraft are designed with different wing shapes according to their function, so evolution has ensured that the forms of birds' wings exactly suit their lifestyle.

In both birds and aircraft, lift, thrust and manoeuvera-bility all depend on the form of the wing and tail, and these properties are related in such a manner that improvement in any one can generally be achieved only by some sacrifice of performance in the other two.

HUMMINGBIRDS *achieve the ultimate in avian manoeuverability: they can fly in any direction without needing to turn in that direction first. All other birds, such as this Great Spotted Woodpecker (above left), are limited to flying forwards.*

IN CONTROL *Just as a pilot uses flaps on the wings of an aircraft (top) to control its speed, so a bird employs certain wing feathers to do the same. Here, a gull uses its alulas to slow itself down during descent.*

EFFICIENCY AND FORM

The most significant feature in relation to flight is of course the wing shape. Generally, a long, narrow wing is more efficient than a short, blunt wing—for purely aerodynamic, non-biological reasons that are well under-stood by aircraft designers. So birds that spend much time in the air, such as swallows, swifts, and migratory shore-birds such as Golden Plovers, have long, narrow wings that provide maximum efficiency.

But, for a bird, flapping long wings is harder work than flapping short ones. Many ground-dwelling birds, such as quail and partridges, need flight for little more than escape from predators. What matters for these birds is rapid acceleration; efficiency is less significant because their flights are generally of short duration. The best possible configu-ration is therefore a short, blunt wing.

Tail shapes also have a bearing on flight perfor-mance and vary for similar reasons. A short tail is aerodynamically efficient but a long tail can improve manoeuverability.

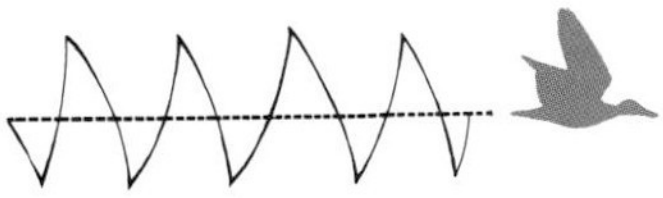

WATERFOWL *fly fast in a direct line, flapping their wings at a steady rate to maintain speed.*

VULTURES *use rising air currents to propel them in an upward spiral.*

WOODPECKERS *alternately flap their wings to gain speed and glide to conserve energy.*

Modes of Flight

This close relationship between lifestyle and wing and tail configuration is manifest in most birds.

Like fighter aircraft, falcons have narrow, backswept wings that provide a high level of performance in open skies. Some other raptors, such as accipiters, operate in more cluttered environments, like woodlands, and rely heavily on surprise. They have broad wings and long tails, offering maximum agility and acceleration.

Large birds of prey, such as vultures and eagles, ride thermals all day to conserve energy. They therefore have little need to flap their wings, which consequently tend to be long and broad, providing maximum lift.

Hummingbirds, on the other hand, flap their wings at an incredible rate that requires a high expenditure of energy. Their wings have more in common with helicopter rotor blades than with conventional aircraft wings, and they share many of the same flight characteristics, especially in the sacrifice of speed and range in return for a significant gain in precision. Like helicopters, hummingbirds can hover in mid-air, or fly backwards or forwards with almost equal ease.

> *O that I had wings like a dove, for then I would fly away and be at rest.*
>
> *Psalms, 55: 6*

DREAMS OF FLIGHT *From the legend of Icarus (right) to Leonardo's designs for flying machines (below right) and more recent visions of "bird-men" (below left), the idea of flight has captured the imagination of humans through the centuries.*

LEONARDO AND THE DREAM OF FLIGHT

The quest for flight is one of humankind's oldest passions. From the fable of Daedalus and Icarus, through the tower-jumpers of medieval times and the "bird-men" of later centuries, history is filled with accounts of people building wings and leaping from hillsides and towers, in the vain effort to fly like a bird.

Among the most noted of early bird-men was the Italian Renaissance artist and engineer, Leonardo da Vinci (1452–1519), whose theories and designs formed the basis and stimulant for actual flight generations later.

The fundamental idea that Leonardo followed was that human flight could be achieved by studying and imitating bird flight. Based on this, he evolved a series of machines with flapping wings, called ornithopters. "Write of swimming in the water and you will have the flight of the bird through the air", he wrote. His fecund imagination also generated the first designs for a parachute and a helicopter.

Leonardo's obsession with flight is reflected in his notebooks, which were filled with sketches of bird flight and flying machines. The most famous of these works, *Sul volo degli uccelli* (On the Flight of Birds), was published in Florence in 1505.

HABITATS *and* NICHES

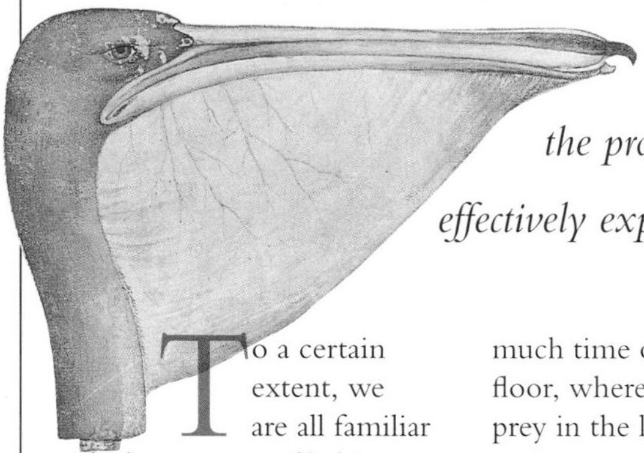

The bird species that have survived the process of evolution are those that have most effectively exploited a niche within a specific habitat.

To a certain extent, we are all familiar with the concept of habitat in relation to birds. We normally associate ducks, for example, with wetland areas and gulls with seashores. But a bird's habitat is more than just a place: it is a complex web of relationships between the bird species that occupy it, the vegetation, the climate, the food supply and predators.

Birds are versatile animals and have come to occupy almost all habitats, from frozen wastelands to deserts, and from swamps to dense forests.

ECOLOGICAL NICHES

Bird species have specialised to such an extent in order to survive that not only do they favour a particular habitat but also a specific slot, or ecological niche, within that habitat. This niche is often associated with the means of gathering food.

Let's take as an example a group of insect-eaters that may be found together in European woodlands. Among them, Song Thrushes spend much time on the forest floor, where they search for prey in the leaf litter. In the understorey, wrens flit from shrub to shrub in search of insects. Common Treecreepers climb tree trunks extracting insects from the bark, while Great Spotted Woodpeckers peck repeatedly at the trunks to get at wood-boring insects. From their perches under the canopy, Spotted Flycatchers dart out to seize flying insects. High in the canopy, Chiffchaffs flick among the branches in search of prey, while Swifts pursue flying insects in the air above.

All these birds occupy the same habitat and share the same basic diet (insects). They differ, however, in the equipment and the techniques they use in order to obtain their food. These differences define each bird's position—its niche—within its community.

HABITAT PREFERENCES *The subtle distinction between habitat and niche becomes most evident in highly specialised birds, such as the Spoonbill (above right) and the Nuthatch (right). Both inhabit very different environments and both exploit their habitats in very particular ways.*

DARWIN'S FINCHES

Undoubtedly, the most famous example of niche adaptation is that provided by a group of finches first discovered in the Galapagos Islands by Charles Darwin (left) during his voyage on the *HMS Beagle* in 1835.

All the finches on the islands are descended from one species—a seed-eating ground finch. Some of the finches have taken up typical seed-eating niches, but others have evolved in quite different ways to take advantage of the niches that were originally available to them in the absence of other landbirds.

One species has developed a longer bill for feeding on cactus flowers and fruits as well as seeds. Other tree-dwelling finches have adapted to feeding on fruits, seeds and insects. Another species—the Warbler Finch—has adopted the habits of a warbler and gleans insects from foliage.

The Woodpecker Finch, on the other hand, has learned to use a twig or cactus spine to dislodge insects from beneath bark or from cracks in rotten wood. Perhaps the most remarkable of all these finches, however, is the Sharp-billed Finch, which pecks at the bases of wing and tail feathers of moulting seabirds and then drinks the oozing blood!

FOOD THAT FITS THE BILL

Bill shape often betrays diet more obviously than any other feature. If you guess from its bill shape that whatever the Avocet (below, top) feeds on, it must be very small and agile, you would be right—it eats tiny shrimps living in shallow water. Similarly, finches (upper centre) have deep, short conical bills for crushing the husks of seeds; eagles (lower centre) have hooked bills that are ideal for tearing flesh; and herons (bottom) have bills that resemble spears in function as well as shape.

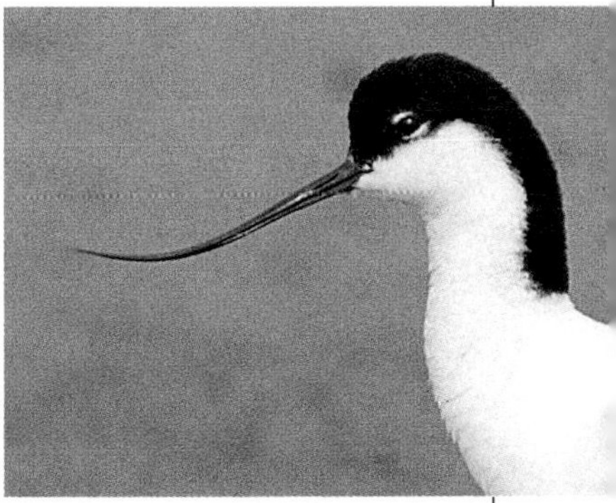

MORPHOLOGICAL ADAPTATIONS

Of all the characteristics that relate to a bird's niche and how it obtains its food, the most obvious are the sizes and shapes of the bill and feet. Indeed, the shape of a bird's bill and feet can tell you a good deal about what and how it eats.

Returning to the insect-eating birds of our European woodlands, we can link physical characteristics to foraging strategies. The Song Thrush has large, strong feet, ideal for kicking leaves aside to reveal insects. The fine, pointed bills of Wrens are suited to gleaning insects from undergrowth foliage.

Both the Common Treecreeper and the Great Spotted Woodpecker have short legs with long claws adapted for grasping the surface of tree trunks, and stiffened tail feathers that serve as props, but their bills reflect different ways of capturing their prey. The straight, stout bill of the woodpecker is used for hammering the trunk to remove bark, whereas the fine, downward-curving bill of the treecreeper serves to probe beneath the bark or into fissures.

Long, pointed wings enable swifts to stay aloft most of the day, and their short, triangular bills with broad gapes are ideal for capturing and swallowing flying insects.

In the introduction to each habitat in the Habitat Birdfinder section of this book (p. 84), you will find further illustrations of the way birds interact with their environment.

LIFE CYCLE

Once it reaches adulthood, a bird follows an annual cycle of events for the rest of its life.

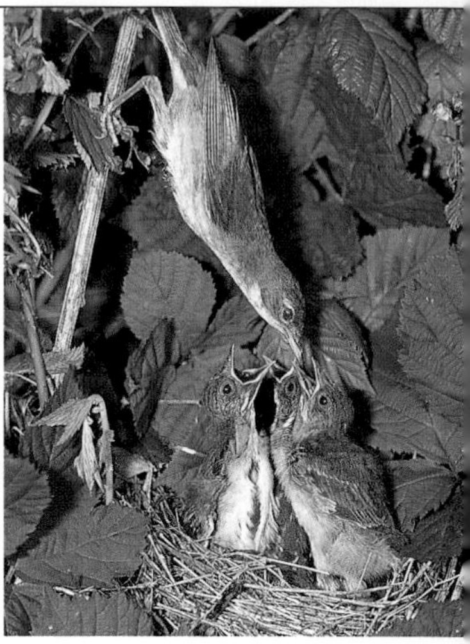

After fledging and leaving its parents' territory, a typical young bird begins a nomadic period that may last several years. If the bird is a male, he probably will not be able to establish a territory (and therefore breed) for some time because most suitable territories will already be occupied by resident males that he has little chance of ousting. He therefore can only slip inconspicuously from one territory to another, always risking hostility from the occupier.

Mortality is generally high during this period. But if the bird can survive long enough, sooner or later he may stumble upon a territory that has been recently vacated by its occupier. He can then establish the territory as his own, attract a mate, and begin his own breeding cycle.

THE ANNUAL CYCLE OF THE WHITETHROAT

The chart on these pages shows the annual cycle of a Whitethroat (see also p. 186) that winters in tropical Africa and breeds in Europe. This chart is obviously a generalisation, even for this species, but it is fairly typical of most European songbirds. Further information on each phase of this cycle is provided elsewhere in this chapter.

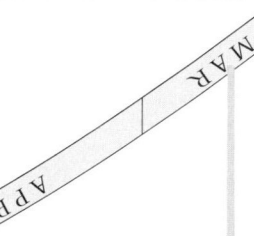

LEAVE AFRICAN TROPICS *Whitethroats migrate by night, covering around 125 miles (200 km) each day.*

ARRIVE AT BREEDING GROUNDS *Timing is critical during spring migration. Fish-eating birds, for example, cannot arrive until lakes and rivers are clear of ice.*

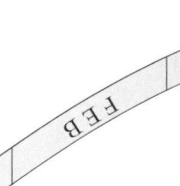

DEPART BREEDING GROUNDS *Timing is less significant in autumn than in spring. In autumn, departure and travel therefore tend to be spread over a broader time frame.*

MOULT *This may last up to two weeks. It precedes migration in most landbirds, but in many other birds may be delayed until after migration.*

ESCORT YOUNG, YOUNG DEPART *Having left the nest, juveniles remain with the adults for only a few days before dispersing (right).*

SING, ATTRACT MATE *Small songbirds often begin breeding in their first spring, but larger birds often take longer to reach sexual maturity: some albatrosses, for example, may not breed until their seventh year. Small migratory songbirds form their pair bonds on arrival at their breeding grounds, but many larger birds, such as wildfowl, mate at their wintering grounds then migrate north together.*

BUILD NEST *The forms of nests seem to have a bearing on mortality rates. Reed Buntings, for example, build open nests and successfully raise to fledging only about 40% of total eggs laid, whereas cavity-nesting birds like the Blue Tits may raise about 80%.*

FEED YOUNG *Typically, this is when male birds get more involved in the process, foraging and supplying food to the hungry young (below).*

MAY

LAY EGGS, INCUBATE EGGS *Among most birds, average breeding success (that is, the number of young raised to independence against the number of eggs laid) tends to rise slightly after the first year or two, showing that learning and experience often play a part in the nesting cycle.*

JUNE

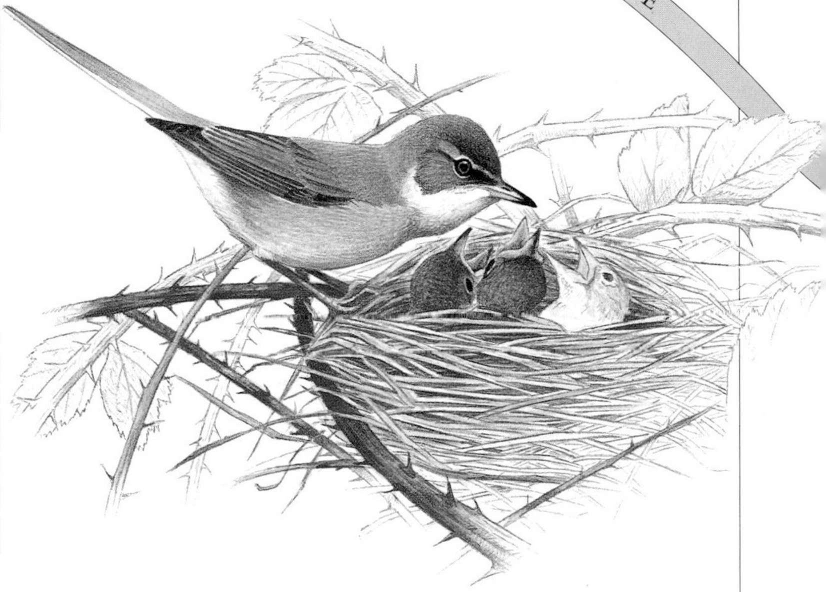

NOV | DEC

RETURN TO AFRICAN TROPICS *Losses during migration are frequently very heavy, particularly among young birds and during long flights over water. However, average life expectancy tends to stabilise after the first successful crossing.*

THE TIMING *of the above events will vary among Whitethroats according to where in Europe the birds breed and how long they spend there. The duration of each phase, however, is relatively consistent. For example, the following timescales will hold true for most Whitethroats:*

Nest construction	4–5 days
Egg laying *(clutch size: 3–6 eggs)*	5–7 days
Incubation	9–14 days
Fledging *(from hatching to departure of young)*	10–12 days

Photographs, clockwise from the top of page 32: female Whitethroat feeding young; male Whitethroat singing; male Whitethroat carrying food; female Whitethroat at pond to bathe.

LIFE EXPECTANCY *As mortality is high in the first months (75% in some cases), figures for average life expectancy are low. As indicated below, larger birds tend to live longer.*

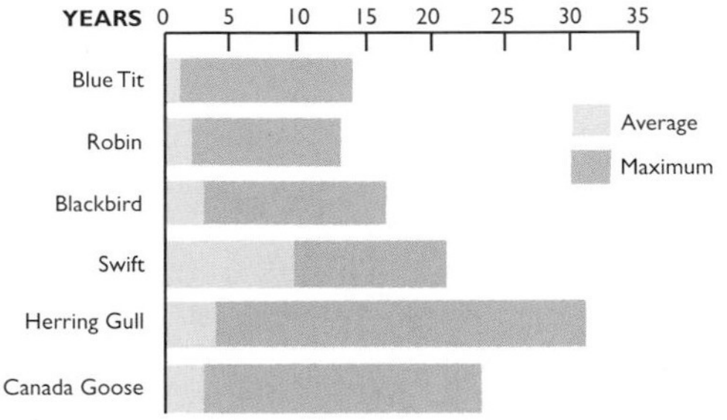

Displays

Like humans, and unlike most other animals, birds respond strongly to visual signs. Much of their communication therefore involves displays, and these convey a wide range of messages.

COURTSHIP DISPLAYS *Displays in sexual contexts often involve plumage features. One of the most remarkable of these features is the male Peacock's tail, portrayed here in a Roman mosaic from Ravenna in Italy.*

In the course of evolution, certain actions by birds have come to have a communicative function. Song, of course, is one such action, but most other communication between birds is visual and often involves plumage displays.

Plumage as Display

Plumage patterns and colours are among birds' most appealing features, and we rely strongly on them for field identification. Among the birds themselves, plumage plays a significant role in communication. When Chaffinches fly up, for example, they flash their white outer tail feathers. This says "follow me" to other birds in the flock.

A wide variety of birds have developed plumage colours and patterns that send messages at certain times of the year. The most common manifestation of this is the colourful breeding plumage that many acquire each spring, often extending to elaborate features that may be used in specific displays. Such features take a variety of forms and usually occur on the most visible parts of the body, especially the head, neck and breast, upper wings, or tail. For example, they may be specialised feathers. Male egrets develop elaborate and colourful plumes, and male sunbirds have iridescent gorgets and crowns that change colour as they move. Possibly the most spectacular feather display of all is the fanning of raised upper tail-coverts by a male Peacock.

In some cases the combination of colour and pattern is particularly important. The male Wood Duck, for example, has glossy, brightly coloured plumage and a sleek crest or hood. This crest can be depressed tightly against its neck and spread to one side so as to accentuate its appearance.

TERRITORIAL DISPLAYS *A Grasshopper Warbler uses song to proclaim its territory. In many other birds, displays may be visual rather than vocal or they may use a combination of both.*

More bizarre features have evolved, purely for display, in other species. For example, during courtship in the adult male Great Bustard, its gular pouch is inflated into a large, pendulous balloon, exposing two bluish stripes of bare skin and pushing moustaches up in front of its eyes. At the same time, the tail is cocked flat on its back, touching the head, which is thrust backwards over its shoulders. As a result, this largely brown bird is quickly transformed into an almost entirely white one.

Display Behaviour

Displays are not confined to the appearance of the bird. While they may be given in conjunction with plumage displays, they can also take other forms. The male Peacock performs as he fans his extraordinary tail. Breeding egrets posture to show themselves to best effect.

Sometimes the behavioural component in the display dominates. Displays by raptors, for example, are almost entirely behavioural, and usually involve some kind of demonstration of aerial agility or power.

A number of other birds also give display flights, including Woodcock, Common Snipe, larks and Fan-tailed Warbler. These flights are often accompanied by singing.

SEXUAL DISPLAYS *In the breeding season, male Black Grouse (above) indulge in elaborate displays that are essentially one-way. Other displays may be mutual, male and female performing them together. Examples include the displays of Great Crested Grebes (top), the "greeting" ceremony of Northern Gannets (right), and the dancing displays of Common Cranes (above right).*

THE FUNCTIONS OF DISPLAY

Most displays, particularly the more elaborate ones, are sexual—they are designed to attract potential mates—and the male bird generally takes the initiative. Males therefore have more colourful plumage and perform most of the display routines (though there are exceptions).

There are various other types of display, such as actions of greeting, threat, and submission, and some birds, such as the Ringed Plover, use displays to distract predators.

SONGS *and* CALLS

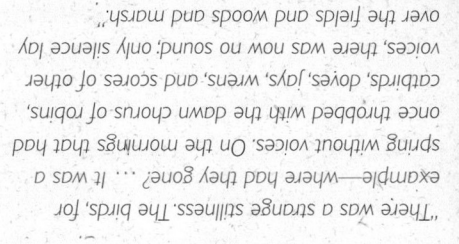

Through the ages, humankind has delighted in the charm of birdsong, but only recently have we developed the technology to find out what these songs and calls signify.

The joyous sound of birdsong is not only a source of pleasure and inspiration, it is also a valuable aid to field identification, and many birdwatchers rely on songs and calls to name more reclusive species in the field.

HOW BIRDS SING

In birds, as opposed to mammals, the larynx lacks vocal cords. Instead, vocalisation is produced by the syrinx, a specialised organ found only in birds, which is situated at the base of the windpipe or trachea. The syrinx is remarkably sophisticated, having two chambers that the bird can use simultaneously to produce extremely complex sounds.

CALLS

Vocalisations are commonly divided into calls and songs. These terms are useful, but they are difficult to define precisely. Generally, songs are used in sexual contexts and calls are used for all other types of vocal communication.

There are calls covering most aspects of social behaviour, including threat, alarm, flight, begging and so on, and some species have calls that have specialised functions. Cave-dwelling swifts, for example, emit a series of echo-locating clicks when flying in the dark.

Although calls are relatively short and simple, there is evidence that they transmit information about the identity of the calling bird.

SONGS

Generally, the male does the singing (but there are exceptions) and the songs function as either territorial announcements or as sexual attractants.

Although each species has a distinctive song, some birds incorporate mimicry of other species in their repertoires. Sometimes a song includes contributions from two individuals, usually a mated pair. This is known as duetting and, at times, the co-ordination between the two singers is remarkable.

Experiments show that while some birds are born with their songs, others learn them from their parents. As with human languages, local dialects occur, with certain characteristics of songs in one population differing from those in other populations. Some first-year males sing a

RACHEL CARSON

"There was a strange stillness. The birds, for example—where had they gone? ... It was a spring without voices. On the mornings that had once throbbed with the dawn chorus of robins, catbirds, doves, jays, wrens, and scores of other voices, there was now no sound; only silence lay over the fields and woods and marsh."

So wrote Rachel Carson (1907–64) in her historic book *Silent Spring*, published in 1962, which alerted the public to the disastrous consequences of the uncontrolled use of chemical pesticides.

A lifelong birdwatcher, Carson conjured images of a countryside without birdsong—a frightening picture of nature in deathly silence. Even people who generally pay little attention to conservation issues are concerned at the thought of losing the concertos and symphonies of nature that emanate from gardens and parklands as winter gives way to spring.

In her warnings, Rachel Carson confirmed birdsong as a precious part of our natural world.

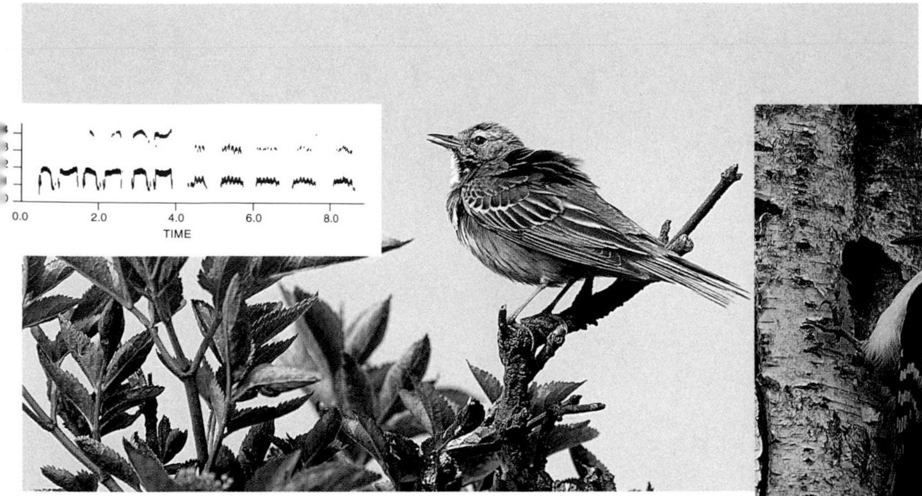

SOUNDING OUT THE BIRDS *Most bird sounds are vocal, as in the songs of the Tree Pipit (above) and the Yellow-hammer (far left). Exceptions include the Great Spotted Woodpecker (top), which uses bill drummings to produce a sound like a distant machine gun. Scientific study of bird sounds was made possible by the work of Dr Arthur Allen (left, in the centre) and his associates. Today a common research tool is the sonogram (inset, above left). This one portrays the call of a Great Northern Diver.*

little differently from adult birds, and different songs may be sung as the breeding season progresses.

Overall, the complexity of vocalisations varies widely. There are, however, a few birds, such as the storks, that never vocalise at all.

Other Bird Sounds

Sounds other than songs and calls are also created by birds in a number of ways.

Some species, such as snipes during display flight, produce loud, distinctive sounds by diving at high speed so that air passes rapidly through stiffened or modified wing and tail feathers. Others, including most grouse, use air sacs on the neck to produce loud booming sounds.

Scientific Study

Only relatively recently have we been able to study bird vocalisation scientifically.

The first-ever recording of a bird was made by Ludwig Koch in Germany in 1889, and in 1898 Sylvester Judd, a biologist, achieved this in America. But it was not until 1932 that scientists at Cornell University, led by Arthur Allen, perfected the techniques and equipment required to successfully record birdsong in the field.

This pioneering work allowed scientists and students of ornithology to study and compare the songs of different species. The subsequent evolution of technology has enabled ornithologists not only to record bird songs and calls but also to modify them electronically and play them back to birds in order to study how they react. Scientists are also able to reproduce bird sounds in graphic form as sonograms: charts that plot frequency, or "pitch", (vertical scale) against time (horizontal scale).

Among the artistic hierarchy, birds are probably the greatest musicians to inhabit our planet.

Olivier Messiaen (1908–92), French composer. Messiaen's music was strongly influenced by birdsong.

Territory *and* Pair Formation

Whether it be a large tract of land or a few centimetres of a branch for roosting, the quality of a bird's territory plays a crucial role in its breeding success.

For a bird, a desirable territory is an area that provides all that it requires in the way of food, shelter and a nesting site, either for its general survival or for breeding. All territories are defended, usually against other birds of the same species, but also—particularly where there is a valuable food resource or nesting site at stake—against other species.

Types of Territories

Those territories that provide all the necessary resources will be occupied by a pair of birds throughout the breeding season, or even throughout their entire lives. Other territories may be used for particular purposes, notably roosting and feeding.

Most territories are well-defined areas, with only minor boundary changes taking place from time to time, but birds may also defend additional territories—a foraging resource such as a berry bush, for example—that are outside their main territory.

Colonial nesters, such as seabirds, herons, egrets and swallows, nest close to each other, and each pair will defend the immediate surrounds of the nest out to a distance at which pecking contact can be made with neighbours. Food may be gathered at a shared foraging site, such as in the sea or at a nearby marsh, or pairs may occupy and defend separate feeding territories.

Sizes of feeding territories usually depend upon the amount of food available. Take certain species of woodpecker, for example. Each bird, or pair of birds, requires access to a certain number of mature trees that can produce sufficient larvae under the bark of dead or dying branches to meet their energy requirements. These trees may be scattered over a wide area or found in a single plot.

BIRD TERRITORIES *may encompass only a single resource, such as the individual nest sites in this colony of Northern Gannets (right), or all the resources needed to sustain a breeding attempt, as in this diagram of a typical songbird territory (left). The highlighted area in the diagram indicates the extent of the territory, and the key indicates the uses of the resources within the territory.*

SOUL MATES *The souls of the Pharoah Ani and his wife depicted as birds (left), from* The Theban Book of the Dead, *c. 1250* BC.

Territories and Courtship

A variety of resources, the most obvious one being food, attracts females to territories held by males for breeding or specifically for courtship and mating. If a resource is scarce or unevenly distributed, then males with better-quality territories are likely to attract a greater number of females.

COURTSHIP *sometimes involves the transfer of a "gift" from one partner to the other, as in the "weed-swapping" display of Great Crested Grebes (left) and the courtship feeding of Common Terns (below).*

For example, male thrushes that defend the best berry supplies attract the most females. Female tits are more attracted to territories with shaded nest sites, as prolonged exposure to the sun often results in the death of nestlings.

Other types of territories play a part in courtship. For example, males of polygynous species (such as Black Grouse) congregate at communal display areas, known as leks, where they compete for patches of ground. Males that win control of central territories are the ones that attract the most females.

Forming a Bond

Generally, when a female first appears in a male's territory she is greeted as an intruder, but in response to submissive behaviour on her part, the male stops being aggressive and begins courting her. This may involve intricate social ceremonies. Courtship feeding, for example, is widespread. Not only is this a means of winning the female, but it also reflects her need for a high level of nutrition to support her through the demanding process of breeding and incubation.

Pair Bonds

Some birds bond for life; some form new partnerships each breeding season; and some do not form pairs at all, the male mating with a number of females and taking no part in the rearing of the young.

Most songbirds form a pair bond for breeding, and the relationship may be resumed in subsequent breeding seasons. However, this may have more to do with convenience—the birds tend to return to the same area after migration and are thus likely to find the same partner again—than with any strong bond with a particular mate.

MARGARET MORSE NICE

One of the most influential studies of territorial birds was carried out in the 1930s by the renowned ornithologist Margaret Morse Nice (1883–1974). For eight years she observed a population of Song Sparrows living in an area at the back of her home near Columbus, Ohio. With painstaking attention to detail, she charted 39 acres (16 hectares), producing maps showing the location and movements of each bird.

Each spring, new maps had to be made almost every day to keep track of new arrivals. The resident sparrows were all trapped, weighed, and fitted with rings for identification. Like many skilled birdwatchers, Nice was also able to recognise each individual bird by its song. One male bird was observed for over seven years as he established and defended his territory, attracted a mate, and reared successive broods.

Nice's pioneering work is widely regarded as one of the most significant contributions to our understanding of bird populations and their territories.

NESTS *and* EGGS

Most birds create a nest of one kind or another in preparation for the physically demanding process of egg-laying, incubation and raising a brood.

As soon as a breeding pair has bonded, work will begin on building a nest. This will serve as a cradle for the eggs and a temporary home for the developing chicks. Selection of the nest site and building the nest may be undertaken by the female alone or in cooperation with her mate.

Most nests are built for a single attempt at breeding. A few birds use nests at other times of the year for sleeping or shelter, but these nests are rarely used for raising young.

DIVERSITY OF NESTS

We usually think of nests as being constructed from twigs, leaves, and grass stems placed in a tree or bush. However, birds use an extraordinary range of techniques to create a wide variety of structures.

Some species, such as Ospreys and White-tailed Eagles, reuse their nests, each year adding new material to their platforms of sticks so that the structures grow larger and larger. Other birds reuse the nests of other species. Long-eared Owls, for example, often use old crow nests, and many cavity-nesting birds use abandoned woodpecker holes.

CRADLES FOR THE YOUNG *Nest materials and structures vary widely, from virtually none, as with tern nests, to the intricate cobweb and lichen structures of Long-tailed Tits (above), and the mud-brick or dug homes of certain swallows and martins (below).*

EGG-LAYING AND EGGS

The batch of eggs laid in a single breeding attempt is known as a clutch and may take up to a week to lay. A complete clutch may comprise only a single egg, as in some seabirds and vultures, or up to a dozen or more in the case of quail, pheasants and waterfowl. Some species will relay if their first nesting attempt fails, even if they normally produce only one clutch a season.

Many birds, especially the smaller songbirds, habitually lay two or more clutches a season, and these re-nestings can sometimes be so rapid that the male will still be feeding young from the first nesting while his mate is laying eggs in a second nest.

EGG COLOUR

Most brightly coloured eggs are laid where their owners can recognise them by daylight. Where their brightness would stand out from the surroundings, the eggs tend to be laid in deep nests or ones well hidden by foliage. Eggs laid in

A NEW LIFE *Using the tip of its bill to first puncture the tough inner membrane and smash a small opening in the hard outer shell, a baby bird struggles to free itself. This hatching process may last up to a day.*

open nests, particularly on or near the ground, are usually coloured and patterned so that they blend in with their immediate surroundings. Eggs that are laid in hollows or burrows are generally white or near-white.

Incubation

In the breeding season, most female birds (and some males that share incubation) have brood patches. These bare patches of skin on the belly permit a more efficient transfer of heat from the bird's body to the eggs.

Incubation is hard work, and the incubating bird may have to double its thermal output. The period of incubation varies from a couple of weeks in smaller birds to over eight weeks in gannets, vultures and eagles.

Care of the Young

The term altricial is used to describe chicks that are born blind and helpless. Chicks that hatch with their eyes open, are covered with down feathers, and are capable of leaving the nest shortly after emerging from the eggs are described as precocial. (Some chicks, however, have both altricial and precocial characteristics.)

During their development in the nest, altricial chicks are fed and cared for by the parents. This nestling period will last from an average of eight to twelve days for some small songbirds to nearly a month for large woodpeckers and about four months for the Griffon Vulture.

Precocial chicks vary in their level of dependence on the parents. Some remain in the nest for a few days after hatching. After leaving the nest, chicks of certain species (grebes and rails, for example) are fed by the parents, whereas others, such as young gamebirds, are merely shown food by the parents. Other newly hatched birds may follow their parents, but find their own food, as do ducklings and young waders.

Brood Parasites

Some species have developed techniques to bypass the tasks of incubating and caring for their offspring. The most widespread are the brood parasites, which lay their eggs in the nests of other birds, leaving these eggs to be hatched and the chicks to be reared by the unwitting foster parents. In Europe, cuckoos are the best known brood parasites.

KONRAD LORENZ AND IMPRINTING

For centuries, people have adopted ducklings, goslings and other types of domesticated fowl as pets, giving little thought as to why the birds accepted them as foster parents. Only in 1935 was the process fully explained by the Viennese zoologist and ethologist, Konrad Lorenz (1903–89).

Lorenz had been interested in this question since childhood when he had adopted goslings as pets and found that he could get them to follow him as if he were their mother. In later experiments he was able to establish that there is a critical period immediately after the chick has hatched from the egg during which the first image that it sees will be imprinted in its mind and henceforth regarded as its parent.

Lorenz's work on this and other aspects of bird behaviour provided ornithologists with a remarkable insight into the socialisation of birds. He was awarded the Nobel Prize for physiology in 1973.

CHICK TYPES *Two broad groups can be distinguished among newly hatched birds. Altricial chicks (below) are naked, blind and helpless. Precocial chicks (left) are alert, mobile and covered in fluffy down.*

MIGRATION

In Western Europe the flux of bird migration is among the greatest in the world, and the arrivals and departures of birds are major signs of seasonal change.

Some sedentary birds remain in the same geographical area throughout their lives. However, nearly half the world's birds divide their year between two main localities and undertake annual migrations.

Most migrations result from seasonal fluctuations in the availability of a particular food. In temperate countries, there tends to be more food around in summer and autumn than in winter and spring. Winter weather causes a reduction in the amount of food available and shörter days mean there is less time to gather it.

This situation is pronounced at higher latitudes in Europe, where the availability of food declines dramatically in winter, particularly in deciduous forest. Among the few insect-eaters that can remain in such areas are some woodpeckers and Nuthatches that are able to extract prey from the trunks of leafless trees.

While most birds travel alone, some migrate in flocks of one or more species. The benefits of travelling in flocks include greater protection against predation (particularly for daytime travellers), and, for younger migrants, in some cases at least (geese and cranes, for example), being guided by more experienced birds.

Some migrants travel by day, while many others journey by night. Typical day migrants include most waterfowl, swallows, pipits, starlings, and finches. Night migrants include many waders, thrushes, warblers and flycatchers.

NAVIGATION

Migratory birds are natural navigators with remarkable homing capabilities. In June 1952, a Manx Shearwater was

ON THE WING *Many birds, such as cranes (top), travel mainly overland, but some of the most dramatic migrations involve ocean crossings by birds, such as waders (above), that cannot land on water and must therefore complete their journey in a single flight. Migration studies have been greatly aided by the use of radar (top left), which can be used to track flocks of migrating birds.*

THE MYSTERY OF MIGRATION

For centuries, the annual disappearance of bird species perplexed humankind. Many primitive peoples considered the departure and return of birds to be a divine manifestation and there are many myths associated with migratory birds. Aristotle and his contemporaries proposed scientific theories to explain the disappearance of some species, suggesting, for example, that Swallows (right) overwintered in burrows in the ground. Not surprisingly, many people believed that the birds that disappeared went into hibernation. As late as the sixteenth century, there was a theory that Swallows formed tight balls under the surfaces of ponds, where they passed the winter.

MIGRATION ROUTES *Migrating birds traverse almost every part of Europe. but the flow is heaviest along the coasts. Land birds, especially, tend to concentrate at places where sea crossings are shortest: via Falsterbo, Gibraltar or the Bosporus and, to a lesser extent, via islands such as Sardinia, Sicily or Crete.*

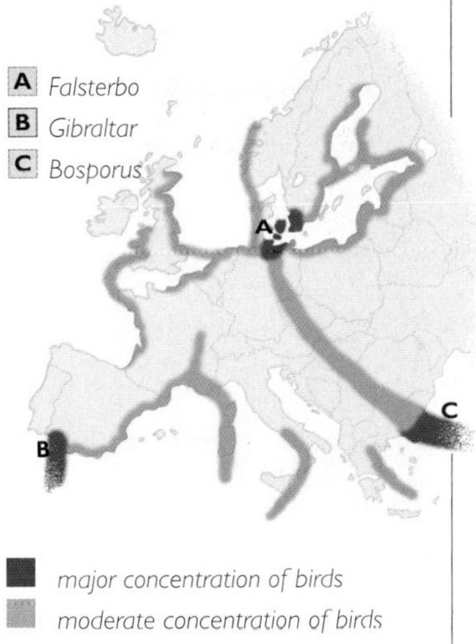

taken from its burrow on Skokholm Island, off the coast of Wales, tagged with a leg ring, and taken across the Atlantic to Boston. Here it was released, some 3,100 miles (5,000 km) from home. It was found safe in its burrow on Skokholm Island 12½ days later.

It is thought that most birds navigate by sight, using the sun to guide them during the day and the stars to lead them at night. Birds also have a built-in "chronometer", or innate time sense, that tells them when it is time to depart, how long the journey will take, and so on. But while these senses and abilities are present from birth, migrants also learn from experience, becoming familiar with territories and flyways. They also learn to follow certain air and sea currents, to use changes in temperature as guides, and to watch the passage flights of other birds.

Is it by thy wisdom that the hawk soareth and stretcheth her wings towards the south?

Book of Job, 39: 26

STRATEGIES

Migration strategies vary widely. Most songbirds, for example, break their journey into short hops of 200 miles (320 km) or so and they may delay their journey in the event of severe or overcast weather. Large groups of birds often find themselves waiting together in one place for weather more conducive to travelling. Consequently, songbirds often migrate in waves, and the arrival of such a wave can be an incredible sight.

Other birds cover distances of up to 1,000 miles (1,500 km) non-stop per day. Many species, including Swallows, make an annual journey of 6,250 miles (10,000 km) from Northern Europe to tropical Africa. Other species, such as the Ruff, migrate from eastern Russia to overwinter in Western Europe or Africa, covering almost the same distances. More impressive still are the Northern Wheatear, which migrates from Alaska to Africa, and the Arctic Warbler, which makes an annual migration from Lapland to Southeast Asia. However, the greatest globetrotter in terms of distance covered each year is the Arctic Tern. Terns that breed in Arctic and North Atlantic regions overwinter on the edge of Antarctica at the opposite side of the globe.

IRRUPTIONS

Not all movements of birds involve migration. Non-seasonal movements, mainly brought about by regular or irregular changes in food supplies, can result in a species appearing in areas well outside its normal range. Such movements are known as irruptions.

The Snowy Owl, for example, leaves the Arctic for the southern Baltic and, sometimes, the North Sea region only when there is a drastic decline in the number of lemmings, its chief prey.

I sat in my sunny doorway from sunrise till noon, rapt in revery, amidst the pines and hickories and sumachs, in undisturbed solitude, while birds sang around or flitted noiselessly through the house.

Walden, HENRY DAVID THOREAU (1817–62),
American writer and naturalist

Chapter Two
Birdwatching at Home

BACK GARDEN BIRDWATCHING

Whether you live in a city flat with a shared back garden or a country cottage with extensive grounds, birdwatching can begin at home.

Through the centuries, people have delighted in observing the activities of the birds frequenting the land around their homes. Their beauty has always been a source of joy and wonder and, at times, a consolation.

Providing food, water and nesting sites for birds in your garden will significantly increase opportunities for observing them. It will also help many species that in recent years have struggled to find suitable nesting and foraging habitats.

Once they have discovered your garden, many birds will keep coming back. Resident species, such as Collared Doves and House Sparrows, may build their whole life cycle around a particular feeder station. Some migratory birds, too, such as Robins and Blackcaps, will return to spend winter in the same garden year after year.

FAST FOOD *Carefully presented food will attract many birds, especially in winter, when smaller species often find it difficult to gather enough food by day to see them through the long nights.*

HENRY DAVID THOREAU

Some of the most interesting accounts of back garden birdwatching can be found in *Walden or Life in the Woods*, written by the nineteenth-century essayist and philosopher Henry David Thoreau. This series of 18 essays explores the relationship between humans and nature and features numerous detailed notes on the activities of the birds found in and around Thoreau's wooded garden.

Rejecting the constraints and conformity of a commercial society, in 1845 Thoreau retreated to the woods to conduct an experiment in basic living. For two years, he lived in a cabin he had built on the shores of Walden Pond, near Concord in Massachusetts. Here he spent many hours contemplating the wonders of nature. With little human contact during these years, the woodland birds became his constant companions and he devoted much of his writing to observations of their behaviour.

In birds, he discovered kindred spirits and he marvelled at the simplicity and freedom of their lives. The experience at Walden gave rise to a lifelong fascination with birds and ultimately shaped Thoreau's philosophy on nature.

SETTING UP A FEEDER STATION

Birds have a number of basic requirements. They need food, water, protection from predators and somewhere to nest. All these needs can be catered for in an average garden, even in urban areas.

For your feeder station to be as effective as possible, it is important that you choose appropriate foods, present them in the right way and make sure your visitors are well protected.

To further assist local birds and increase opportunities for observing bird behaviour, you

BIRD GARDENS *Since antiquity, birds have been seen as a necessary adjunct to any fine garden, as shown in this mural from Pompeii.*

may also decide to put up a nestbox or two. And, if you have the space, cultivating trees and other plants will help turn your garden into a veritable wildlife refuge.

There is sufficient guidance in the following pages to get you started with back garden birdwatching, but always try to learn from the birds themselves. Each area has its own species, every species has different requirements and individual birds will act in different ways. Creating the perfect environment will involve trial and error. But don't become discouraged. The rewards for both bird and birdwatcher are great.

Observing Birds in the Garden

Back garden birdwatching can provide you with a rich insight into the life cycle of birds. Birds generally follow a regular routine. They do the same things—feeding, preening, bathing—at the same time, and for the same length of time, each day. Even if you only attract a few common species, being able to watch them at different times of the day, for as long as you want, is a great way to learn more about them.

Watching birds in the garden will also help you hone your identification skills. In the field, most songbirds move quickly and keep their distance from humans. Difficult to see, they are even harder to name. Feeders and nestboxes bring the birds to the observer, and if the birds feel well protected, they will become confident enough to spend long periods close to buildings and people. This makes it far easier for you to identify them and learn more about them by consulting field guides such as our Habitat Birdfinder (p. 84).

BITE TO EAT *Birds are curious when there's food involved. This female Great Spotted Woodpecker, for example, is trying to find out if there's something edible inside one of the baskets.*

Bird Food Basics

Knowing something about the eating habits of birds in the wild will help you choose the right foods for the species you wish to attract to your garden.

In its natural habitat, each bird occupies a niche in the food chain based on the type of food it eats and the way it obtains this food.

Among seed-eaters, Collared Doves, Chaffinches and Bramblings normally feed on the ground, scavenging seeds that have fallen or been blown there. Greenfinches, Goldfinches, Siskins, Bullfinches and Hawfinches harvest seeds from docks and thistles, and catkins from birch and alder trees. Crossbills work seeds from pine, fir and spruce cones.

HULLED SUNFLOWER SEEDS *Enjoyed by most seed-eaters, such as finches, and some insectivores, like this Great Tit (top).*

The natural diet of warblers, tits, treecreepers, crests, wrens and most woodpeckers is insects and spiders and their eggs. Thrushes like Blackbirds, Redwings, Song Thrushes, Mistle Thrushes and Fieldfares are fruit-eaters that depend on the fruit of native plants like elderberry, raspberry, madrone and toyon, though all of these species also eat flying and terrestrial insects and even molluscs and slugs.

Birds will be attracted to feeding stations because they offer food in concentrated doses and require little expenditure of energy. To attract a range of species, you need to supply a range of the above foods, or their nearest equivalents.

Kitchen scraps will attract birds, but it is questionable as to whether these are good for them, and scraps give you little

BLACK-OIL SUNFLOWER SEEDS *Expensive, but highly nutritious and popular with most birds—the best all-round seed.*

I value my garden more for being full of blackbirds than of cherries, and very frankly give them fruit for their songs.

Joseph Addison (1672–1719), English writer

HIDDEN DANGERS

Be wary of the dangers lurking in some foods you may think suitable for birds.

What may be considered low-level pesticides by farmers using them on human food can turn out to be poisonous for small wildlife. All seeds and fruit left out for birds should thus be purchased from suppliers of pesticide-free produce.

Sticky food like peanut butter can be a danger as it clogs the nostrils of messy eaters like tits. Serve this and other butters sparingly, or mix them into suet cakes (see p. 49).

STRIPED SUNFLOWER SEEDS *The next best thing to the more costly black-oil sunflower seeds.*

control over which species you attract. It is better to select foods that correspond to birds' natural preferences. That means seeds for seed-eaters, suet for insect-eaters and fruit for fruit-eaters.

The foods illustrated here are among the most effective and are available at almost any pet shop or supermarket.

SHELLED PEANUTS *Favoured by Jays, tits, and some woodpeckers.*

THISTLE SEED *The best way to attract Goldfinches and Siskins.*

WHITE PROSO MILLET *A favourite with finches and sparrows.*

MILO (SORGHUM) *Commercial seed mixes with a strong orange colour probably have too high a level of milo. Such mixes are unpalatable to most birds and should therefore be avoided.*

FRUIT *Treats for fruit-eaters include raspberries, grapes and bananas, and dried fruit such as raisins.*

K SCRATCH *racked corn is inexpensive and will be by most sparrows. Pigeons and doves love it.*

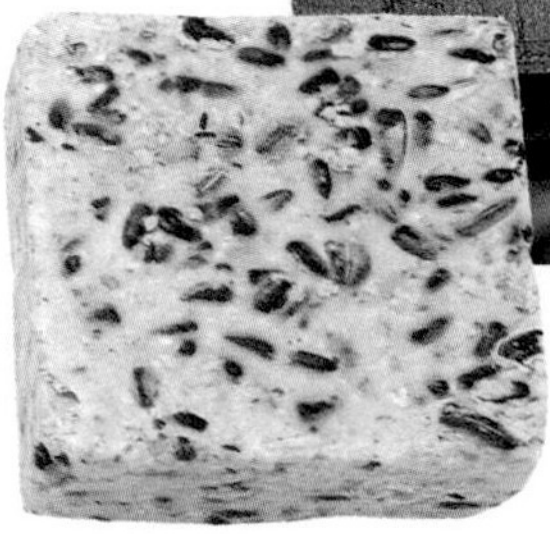

SUET *Ideal food for Starlings, Nuthatches, and woodpeckers. Ready-made suet cakes that fit suet feeders are available. Suet is primarily a cold-weather food. In warm weather, it can melt and transfer to a bird's feathers, causing loss of insulation and flight form, and possibly loss of feathers.*

MAKING SUET CAKES

There are a number of advantages in making your own suet cakes. First of all, it's a fun activity that even children can become involved in (under close supervision, of course!). Secondly, it means you can control exactly what is going into your "cakes" and add extra ingredients to increase the variety of birds that will feed on them. And finally, making your own cakes adds a personal touch to what you offer your feathered friends.

Rendering suet can be done on a stovetop or in a microwave. Suet is available in large chunks from butchers and supermarkets. Usually it is free, but some outlets may charge a small fee.

Cut the suet (5½ pounds [2.5 kg]) block into one-inch (2.5 cm) squares (or ask the butcher) and heat the squares, stirring occasionally, until they have melted. Drain off the liquid into a container. Discard any crispy chunks or leave them out in your garden for nocturnal mammals. Repeat the process until you have 2 quarts (2.5 l) of liquid.

Then stir in a pound (500 g) of chunky peanut butter and a couple of cups of corn-meal or flour. These dry materials will help keep your suet cakes from melting in the sun or during a hot spell. Also add some raisins or other dried fruit. It is better not to add seeds as these will entice Jays and sparrows, which will crowd out the insectivores that the suet is intended for.

You can use the warm suet mixture for log or cone feeders (see p. 51). Otherwise spoon the mixture into pie tins (½–¾" [1–2 cm] deep) and refrigerate. When firm, cut it into chunks that will fit your suet holder, serve some immediately, and freeze the rest for future use.

BIRDFEEDERS

Most birds will come to a handful of food thrown onto the ground, but feeders and bird tables offer the birds protection and comfort, and give the birdwatcher a clearer view of the bird.

Birdfeeders offer a number of advantages over ground feeding. They let you choose where you view the birds, and at the same time keep your garden tidier by holding all the food in one place. They also allow you some degree of control over which species you attract. You can use a variety of foods and feeders if you want to draw in as many birds as possible, or you can select from a wide range of specialised feeders in order to target individual species.

Some species—sparrows, for example—like to feed on the ground, but most prefer feeders because they simulate their natural foraging conditions. For finches, tube feeders are just like the stalks of the thistles they feed on.

Other birds find feeders attractive because they allow them to feed at a safe distance from predators (see p. 52).

The following types of feeders are the best known and most effective. Each is available in a variety of styles.

Platform feeders These simple wooden platforms with raised sides are suitable for all types of food, will hold large quantities and are easy to clean. A canopy to keep the seeds dry and shelter the birds, and a mesh base to allow water to drain away are desirable features. Platforms are good for attracting feeding flocks and larger birds.

Hopper feeders These can be hung up or mounted on a pole. Look for models with even-flow seed distributors that ration seeds—thus avoiding the need for frequent refilling—and a canopy.

Tube feeders The best of these have dividers below each portal so that only one section at a time is emptied and you can fill each compartment with a different type of seed.

Tube feeders are usually hung but can also be pole-mounted. Often they feature a tray under the bottom portal to catch any seeds that are spilled.

Some tube feeders are made specifically to hold thistle seeds.

Bowl feeders These normally consist of a clear plastic bowl and an adjustable dome that will keep out larger, more aggressive birds and squirrels. They are easy to clean and hold a considerable amount of seeds. Most have perches for small birds.

Tube fe

PLATFORM FEEDERS *and bird tables (right) hold large quantities of food and will accommodate larger birds and whole flocks. Tubefeeders (above) will also allow whole flocks, like these Greenfinches, to feed together in one place.*

Hopper feeder

Window feeders These clear plastic seed feeders can be attached to your window by means of suction cups, bringing the birds as close to you as possible. To prevent nervous birds flushing every time there is movement inside your house, install one-way glass or hang see-through curtains.

SUET *can be presented in any number of ways.*

Suet feeders Suet can be presented in a ready-made feeder (a variety of models is available), or in a simple net or mesh bag hung from a line or a tree. Another type of suet feeder can be made by drilling ½ to 1 inch (1 to 2.5 cm) holes in a log or a wooden stump and plugging them with homemade suet, or by dipping a pine cone in warm suet.

PEANUT LOVERS

In squirrel-free areas, unshelled peanuts strung together are often supplied as food for Great, Blue and Coal Tits. Other species, even Jays and Jackdaws, may also succeed in learning how to get a grip on such strings and how to unwrap the peanuts.

Peanuts can also be presented in bags. There are several types of shelled peanut bags. Some are made of red nylon and seem to be especially attractive to Siskins and, naturally, tits. After a while, Jays or woodpeckers may develop the habit of destroying these bags before much of the contents has been eaten. In such situations, a wire peanut feeder is better value.

PEANUT BAGS *will attract many birds, such as this Great Spotted Woodpecker. Unfortunately they will often destroy the bags before other birds have had their share.*

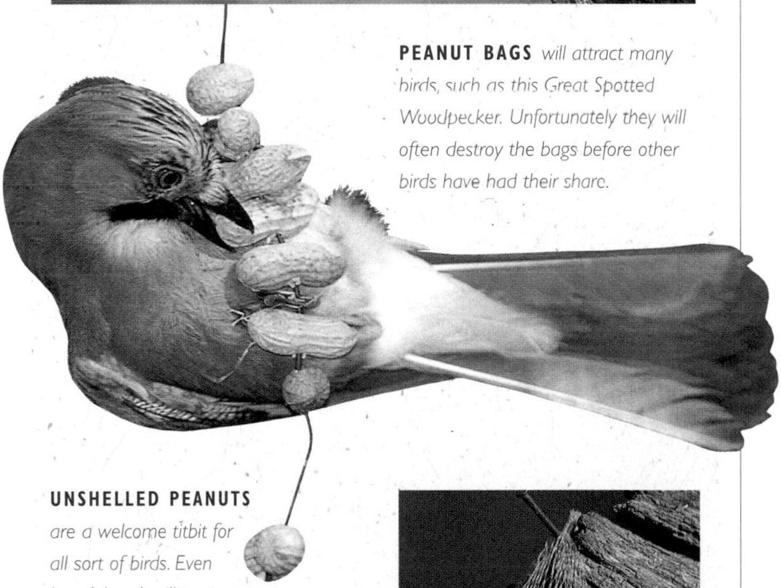

UNSHELLED PEANUTS *are a welcome titbit for all sort of birds. Even Jays (above) will try to get them out of their shells.*

NYLON BAGS *seem to be especially attractive to tits, like this Marsh Tit (right), which is a real acrobat when it comes to eating.*

Taking Care *of* Your Guests

While feeders offer birds a concentrated supply of food, they also expose them to a number of risks. A responsible feeder steward makes sure that these risks are minimised.

Like having children or buying a puppy, establishing a bird feeding station requires commitment. Try to have fresh food available at all times (or at least at regular intervals). Birds can tolerate some change in food availability but try to be consistent, especially in cold weather.

Some birds become partly or wholly dependent on a particular feeding station. If their supply of food suddenly stops or is erratic, it can leave them in a precarious position, particularly in winter when millions of feeder visitors move from northerly nesting grounds to temperate winter locations. If you have to be away, make sure you get someone to take your place as feeder steward.

Make sure that all food is fresh and clean. Check suet occasionally to make sure that it is not rotting. Scrub containers and thoroughly dry those which will contain dry food like seeds or nuts. Wet seeds are not as nutritious and are likely to be rejected.

Placement of Feeders

Of course, you will want to place your feeders where you can see them, but bear in mind that the placement of feeders can also affect the well-being of the birds.

Particularly in cold areas, try to place feeders in sheltered parts of your garden where there is a reasonable amount of sun. This will help the birds stay warm and keep the seeds dry.

Coming to the same spot every day makes birds vulnerable to attacks from predators. Careful placement of your feeders can minimise these risks. Most ground-feeding birds like to be near shrubbery so that they can take cover as soon as they perceive a threat. Low platform feeders and ground-feeding areas should therefore be within reach of cover but not so near that predators can creep up on the birds unawares.

Other seed-eaters that take flight when disturbed, such as Greenfinches, Hawfinches and Siskins, will only feed in comfort from elevated structures that provide them with a good view of their surroundings. Hopper feeders and tube feeders should therefore be at least 3 feet (1 m) off the ground.

Insect-eaters dislike flying through wide open spaces and will feel safer coming to suet feeders on or close to trees.

WINTER FEEDING *Birds often become dependent on winter feeders, bringing responsibilities as well as rewards for their human carers.*

DETERRING PREDATORS

You may need to take certain steps to protect your visitors from a range of predators.

Cats are the most common threat to birds that visit gardens. If a cat enters your refuge, you should chase it away. Squirting cats with water may keep them away, and of course a dog—particularly one that barks a lot—can be effective. You may have to talk to cat-owning neighbours and ask them to keep their pets away.

PREDATORS WITH PURR *Finding effective ways of discouraging feline hunters is a challenging aspect of back garden bird-feeding.*

Birdfeeders provide Sparrowhawks and Kestrels with a concentrated source of prey, as well. While it may be painful to watch a bird of prey take a Chaffinch or House Sparrow, these magnificent raptors are protected by law and need nourishment as much as the local passerines. Remember that a bird of prey has to get its meals somewhere. If it happens to be at your feeder it can be a spectacular sight to witness, and a reminder that birds face a constant struggle for survival.

If, however, you find the prospect of one of your visitors being taken too distressing, try scaring the raptor away by making a loud noise when it appears. If that does not work, consider downgrading the amount of food offered so that the abundance of prey is reduced.

SQUIRRELS

Squirrels are cute and fun to watch, but where they occur even one can terrorise the entire bird population of a back garden. This is especially the case with Grey Squirrels, which are introduced from North America into Britain, Ireland and some parts of northern Italy.

Keeping them away from feeders and nestboxes is an eternal problem as squirrels are remarkably adept at overcoming obstacles and out-witting all attempts to thwart their activities.

In particular, platform and suet feeders that aren't protected are constantly in danger of being ambushed. Squirrel-proof feeders, special squirrel baffles (impassable cones that attach to the pole or post supporting feeders and nestboxes) and unclimbable poles are all available.

One diplomatic solution is to give your squirrel its own feeding station, pos-itioned well away from the birdfeeders, and stocked with favourites like cracked corn, corn-on-the-cob, pine nuts, walnuts and whole peanuts. In exchange, it should keep its distance from the birds. The drawback is that when the squirrel realises what a good deal this is, it is likely to return with its friends and family!

WINDOW KILLS

Estimates suggest that over 100 million songbirds are killed each year as a result of collisions with windows. Resident birds normally know the where-abouts of windows in their territory. Migrants and recently fledged birds run the highest risk of colliding.

Most strikes happen during panic flights caused by the appearance of a predator. The birds are either confused by the reflection or decide that what they see through the window would be a good place to lie low for a while until the danger has passed.

To reduce the chance of birds colliding with your windows, consider placing some prominent decals (including bird-of-prey transfers) on windows that are near feeders, or hang nylon netting in front of them.

Nestboxes

Attracting birds to nest in your garden will help species that are struggling to find suitable nesting sites, and give you an insight into the fascinating events that take place during breeding.

Whether it is as a result of habitat destruction or competition with introduced species, many birds have trouble finding places to nest. One way to help birds in this predicament and entice more species to your garden is to provide nestboxes.

Choosing a Nestbox

Different types of nestboxes are available.

A basic shelf suits birds like Robins that, in the wild, place their mud-based, grass-cupped nests in the fork of a tree or on a stout limb.

An enclosed box is favoured by most species. Preferred dimensions vary (see the table below) but the basic shape is the same. Some birds, such as tits and Nuthatches, like to pause before entering the nest and therefore prefer boxes that have a front porch perch. Others—woodpeckers, for example—dive directly into the nest.

Specially designed tiles to put on roofs for nesting Swifts, or imitation mud cups underneath a high gutter for nesting House Martins, can be useful when placed in the right position. For more information, contact the Royal Society for the Protection of Birds.

Siting a Nestbox

Finding the right spot for a nestbox is to some extent a matter of trial and error. Generally, it should be hung at least 6 feet (2 m) off the ground in a sheltered and secluded part of your garden. Try to find a place that will receive enough sunshine to keep the box dry, but not so much that the birds will suffer from the heat. Give some thought to protecting the box from predators (see p. 53).

Open-shelf boxes should be placed on the trunk of a tree, and will be all the more attractive to birds if overhanging leaves provide extra cover.

To discourage House Sparrows, hang nestboxes away from buildings—their favoured habitat. If species like Starlings or House Sparrows do take up residence and you do not welcome them, you can evict them at the nestbuilding stage without causing them any great harm.

TYPES OF NESTBOXES *Open shelf (above left); enclosed box (above and top left); Swift-tile (below left)*

SPECIES PREFERENCES

Species	Floor	Height of hole above floor	Entrance hole	Remarks
House Sparrow	6" x 6"	7¾"	1¼"	Easily disturbed
Jackdaw	7¾" x 7¾"	15¾"	6"	Place in a high, safe spot
Little Owl	47¼" x 7¾"	11¾"	2¾"	Divide the box to make it dark
Mallard	11¾" x 11¾"	7¾"	6"	Place on a raft or an island
Nuthatch	6" x 6"	7"	1¼"	
Starling	6" x 6"	11¾"	2"	
Rock Dove	7¾" x 7¾"	4"	4"	Place on a board, so that the birds can walk in and out
Great Tit	6" x 4¾"	7"	1¼"	Tits also use bigger boxes
Redstart	6" x 4¾"	7¾"	1¾"	Will also attract Starlings
Woodpeckers	6" x 6"	13¾"	2½"	Place high on a tree trunk

BUILDING A BASIC NESTBOX

Anyone who can saw, turn screws, drill and hammer nails can build a basic nestbox. If the end result is less than perfect, don't worry—the birds won't notice!

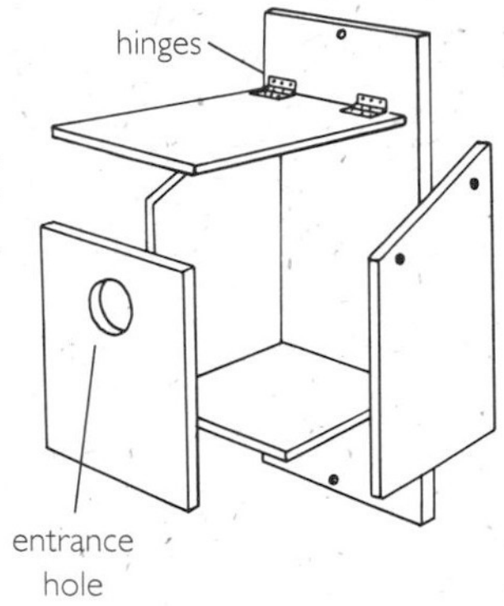

First of all, decide what kind of birds you want to attract and refer to the chart opposite for the appropriate dimensions. Use insect and rot-resistant wood like cedar or pine from ½ to 1 inch (1 to 2.5 cm) thick. Cut the wood to the required lengths. Drill ventilation and drainage holes, and partly screw in the hinges.

Use galvanised box nails to hammer the pieces together as shown in the diagram (left) and screw in the hinge to the top.

Be sure any rough areas are sanded smooth—especially the entrance hole. Do not use chemical finishes or paint. Leave the wood untreated. Weathering and aging will give the birdbox a natural look.

Attach the back-board firmly to your chosen tree or post.

Put nestboxes out only when you know your preferred species will be looking for a nesting site (see The Habitat Birdfinder). Don't be discouraged if your nestbox isn't occupied straight away. Try moving it, and carefully consider the needs of the species you are targeting. If birds do take up residence, do not approach the nest as this may cause the birds to abandon it or may direct predators to the nest.

Leave the nestbox in place until the nesting season is over, as many pairs will try to raise two or even three broods a season, or another species might move in. Once the season is over, however, take the nestbox down and clean it for the next year.

OBSERVING NESTING

The presence of a single bird or a pair near a nestbox may be the first sign of future occupancy. After a few hours or days of inspection of the area and the box, one or both parents may start lining the box with sticks and grasses. Most hole-nesters build a cup-shaped nest in the cavity.

Things will then slow down and you may only see the male bringing food to the incubating female. Once the eggs have hatched, the female will reappear and both parents will make trips to find food for the chicks, increasing in frequency as the chicks grow.

Often, after entering the box with food, the adult will leave with a white ball in its beak. This is a faecal sac containing nestling faeces. To keep the nest clean, clear of parasites, and free from smells that may attract predators, the adult will dispose of the sac well away from the nest.

After fledging, some family groups will remain in the garden, so you can observe parent birds caring for their young.

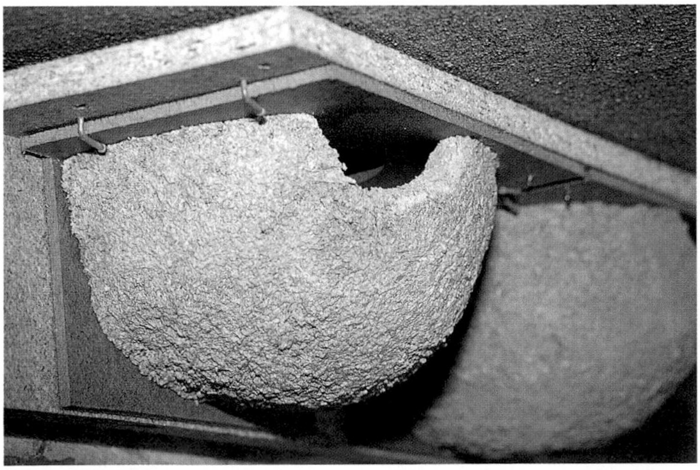

HOUSE MARTINS *are attracted to artificial nest sites resembling their mud nests. They may make their own nest beside it, or move into the artificial cup.*

Nestboxes (above right) can help Pied Flycatchers, Great Tits, and other cavity breeders to nest in areas where old trees and natural cavities are absent.

PLANNING *a* GARDEN *for* BIRDS

Creating a haven for birds can entail more than providing feeders and nestboxes. A little extra effort can turn your garden into an attractive wildlife habitat.

Exactly how you plan your birdwatching garden will, of course, depend on what kind of garden you have and your geographical location. There are, however, three elements that are crucial in attracting birds: cover, in the form of trees and shrubs; food, in the form of native plants; and water for the birds to drink and bathe in.

COVER

Dense vegetation will attract birds as it is likely to provide shelter, nesting sites, and protection from predators. Coniferous trees and denser deciduous species will attract many species.

Cover should include both live and dead vegetation. Planting a dead tree or hanging up some attractive leafless branch can add stark beauty to the garden and provide perches for birds.

In most areas, trees will be the main features in a garden, but remember that many seed-eating birds live near or on the ground and will therefore prefer undergrowth, bushes and flowers.

PLANTS AS FOOD

Food in the form of native plants should be the mainstay of a bird's diet, and, as far as possible, the food you place in feeders should only supplement natural feeding.

Most coniferous trees are attractive to insects and these, in turn, provide food for many birds. Fruit-bearing trees and berry-bearing shrubs provide food for Blackcaps, Blackbirds, Redwings and Waxwings.

Use only native plants in your garden. Native deciduous trees like maples, alders, some oaks and beeches provide much better general feeding for birds than do exotics. Birds tend to avoid non-native species such as acacias because they fail to attract native insects.

The chickadee and the nuthatch are more inspiring society than statesmen and philosophers.

A Winter Walk,
HENRY DAVID THOREAU (1817–62),
American writer and naturalist

PLANTING FOR BIRDS

Plant	*Provides*	*Favoured by*
Shrubs and Vines		
Elderberry (*Sambucus*)	Fruit, insects, shelter	Warblers, thrushes, Starling
Honeysuckle (*Lonicera*)	Fruit; flowers, insects	Warblers, wrens, thrushes
Blackberry/raspberry (*Rubus*)	Fruit, dense cover, insects	Warblers, wrens, thrushes, buntings
Ivy (*Hedera*)	Fruit, dense cover, insects	Woodpigeon, thrushes, Blackcap
Hawthorn (*Crataegus*)	Fruit, cover, insects	Warblers, thrushes
Trees		
Oak (*Quercus*)*	Acorns, insects, cover	Woodpigeon, Jay, tits, Nuthatch, woodpeckers
Pine (*Pinus*)*	Nuts, insects, cover	Crossbills, Goldcrest, treecreepers, woodpeckers
Plum/cherry (*Prunus*)*	Fruit, insects	Warblers, thrushes, tits, Bullfinch, Hawfinch
Holly (*Ilex*)	Fruit, dense cover	Thrushes
Yew (*Taxus*)	Fruit, dense cover	Thrushes, crests

* Make sure you use the right species for your area.

Eucalyptus trees can even be dangerous, as native birds have not evolved the subtle adaptations required to forage from this source. Many short-beaked nectar feeders, such as the occasional *Phylloscopus* and *Sylvia* warblers, have trouble removing the pitch of eucalypts from their bills and may even suffocate as a result.

Try to avoid using pesticides. These may have little effect on humans, but they can be extremely harmful to birds.

Birdbaths and Ponds

Water is an important factor in attracting birds to your garden. On larger properties, a pond may attract ducks, geese, herons and even some migrating waders in late summer and autumn.

In more restricted areas, a small pond with a recirculating stream will bring migrant warblers, as well as the resident Jays, Robins, thrushes and finches to bathe and drink. Overhanging branches and thick cover nearby will keep them coming back.

Birdbaths are an attractive addition to almost any back garden. Those which recirculate dripping water are much more appealing to birds than those with still water.

Many commercial ponds, pond and stream liners, recirculating pumps, pond and bath heaters and even waterfalls are available, but it can be much more fun to design and build your own.

A GARDEN HAVEN *for birds involves water, food, shelter, and safety from predators. A mixture of carefully chosen ornamental shrubs can fill several of these roles.*

MAKING A BIRDBATH

A simple birdbath can be made out of almost anything that is non-toxic and can hold shallow water. To accommodate several birds at one time, a surface diameter of at least 20 inches (50 cm) is best. Nearly any dustbin lid will do, and the dark-coloured plastic ones are best.

Place the lid on the ground or on a solid foundation above ground level. To avoid puncturing it with nails, use rocks or branches to weigh the lid down. If placed in the water, these objects will be used as perches by the birds.

Since birds find moving water particularly attractive, something like a dripping garden hose supported above the edge of the bath on a forked stake will be very effective.

Overflow can easily be channelled so that it irrigates nearby plants. You can even create a waterfall effect by placing another lid at a lower level below the first and increasing the water supply. However, it may then be necessary to recycle the water.

MAIN ATTRACTIONS *A homemade birdbath like this one (above) will be almost irresistible to small birds. Feeders (left) are all the more attractive if positioned close to cover.*

The more people who become interested in the natural world and committed to it, the greater the chance that wild nature will continue to exist.

Travel Diaries of a Naturalist,
SIR PETER SCOTT (1909–1989), English artist and naturalist

Chapter Three
Going Birdwatching

PREPARATIONS

Good preparation and some thorough groundwork will help you make the most of your birdwatching trips.

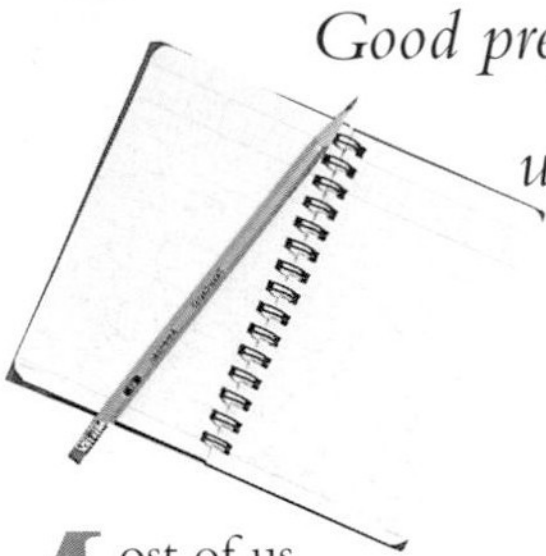

Most of us are birdwatchers of a kind, in that we are bound to notice the birds around us from time to time. It is unusual to find a person who cannot tell the difference between a pelican and a hawk, for instance, or who has trouble identifying a sparrow. Really, we are all just a step away from the great enjoyment bird-watching can bring.

And what an array of birds there is to become acquainted with! In Europe there are two species of pelicans, eight "flocking" species of wild geese, more than thirteen species of owls, ten of wood-peckers and ten of tits.

In total, more than 900 species of bird have been recorded north of the Sahara. This is a daunting number for a beginning birdwatcher.

But, of course, many species have only small populations, and are found in remote places, so you are hardly likely to encounter more than a small proportion of all European species in a single outing. On the other hand—and this is one of the joys of birdwatching—you never know what you are going to find. In northern Scandinavia in winter you may struggle to see 10 species in an entire day, while a summer visit to the same spot may yield over 100. The key to getting the most from any outing is to be well prepared.

FIRST STEPS

It's best to begin slowly. Start by browsing through The Habitat Birdfinder (p. 86) at home to become familiar with the various groups and species you are likely to come across. Don't be discouraged by the great diversity. Think about the kind of environment you live in, select a corresponding habitat in The Habitat Birdfinder, and read the entries that relate to the birds you are most likely to see.

FIELD GUIDES *The prime purpose of a field guide (left) is to help you through the vital first step in birdwatching: to identify your bird.*

A BIRDWATCHER'S JACKET *(above) is useful item of clothing. Its many pockets are ideal for field guides and other birdwatching paraphernalia, such as a notebook, pen, maps and so on (top).*

The next step is to study an area in your neighbourhood, such as a park, using the information in this chapter to help you develop your identification skills. Parks with lakes are particularly rewarding as most waterbirds are large, easily observed and distinctively marked—three desirable attributes. You are also likely to find exotic visitors in such parks, which might be a little confusing, but don't be put off.

Once you have mastered some basic skills you will be ready to go further afield. Be thorough, but don't get frustrated when birds disappear before you have clinched their ID! Another new bird will be nearby.

O to mount again where

erst I haunted;

Where the old red hills

are bird-enchanted...

ROBERT LOUIS STEVENSON (1850–94), Scottish novelist and poet

FIELD GUIDES

The Habitat Birdfinder introduces you to over 200 of the most commonly encountered European species and is a great place to start your birdwatching. Fairly soon, however, you are likely to want to acquire a complete field guide to European birds. After binoculars, a good field guide will be your most important birdwatching tool. A wide range is available (see p. 274).

BIRDWATCHING GEAR *As in any other out-door activity, staying warm and comfortable is an important consideration. A wide range of clothing and accessories is readily available for birdwatching, from rain-proof jackets, back-packs and sturdy boots (far right) to field bags and carry-pouches (right) for your field guide.*

At first the organisation of a field guide may seem odd, as the birds will not be presented in any obviously logical order, such as alphabetically or large-to-small. This is because birds (and other vertebrate animals) are classified by scientists in taxonomic order (see p. 20).

Out in the field you will become aware of the usefulness of this in at least one respect: physically similar birds are grouped together, and these, of course, are the ones that you are most likely to confuse.

A STARTING POINT *A good place to start birdwatching is at a local pond or lake, as waterbirds are often fairly easy to identify. However, particularly if you are in a park, watch out for exotic species that may mislead you.*

Once you identify a bird and know its name, you will find that more information is available in your guide.

GETTING EQUIPPED

A particularly essential piece of equipment for a birdwatcher is a good pair of binoculars (see p. 62). Otherwise, use the clothing and provisions that you would take on any hike or field trip.

Bear in mind, however, that birdwatching may involve sitting or standing in one spot for long periods. Warm clothing will therefore be important in colder areas. If it's hot, be wary of the sun's rays: brimmed hats and sunscreen will protect you but if you are at sea, remember that the sun may be twice as intense as it is on land.

If you are likely to be out in the rain, remember to take something along to dry the lenses of your binoculars, spotting scope or spectacles. Even a baby's nappy can be extremely effective—after all, it was invented to soak up moisture. Avoid rainwear that squeaks or "swishes", as it will alert the birds to your presence.

CHOOSING BINOCULARS

As your most important piece of birdwatching equipment, binoculars should be chosen with a good deal of care.

SIZE AND WEIGHT *are important considerations in choosing binoculars, but the pair you buy must also deliver a bright, crisp image at both short and long ranges.*

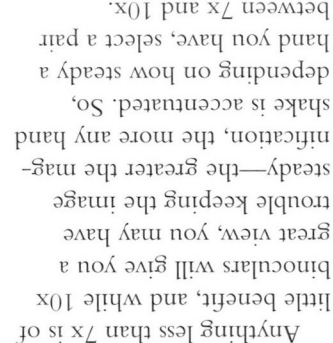

Many people have an old pair of binoculars at home, but if they have been lying around for some time they may well have been knocked out of alignment. Unless they are particularly valuable, you may be better off investing in a new pair rather than paying for expensive repairs.

When buying binoculars, the following features should be considered carefully.

MAGNIFICATION

All binoculars feature a set of numbers such as 7x40. The first number denotes the power of the binoculars: a 7x pair of binoculars will make a bird look seven times larger than it appears to the naked eye; a 10x pair will make the bird look 10 times larger, and so on.

Anything less than 7x is of little benefit, and while 10x binoculars will give you a great view, you may have trouble keeping the image steady—the greater the magnification, the more any hand shake is accentuated. So, depending on how steady a hand you have, select a pair between 7x and 10x.

BRIGHTNESS AND WEIGHT

The second number that appears on your binoculars—40 in the above example—denotes the diameter of the objective (front) lenses. The larger these are, the more light will enter the binoculars and the brighter the image will be. However, the larger the objective lenses are, the heavier the binoculars will be.

CONSTRUCTION AND WEIGHT

There are two types of binoculars—porro prisms and roof prisms (see below)—and their designs have a bearing on their weight and price.

Until the 1980s, the best binoculars were porro prisms. Porro designs are still popular and, in general, dominate the lower end of the price range (£45 to £450). Many provide bright, clear viewing and, in some cases, good close focus.

Recently, however, new technology has allowed manufacturers to create roof prisms that provide the same power and clarity in a more compact design. Roof prisms are therefore lighter but tend to be more expensive.

DURABILITY

Porro designs tend to be frailer than roof prisms. Even with average usage, some part

IN CLOSE-UP *A 7x pair of binoculars will magnify the image you see seven times (top inset). A 10x pair will give you a larger image (bottom inset), but at this magnification you may have trouble keeping the image steady.*

of the frame may eventually break or a prism may slip out of alignment.

Many binoculars now feature rubber armouring for protection. However, there is a tendency for some rubber eyecups to crack and break, and for bubbles to form in armoured panels.

Close Focus

A good pair of birdwatching binoculars should focus on objects that are as close as 14 feet (4.2 m), and the closer they can focus, the better. Some roof prism models, designed for birdwatching, will focus to 12 feet (3.7 m), but some binoculars have a minimum viewing distance of 23 feet (7 m) or more, which is totally impractical.

Price

There are good, robust binoculars available at the lower end of the price range, but, as with most equipment of this kind, you get what you pay for and top-quality binoculars are a joy to use. On the other hand, as binoculars are easily damaged, you should buy only what you can afford to replace.

Comfort

Before buying binoculars, talk to someone who owns the model you have in mind, or try to find a salesperson who is a binocular specialist and ask them for guidance.

In the shop, hang the binoculars around your neck to check their weight: if they feel heavy, they'll feel a good deal heavier at the end of a day in the field. Look through them and roll the focus wheel to be sure all parts operate smoothly. Check how well they focus on objects close by. How well do the eyepieces fit your eyes? If you wear glasses, can you use them with your glasses? Comfort and ease of use are as important as power. Last but not least, check what kind of warranty the manufacturer will provide.

Maintenance

Binoculars must be properly aligned and kept clean. Use a soft cloth to wipe oily dust and lunch crumbs from the lenses. Q-tips are good for small, hard-to-reach crannies.

USING BINOCULARS

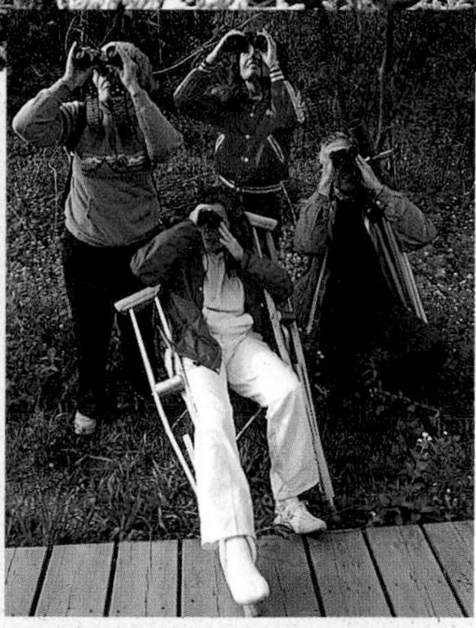

When aiming binoculars, it is important to find an object (or at least a specific area) first with the naked eye and to keep watching it while bringing the binoculars up to the appropriate line of vision. Practise aligning your binoculars to what you are looking at. You will take longer to find what you want if you search the landscape aimlessly.

By the way, you may not have realised that if you turn your binoculars around, they can function as a microscope for making monsters out of ladybirds or examining the details of flowers.

ROOF PRISMS

PORRO PRISMS

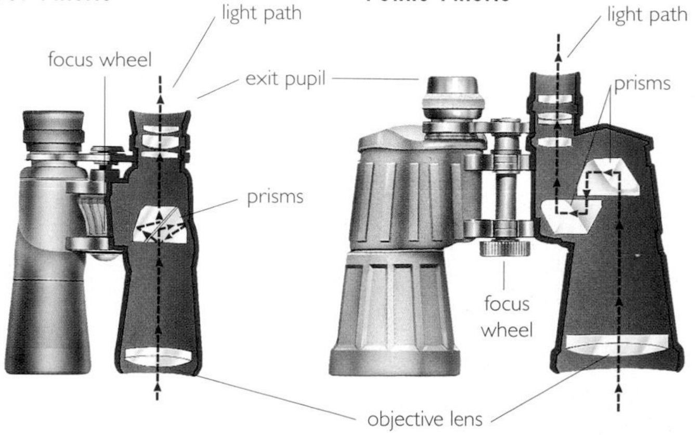

ROOF AND PORRO PRISM *binoculars both use prisms to fold the light path passing through them. However, the roof prism design (far left) achieves a slimmer style and reduced weight by means of a more complex prism configuration than that found in the somewhat simpler (and consequently less expensive) porro prism design (near left).*

CHOOSING *a* SPOTTING SCOPE

If you plan to do a good deal of long-range viewing in open areas, such as in grasslands or at the seashore, you may find it worthwhile to invest in a telescope.

Having used binoculars in the field for a while, you may decide you would like to buy a telescope, or spotting scope. This will complement your binoculars, rather than replace them, as only in certain environments and for particular activities will a spotting scope prove more effective.

In particular, spotting scopes are excellent for identifying distant, perched raptors or for scanning flocks of waders. They are also useful for close scrutiny of nesting activity and birds at feeders. They are less effective for observing small, fast-moving forest birds.

A wide range of brands and models of spotting scopes is available and, as a general rule, you get what you pay for—the more expensive ones give brighter, sharper images and their optics and construction are more rugged. Given the expense, it's a good idea to talk to other birdwatchers about the spotting scopes they like to use and even try looking through them.

After settling on a make and model, you still need to consider configuration and eyepiece power.

THE RIGHT FIT *You may find that scopes with offset eyepieces (below) are more comfortable to use as you don't have to stoop so low to see through them. On the other hand, straight scopes (below left) are generally easier to aim.*

CONFIGURATION

Spotting scopes are available in two forms: either with an eyepiece aligned with the barrel, or one that is offset by 45 degrees.

You may find straight scopes easier to aim, but, on the other hand, offset scopes are often more

TRIPODS

Choosing a tripod is a matter of finding just the right compromise between stability and weight. The heavier your tripod is, the more stable it will be, but, on the other hand, the heavier it is, the less convenient it will be to take on birdwatching outings. There are also a number of other features that may have a bearing on your decision.

Probably the most important single element is the head. Tripods are mostly made for cameras and have all sorts of knobs and screws for adjusting the head to various positions. Birdwatchers need rapid-action controls, and the fewer there are the better. A single handle with a grip-tightener for locking, and vertical and horizontal lock screws are all you need. The handle should be on the opposite side of the head from the eye you normally look through.

The fixtures at the junction of each telescoping section of the legs of your tripod must be sturdy. Screw locks are usually stronger and last longer than flip-locks, but flip-locks allow quick set-up and collapse. Tubular legs are normally steadier than square ones and you may appreciate the difference when birdwatching on windy days.

SMALL FRY *Setting the tripod low is not merely a convenience but it also makes the spotting scope more stable, so the view will be improved.*

WELL EQUIPPED *With spotting scopes, birdwatchers can deal with even the most challenging of identification problems, such as those which arise with some migratory waders (left).*

comfortable to use as you may not have to stoop so low to look through them. Try the different types out and think about how you will be using your scope. Weigh up carefully the pros and cons of the two types before you buy.

Eyepiece Power

The most common magnifications are: 15x; 22x wide angle; 30x; 40x; and 20x to 60x zoom.

A spotting scope at lowest power (15x) is hardly worth the expense if you are proficient with 10x binoculars. A 40x eyepiece may give a nice view of a raptor ¼ mile (300 m) away, for instance, but will not be particularly effective for scanning shorebird flocks.

A zoom lens may seem a good compromise, and there are many worthwhile models available, but some cheaper zoom eyepieces are optically incorrect, giving fuzzy images, and most of them lose their light-gathering ability quickly as the power increases.

All things considered, the best all-round magnification is in the region of 25x to 30x.

Using your Spotting Scope

Spotting scopes have a smaller field of view than binoculars and are, therefore, even more difficult to master. Once you have your scope, it's a good idea to practise using it at home before you go on a birdwatching trip.

Aim at a stationary object like a telephone pole or your neighbour's fuchsia, trying to locate the object and focus on it as quickly as you can.

ON THE ROAD *Car window clamps for spotting scopes (above) facilitate birdwatching on the move, allowing you to stop and take a close look at birds such as this Little Bittern (right). If you don't have a clamp, a plump beanbag flopped over the open window will do much the same job.*

I find it hard to see anything about a bird that it does not want seen. It demands my full attention.

Annie Dillard (b. 1945),
American poet and essayist

Going Afield

An effective birdwatcher is one who has a good idea of when and where to go looking, and who causes the birds a minimum of disturbance.

From the beginner's viewpoint in particular, birds can seem very difficult to even get close to. However, providing you go looking for them within their range and at the right time of year, and keep in mind the following information, you will find that a large number of birds can be located with just a little careful planning.

Birds are always more conspicuous first thing in the morning, for then they are at their most active, and are generally in full song, often singing from prominent perches. This is particularly the case in spring, when most male (and some female) landbirds sing from perches or perform showy displays.

In winter, swimming birds gather together on oceans, bays, lakes and rivers where various species may be studied side-by-side. During spring and autumn migration, waders, birds of prey, seabirds and many small songbirds become gregarious and may be observed in single-species and mixed flocks.

GONE BIRDWATCHING *The father of the modern outdoor movement, John Muir (right), pictured on a field trip with Theodo Roosevelt, another keen birdwatcher.*

Fields, meadows and particularly forests may seem birdless until you find a flock. To locate flocks, scan open ground near brushy areas or weedy fields, or listen for the calls of the birds—as they forage they remain in constant vocal communication.

Habitats

The best first step to take in a search for a particular bird is to find out what kind of habitat and niche it favours (see pp. 30 and 86). Within habitats, often the best places to look for birds are what could be termed "boundary areas", such as forest edges, the fringes of meadows, riverside vegetation and reed beds on lakes, as many species prefer to remain constantly within reach of cover.

Approaching Birds

While some birds may be approached openly, many are timid and will flee at the first hint of danger. To many, such a hint is the sense of some-

BIRDWATCHING ETHICS

It is important that all birdwatchers are aware of their responsibilities in relation to birds and to the natural environment in general. Guidelines of good birdwatching behaviour such as those embodied in the Birdwatchers' Code of Conduct should be followed by birdwatchers all over the world.

- Birdwatchers must always act in ways that do not endanger the welfare of birds or other wildlife.
- Observe and photograph birds without knowingly disturbing them in any significant way.
- Avoid chasing or repeatedly flushing birds.
- Only sparingly use recordings and similar methods of attracting birds and do not use these methods in heavily birded areas.
- Keep an appropriate distance from nests and nesting colonies so as not to disturb them or expose them to danger.
- Refrain from handling birds or eggs unless engaged in recognised research activities.

WATCHING *treetop birds in level woodl (left) is often uncomfortable. Look for a slope or similar vantage point from which watch with greater comfort. Always keep your distance from nests or hatchlings like these Montagu's Harriers (above left).*

FIELD TACTICS *An experienced birdwatcher will look first along the edges of habitats, where visibility is least obstructed and the greatest variety of birds is to be found. In grasslands (above left), this tactic may reveal birds such as the Great Grey Shrike (above), while the edges of wetlands (left) are the haunt of birds like the Grey Heron (below left).*

Your first observations of birds and their behaviour can be done by simply learning to drift gently through a wood: a naturalist in a hurry never learns anything of value.

GERALD DURRELL (b. 1925–1995)
English naturalist and writer

thing unusual happening in their environment. A sudden movement, an unfamiliar sound, a flash of light or the shape of a predator (you) outlined against the sky can all alarm the birds and result in their departure.

When arriving at a birdwatching spot by car, turn off the engine at once. If possible, remain in the car. Birds are much less fearful of a car that does not move than they are of people running or cycling around and aiming things at them. If you get out, try not to slam the doors.

In a new habitat, look around and plan your approach before advancing. Avoid walking into the sun as this will make it hard for you to see clearly. Move slowly and avoid talking loudly or snapping twigs. Look into a clearing before you step into it. Standing still in one spot for some time is often the most effective tactic, particularly in woodlands.

Try to avoid breaking the horizon line with the outline of your body. Earth-toned clothes may camouflage you to some extent. Use cover wherever possible: hide behind vegetation, a rock or even a car. Remember, however, that the bird's observation skills are far better than yours and it will almost always know you are there. The key is to move around in a way that will not alarm it. If you can assure the bird that you pose no threat, it will usually tolerate your presence.

Once you have obtained a good view, back off and leave quietly. Birds have a hard enough time finding places to rest and forage in peace without birdwatchers putting them under more pressure.

HUNTERS

Be very careful during the hunting season as, on rare occasions, people have been wounded by hunters mistaking them for quarry. If you do hear hunters, try to head away from them. If they are already close to you, shout to them to warn them of your presence. Do not try to hide—if you do, you are far more likely to be shot at.

IDENTIFYING BIRDS: *the* BASICS

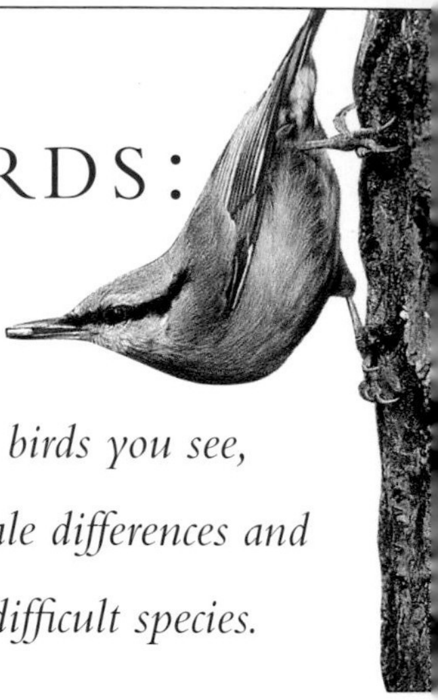

By learning to focus on particular features of the birds you see, you will soon learn to recognise the subtle but tell-tale differences and become proficient in identifying all but the most difficult species.

Frequently, novice birdwatchers are dismayed by the huge number of species listed in field guides. But of the total species list of any given locality, less than half the species of regularly occurring birds are likely to be present at any given time.

FAMILY TRAITS *Most people are able to recognise an owl and a duck (above) when they see them. Once you have established which family a bird belongs to, you are well on your way to making a positive identification.*

When you are trying to identify a bird, always start by considering what you see in front of you. Don't reach immediately for your guide to see what you ought to be seeing or whether the bird looks like any others in your book. Describe the bird to yourself and try to draw on information you already have in your head. Consider the following questions.

FAMILY TRAITS

What family or group does the bird belong to?
Most families of birds share certain physical characteristics, and if you can be sure what group a bird belongs to you are well on your way to making a positive identification. Familiarising yourself with the information on pp. 88–93 will assist you greatly in this respect.

What size is the bird?
The size of a lone bird may be hard to deduce, but try matching it to one you know. Is it bigger or smaller than a Robin? Is it similar to the size of a crow? Size comparisons are, of course, easiest when the mystery bird is with something you know.

BEHAVIOUR

What is the bird doing?
Because different groups of birds demonstrate different behaviour, what a bird is doing may help to identify it. Is it pecking at the ground, leaf-gleaning in a tree or making short flights to and from an exposed perch? Is it swimming and surface diving? Probing mud at the edge of a pond, or flying in a V-formation?

BEHAVIOUR *Only Nuthatches (above) move down tree trunks head first, a behaviour so distinctive that the family can be identified by this feature alone.*

Is the bird alone or in a group?
During autumn and winter, most small sandpipers join huge flocks of their own and similar species. Insect-eaters such as tits, Goldcrests, treecreepers and Nuthatches, come together to increase foraging efficiency and predator avoidance. Other birds are solitary, except during the breeding season.

How much it enhances the richness of the forest to see in it some beautiful bird which you never detected before!

HENRY DAVID THOREAU (1817–62), American naturalist and writer

Physical Features

What distinguishing features does the bird have?

To really pin down a species you have to learn to recognise its field marks.

Field marks are those characteristics of a species that, taken together, distinguish that bird from others. Usually they are plumage features. Pay particular attention to the following parts of the bird:

- eyebrow (supercilium)
- rump
- outer tail feathers
- wingbars

Make sure you are familiar with the names used for the different parts of a bird's body and the tracts of feathers that make up its plumage (see p. 24). In The Habitat Birdfinder, the identifying marks are highlighted in the Field Notes boxes. Always bear in mind that patterns are more significant than colours.

Time and Place

Where are you and what time of year is it? What kind of habitat are you in?

Always make a note of where you are, what time of year and day it is and what kind of habitat the bird is in. It is important that you have noted these details as they may help you confirm a sighting. Many birds are common only within a particular range at particular times of year and favour a specific habitat. Most field guides indicate the distribution of species and their habitat preferences.

ROGER TORY PETERSON *Author of the first compact field guides, Roger Tory Peterson (right) has probably done more to introduce people to birdwatching than any other single person.*

EYE MARKINGS *The pattern of the eyebrow (supercilium) or eye-ring often distinguishes a species, as with the Ortolan Bunting (left), the Northern Wheatear (centre), and the Aquatic Warbler (right).*

WINGBARS *are often important field marks. For example, they help to distinguish this Yellow-browed Warbler (left) from the Willow Warbler (right).*

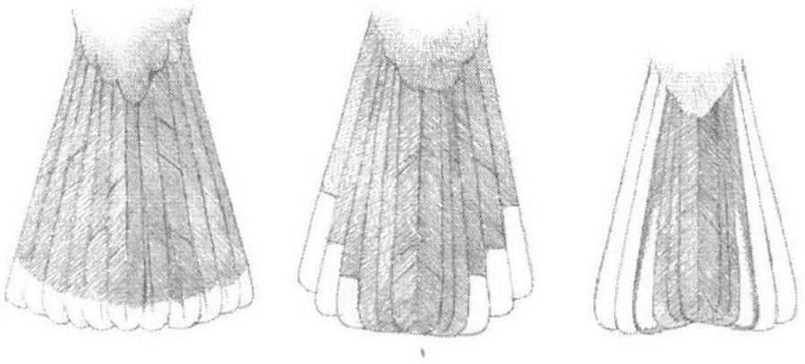

OUTER TAIL FEATHERS *are field marks in many species. Frequently the distinguishing mark is a lighter tip or sides.*

ROGER TORY PETERSON

The first compact, mass-market field guides were written and illustrated by Roger Tory Peterson, and were first published in 1934. These guides introduced the innovative and influential system of "field marks".

A bird's field marks are those physical features that distinguish it from other species. In Peterson's guides, these marks are highlighted both in the text and in the accompanying illustrations.

Peterson's system was so successful that its principles were adopted during the Second World War to assist allied troops in identifying aircraft. Almost all contemporary field guides use field marks to assist in identification.

Identifying Birds: Examples

The following six examples—one from each of the six habitats in The Habitat Birdfinder—show how to put the advice on the previous pages into practice.

Blackbird

An entirely black bird hops about on the lawn, stopping regularly to peer or listen. It flies up and lands on a branch. There are several black species in the urban environment, but crows and Jackdaws are much bigger. Perhaps we should consider the Starling. However, that bird walks step by step, usually fast and hastily and often in flocks. When we watch more carefully, not only does a yellow bill becomes obvious, but also a yellow ring around the eye, which is characteristic of male Blackbirds. Besides, while Starlings have yellow bills, they should also have a metallic gloss in their plumage and, in winter, much white spotting. When we see a male Blackbird, the dark-brown female will often be around as well.

Blackcap

During a walk through woodland, we hear a melodious, fluty song, wavering at first, but then loud and articulated. With luck, we may glimpse a slim, mouse-grey bird. Immediately, we try to see some obvious features and, yes, there is a jet-black cap. What pale greyish, black-capped forest birds can we choose from? There are two look-alike tit species, Marsh and Willow Tit, with similar grey colouring ánd a black cap. However, both have a distinctly thickset, rounder appearance, much white underneath the black cap, and no melodious fluting song. There is just one possibility: our bird is a male Blackcap. In spring, its brown-capped female may be nearby. In winter, some remain to feed on fruit in gardens.

Golden Plover

A flock of well-camouflaged, brownish, long-legged, dove-sized birds stands in the middle of an arable field. The birds suddenly run forward a short distance and then stop abruptly. This action is characteristic of plovers. The upperparts are densely spotted, pale golden-yellow and dark brown or black, while the underside may show black. The Golden Plover is the only plover with these features, and, in flight, white "armpits". The very similar, but bigger, Grey Plover prefers mudflats, lacks yellowish colours and has black armpits. Two smaller, very rare species of golden plover from Asia and America have grey armpits.

Shoveler

As we pass a marshy pond in the countryside, we note a group of birds swimming and splashing in the water. About half of the group is brown and mottled. The shape of their bills instantly identifies them as ducks of some kind. (All other birds found on open water have pointed bills.) This should be easy! The birds we are observing are either up-ending or "dabbling". As they tip forward, we can see that they are kicking at the surface to keep themselves submerged. This is significant, as ducks can generally be divided into two groups—those that dabble and those that dive. Among the dabblers, the males are more distinct than the females for much of the year. The brown birds must therefore be females. The rest have green heads, white breasts, chestnut flanks and pale eyes. They all have an exceptionally large bill with a broad tip, making them rather front-heavy. The combination of dabbling behaviour, colour and, especially, the odd bill confirms beyond doubt that these are Shovelers.

Herring Gull

On a walk along the seashore on a pleasant winter afternoon, we notice several crow-sized birds squabbling over scraps of fish thrown to them by fishermen on the pier. The birds have a white head and body and a yellow bill. The seashore environment, the plumage features, the scavenging behaviour of the birds and their tolerance of humans all tell us that these are gulls.

Immature gulls are tricky to identify (see p. 232), but adults are more straightforward. The pale grey back and white head of these birds indicate that they are adults. The next things to check when looking at gulls are the bill, the legs and the wingtips. Looking through our binoculars, we see that these gulls have a red spot on their yellow bills, pink legs and white-spotted black wingtips. These features identify the birds as Herring Gulls.

Alpine Accentor

Near the rocky summits of the highest mountains in Central Europe, where no tall vegetation can grow, our attention may be drawn by a double, rolling sound like a low-pitched penny whistle. If we are lucky, we may see the bird approaching with an undulating flight. It is larger than a House Sparrow or Chaffinch, but this is not so obvious when direct comparison is impossible. When we look more carefully, we see an outsized Dunnock with some yellow on the bill, a bit of brownish red on the flanks and a row of neat pale or white dots on the folded wing. The Alpine Accentor is the only bird in this environment fitting this description. In summer, it inhabits the highest mountain slopes. In winter, it is one of the few birds remaining near chalets or other buildings in the high mountains.

BIRDWATCHING *by* EAR

If you are able to learn the vocalisations of the birds in your area, you will be able to identify many more of them than if you were relying on your eyes alone.

Birdwatching by ear is a learned discipline. Because each bird species has its own range of vocalisations and because birds frequently vocalise in areas of thick vegetation, a person who can identify each voice will be able to record many more birds in a given area than one birdwatching only by sight.

During spring, each territorial male sings persistently from several perches, seldom leaving his area. At such times, an experienced birdwatcher can estimate the number of territories in an area simply by counting singers.

LEARNING

People gifted with a musical memory and perfect pitch can remember a bird's song or call after hearing it only once. The rest of us have to work at it! Listening to tapes may be helpful—many commercial cassettes are now available—but listen to only a few songs at a time. If you try to learn too many in a session, they tend to sound very much the same.

The best method for learning bird sounds is to go where the birds are and to watch them vocalise. You will probably find that you are able to retain the visual and audible connection—at least for a while.

REMEMBERING

The easiest way to remember a song or call is to compare it with one you already know. For example: "This song sounds like a Robin's but is more abrupt and rolls along through shorter phrases," or "This call note is like the Song Thrush's but is louder and more metallic."

Occasionally, when you hear an unfamiliar bird, you may find it useful to record it in the field for later identification at home, by comparing it with tapes of known species.

Some field guides contain sonograms—graphs representing bird calls—(see p. 37), which some people find very helpful.

It is truly wonderful how love-telling the small voices of these birds are, and how far they reach through the woods into one another's hearts and into ours.

JOHN MUIR (1838–1914), Scottish-born American naturalist and writer

PARABOLIC REFLECTORS *are often used in the field to obtain high-quality recordings (above). A Bluethroat in full song (top).*

TED PARKER

Far-and-away the world's expert on the birdlife of South America, the late Ted Parker was able to identify over 3,000 species of bird by ear.

Many tropical birds live in thick vegetation (either beneath ground cover or within the dense canopy of tall forest) and are very hard to see, so visual censusing simply does not work. Identifying the voices of birds in the jungle is the only way to know what's there.

Ted could be dropped into a rainforest containing hundreds of birds and emerge an hour or two later with a thorough analysis of the avifauna.

A chief scientist for Conservation International, Ted was working on a program assessing the faunal and floral qualities of tropical rainforests when, in August 1993, the plane that had been leased for aerial surveys hit a fog-veiled mountain, killing him and a number of other team members. With his death, a large part of our knowledge of South American birds was lost.

RECORDING BIRDS

As recently as 20 years ago, to record a bird song or call one needed an umbrella-sized cone called a parabolic reflector, a microphone and a cumbersome reel-to-reel recorder. Nowadays, of course, small, lightweight directional microphones and digital recorders do the same job far more effectively.

For best results when recording bird sounds, try to find a bird that is vocalising where there are no other sounds. Running water, other birds, wind, aeroplanes, whispering humans and rustling leaves will all cause interference. Indeed, it's only when you try to record a bird singing that you fully appreciate just what a noisy world we live in!

It is a good idea to find a quiet spot in advance and then, on recording day, have your equipment set up and ready to go before dawn.

ATTRACTING BIRDS WITH SOUNDS

Many birdwatchers play tapes of bird calls in the field in order to attract birds, and this is often very effective. However, as birds will assume that the recording is the call of a territorial rival, repeated playing can place them under extra strain. You should therefore use tapes sparingly.

Another way of attracting birds with sounds is by using techniques known as pishing—making a *pssh, pssh* sound with your lips—and squeaking—kissing the back of your hand to produce crude but effective imitations of calls. Small birds, such as warblers, buntings, wrens and tits, will gather round, apparently fascinated by these sounds.

For a similar effect you can also use a "squeaker", a gadget, available from specialist outlets, consisting of a cylinder with a resin-coated wooden plug that squeaks when the plug is rotated.

INSTANT REPLAY *Portable recorders (left and far left) allow you to record the calls of birds—such as this Marsh Warbler (above)—in the field and then listen to them at home. One way to learn more about recording is to attend a course like the ones annually organised by Cornell Laboratory of Ornithology in Ithaca, New York, USA.*

KEEPING NOTES *and* RECORDS

A birdwatcher's records can take many forms, from short notes on scraps of paper to exhaustive, computerised compendiums.

Some birdwatchers become habitual listers. Almost all keep at least one list of all the species that they have seen.

A list may take the form of scribbled notes in the margin of one trusty field guide, or it may be checked off in one of the many printed lists available from birdwatching organisations. It may record all the birds you have seen on your travels, or only the birds you have seen in your region, local park or even just your back garden—a local list can be every bit as challenging as a national or world list.

Many active birdwatchers start a new list each year, month or even week. Breaking out a clean, unmarked checklist on January 1st can instill a good deal of vigour in even the most jaded birdwatcher.

Nowadays a good national life list might cover 300 to 400 species, depending on where you live. Many avid, well-travelled birdwatchers have been able to notch up 1000 or more for their world list. At the top end of the scale, a few listers have managed to see more than 7000 species.

JOURNALS

One way to get more out of your adventures in birdwatching is to keep a journal recording the details of places visited and wildlife observed.

Use a robust and, if possible, waterproof notebook. Write in it in pencil rather than pen. Pencil is more appropriate for sketching and won't run if the journal gets wet.

Use your journal to record not just the species seen but an estimate of the numbers present, the time and weather when you saw them, and any other relevant observations (see p. 68). Such notes will help you if you wish to do further research on a bird's identity at home, or if you intend to report a rare sighting to your local birdwatching organisation.

Many people choose to enliven their birdwatching notes with sketches, pressed flowers and other jottings. All of this will make your journal a valuable reference source and something to treasure throughout your birdwatching career.

OTHER TYPES OF RECORDS

In addition to maintaining a running narrative on trips afield, many birdwatchers also keep a computer file, loose-leaf

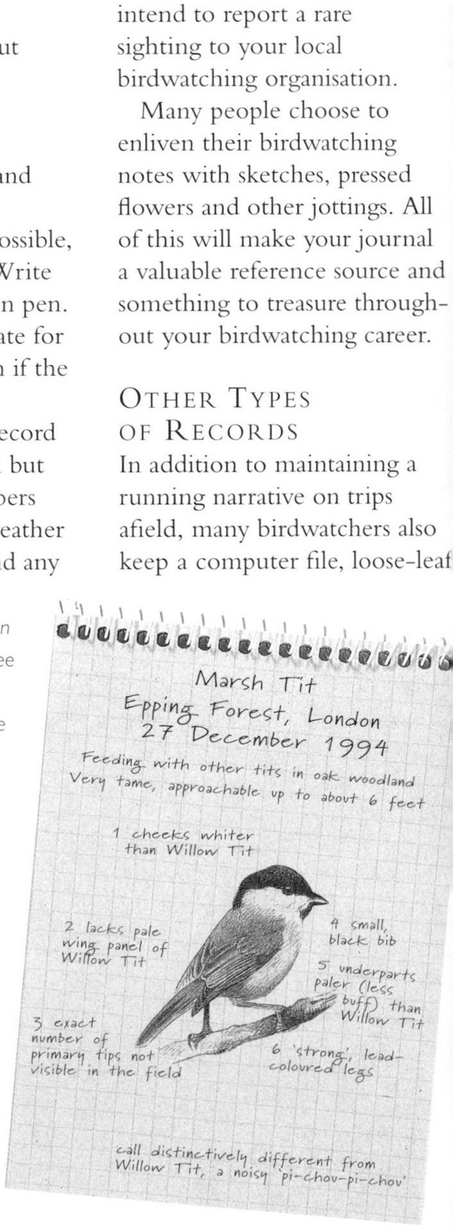
Marsh Tit
Epping Forest, London
27 December 1994
Feeding with other tits in oak woodland
Very tame, approachable up to about 6 feet
1 cheeks whiter than Willow Tit
2 lacks pale wing panel of Willow Tit
3 exact number of primary tips not visible in the field
4 small, black bib
5 underparts paler (less buff) than Willow Tit
6 'strong', lead-coloured legs
call distinctively different from Willow Tit, a noisy 'pi-chou-pi-chou'

A VISUAL REFERENCE *When you are out birdwatching and see a bird that you are unable to identify, it's a good idea to make notes and even do a quick sketch of the bird in your notebook. Note the time and the place, what kind of habitat you are in and any distinctive plumage or behavioural features of the bird (right). With this information at hand, you can then take time at home to consult field guides and other reference works in order to positively identify the bird—and add another species to your life list.*

BIRDWATCHER'S LISTS *Printed "tick" lists (below) are now available for most regions, but many birdwatchers still prefer a traditional notebook (left).*

binder or card index arranged according to species. Looking, for example, under Red-necked Grebe, a well-travelled birdwatcher would find several entries detailing encounters with this species.

Computers

There are many software programs designed for recording bird sightings. Some incorporate complete world or European species lists. Some feature information on the abundance of species in different areas at different times of year.

Many field guides, birdwatching reference books, and encyclopedias of birds are now also available on CD-ROM.

GREAT BIRD ARTISTS

European ornithologists played a major role in the early development of ornithology in North America. The English artist and naturalist Mark Catesby (1683–1749) created the first serious American ornithological work and one of the great works of bird art, *The Natural History of Carolina, Florida and the Bahamas.* Catesby undertook two extended journeys to the Americas between 1712 and 1726, and ultimately succeeded in illustrating around one quarter of all species found in the eastern United States. His two sumptuously illustrated folios were published in London in 1731 and 1743.

Not until the beginning of the nineteenth century was Catesby's work bettered: by Alexander Wilson (1766–1813), a Scottish weaver, school master, and poet, who lived in America. He was so overwhelmed by the beauty and variety of the birdlife that, despite little training in either art or ornithology, he began work on a large-scale guide. The first volume of Wilson's *American Ornithology* was published in 1808, with eight other volumes appearing subsequently.

To finance his work, Wilson sought sponsors by displaying published volumes wherever he went. On one of his trips, he approached John James Audubon (1785–1851). Audubon had arrived in America from France in 1803 and, unknown to Wilson, was at work on a similar project. Initially dismayed, Audubon was subsequently inspired by the meeting to work even harder at his plan to paint every bird in America.

Published serially from 1827 to 1838, to great acclaim, the four volumes of *Birds of America* were a landmark in bird art and are now among the most valuable books in the world.

PORTRAIT PAINTERS TO THE BIRDS *An illustration of a Bald Eagle by the English artist Mark Catesby (top). America's first great ornithologists, Alexander Wilson (above right) and John James Audubon (right), alongside a more recent successor, Louis Aggassiz Fuertes (above).*

Like Audubon, Louis Aggassiz Fuertes (1874–1927) was not only an exceptional artist but an avid and observant naturalist. One ability that set him apart from his peers was his acute memory. After studying his subjects closely in the wild, he would draw them hours later with astounding accuracy. Fuertes' publications are now among the most highly regarded of all bird books.

Photographing Birds

Bird photography can be immensely satisfying, but for beginners it can also be frustrating. Good results require a significant investment in time, money and patience.

The sense of satisfaction achieved by taking a good colour slide or print of a bird—perfectly composed, accurately exposed, pin sharp and with good saturated colours—is enormous, and most bird-watchers want to try their hand at capturing their quarry on film at some time or other.

Bird photography is, however, harder than it might seem. Suitable equipment is quite expensive, and outstanding results need technical commitment. Perhaps the best single piece of advice is to choose your equipment with great care.

Cameras

Cameras come in two basic styles, usually referred to as rangefinders and single lens reflexes (SLR). Rangefinder cameras are unsuitable for bird photography for several reasons, but especially because you cannot normally change lenses with this type of camera, so you cannot use a telephoto lens.

The recommended style and format is therefore an SLR that uses 35mm film, preferably one with automatic exposure control and focusing capability.

Focal Length

The most important factor to consider when choosing a lens for bird photography is its focal length. Usually expressed in millimetres, this is what governs the size of the image of the bird on the film. With a 35 mm camera, you can roughly equate this with the magnification of your binoculars by dividing the focal length of the lens by 50: a 400 mm lens, for example, is roughly the equivalent of 8x binoculars. (This only applies to 35 mm cameras; for other formats the formula is different.)

In a simple lens, the focal length is roughly the same as the length of the barrel, which means that a 1,000 mm simple telephoto lens would be about 3 feet (1 m) long. Sophisticated design in modern lenses has resulted in substantial improvement in this respect, but lenses suitable for bird photography are nevertheless long and heavy.

The greater the focal length, the harder it is to maintain focus and to "target" your bird in the viewfinder. Beyond about 400 mm you will need a tripod (see p. 64), as you will find that you simply cannot hold the lens steady enough by hand to get worthwhile results.

A QUESTION OF BALANCE

A Night Heron (above right) perches on some high-quality camera equipment. Experienced bird photographers use a tripod whenever possible, even with birds as tame and cooperative as this Brown Pelican in the southern USA (left).

THE F-STOP

The second critical parameter is the F-stop, which measures the light-gathering capability of the lens. The smaller the number, the wider the lens opens, the more light is let into the camera, and the quicker the image will be processed. An F4 lens is therefore better (that is, faster) than an F5.6. On the other hand, the smaller the number, the bigger, heavier, and more expensive the lens.

ZOOM AND MIRROR LENSES

Zoom lenses are those in which the focal length is variable (75 to 125 mm is a typical range). Mirror lenses (so-called because the wizardry inside is largely done with mirrors, not lenses), are much smaller, lighter, and more compact than normal telephoto lenses, but their F-stop is fixed. Such considerations are not that important in bird photography, however, as you will usually find yourself operating the lens at maximum zoom, in order to get as close as possible to the bird, and with the aperture wide open (that is, at its lowest F-setting), in order to record the image as quickly as possible.

MIRROR LENSES *(top) are more compact than other lenses, whereas zoom lenses (centre) provide increased flexibility. If you can afford it, this 600mm lens (right) will provide the ultimate in power and image clarity.*

You can extend the focal length of your lens by using a teleconverter, a small lens that attaches to the back of your telephoto lens before you attach it to the camera. These are convenient, but you pay for the increased range with some reduction in image quality and speed. You can also buy a photo-adaptor that allows you to mount your camera onto a spotting scope.

FILM

The most important difference in film types is in speed. High speed films (indicated by higher numbers) allow you to use a faster shutter speed and are therefore better for catching birds in motion, but they tend to give you grainier pictures.

Store film in the coolest place you can find (the refrigerator is fine), and protect it from marked temperature changes when you use it. If you want the very best results, get it processed by a custom lab (check your phone book for one near you) rather than a high street chemist.

VIDEO

Something to consider carefully before investing in photographic equipment is whether you wish to opt for a video camera instead. The latest video cameras are small and easy to use, and you may feel that capturing a bird's appearance, sound, and motion outweighs considerations of image quality.

You may well find yourself getting much more enjoyment out of your video tapes of birds than from still photographs. With a few video cameras (the more expensive models) you can even interchange lenses with your SLR camera, thus getting the best of both worlds.

FIELD OF VIEW *A group of budding bird photographers (above) sets its sights on a Great White Egret (right).*

Beyond Basic Birdwatching

The best way to broaden your birdwatching experience is to get to know other birdwatchers through clubs, birdwatching tours, and other group activities.

In most areas of Western Europe, there are local birdwatching organisations, ranging from ornithological societies to small birdwatching clubs. Most of these groups organise meetings and field trips, and they may help you to become involved in other aspects of birdwatching, such as censuses and research projects.

MOVING ON *Joining a club (above) is the first move to make if you are serious about birdwatching. Organised tours will take you to a wide range of places, from mountain-top raptor watches (below) to tropical wetlands (bottom).*

Many reserves, too, offer a range of naturalist-led walks, some specialising in birds. Some city museums, colleges, and universities offer classes in ornithology or birdwatching (field ornithology).

The principal organisations for birdwatchers in Britain and Ireland are listed on p. 277. Joining a few of these organisations will put you in touch with thousands of other like-minded bird-watchers and provide you with a variety of useful resources in the form of journals and newsletters.

Travel

A continent filled with superb and diverse birdwatching areas awaits you. For a selection of top sites, see p. 82. If you want to explore these and other areas on your own, there are many reports and books on "where to watch birds" which provide the necessary details for almost any place in the world. Good addresses to obtain travel reports are: Dutch Birding Travel Reports Service, PO Box 737, 9700 AS Groningen, Netherlands, and the Foreign Birdwatching Reports and Information Service, 6 Skipton Crescent, Berkeley Pendesham, Worcester WR4 0LG, England. Write for catalogues.

If you prefer to go on an organised tour, there is a huge range of companies and trips from which to choose. Most are inclusive, with similar travel arrangements. The big difference will probably be in the leader or tour guide—some are excellent, some can be a disappointment. To avoid the latter, you can ask other bird-watchers for recommendations.

Speciality Birdwatching

Some people focus their bird-watching activities on one kind of bird. For example, raptor-watching is a popular form of specialised birdwatching. Diurnal raptors (harriers, eagles ospreys, kites and so on) follow well-established migration routes (often over mountains where these birds ride the rising air currents, or at narrow sea-crossings), and along these routes there are localities, known as watchpoints, where hundreds, even thousands, of raptors may be seen in a single day.

COUNTING BIRDS *Researchers often welcome the help of volunteers in the routine work of censusing (above).*

Open sea trips to watch seabirds are especially popular in Ireland and south-western England. Many species of seabird that cannot normally be seen from land may be observed from ocean-going boats on one- or two-day trips. Again, a wide range of trips is on offer, but if you are planning your first pelagic birdwatching trip, be sure the organiser tells you exactly what is involved and how to prepare for it.

Birdwatching as Sport

One fun activity undertaken by many birdwatchers is known as a "bird racing". The aim is to record as many species as possible between one midnight and the next within a clearly defined area and following strict rules.

This can be done as a competition between members of a group or as a group effort aimed at improving on previous tallies. Especially in Britain, the USA and eastern Asia, this is frequently done to raise money for a birdwatching group or for conservation efforts, with each species recorded bringing in a small sum from sponsors.

Research

A number of national censuses and feeder-watch programs are organised each year and all birdwatchers can participate. Perhaps the best known censuses in the world are the Audubon Society's Christmas Bird Counts (CBCs).

Each CBC takes place on one day between mid-December and the first week of January and covers one of nearly 1,700 circles around North America, each of them 15 miles (24 km) in diameter. Participants record all the species they see that day within their circle.

The information gathered during the CBCs has given rise to a database that is one of the most important birdwatching resources in the world.

In Western Europe, most countries have organisations set up for censusing breeding birds, wintering waterfowl, migrating raptors and migrating seabirds, and also for documenting rarities.

Observatories and ringing stations also conduct research that requires volunteer participation. Ask your national bird society or local bird club for information on how you could participate in such work. For information and addresses, see p. 277.

Birds are Nature's most vital and potent expressions.

Frank M. Chapman
(1864–1945), American ornithologist

FRANK M. CHAPMAN *(above), curator of ornithology at the American Museum of Natural History and editor of various journals, organised the first Christmas Bird Count in America on Christmas Day 1900, as a protest against traditional Christmas bird shoots.*

BIRD AID *Many regions have organisations dedicated to nursing back to health injured and abandoned birds (below). One way of monitoring the movements of birds is by ringing (right). A metal ring bearing an address and a number (above right) will identify a bird if it should be found again.*

BIRDS *in* DANGER

Although public attitudes to conservation have changed radically in the past one hundred years, many bird species are still in grave danger of extinction.

For early ornithologists, the gun was as important a tool as writing and sketching materials, as most of their studies were based on dead specimens. Early in his career, John James Audubon (see p. 75) said, "I consider birds few if I can shoot less than a hundred a day."

Even in the nineteenth century, the wholesale slaughter of birds continued in the name of sport and fashion, but the attitude of the ornithological community began to change.

OVERHUNTING *exterminated the Passenger Pigeon, a species once so numerous that flocks of millions (below right) were a common sight. At the height of this destruction, in the 1880s, Frank Chapman (see p. 79) undertook a survey of headwear in New York and found that of the 700 hats that he counted, 542 sported mounted birds. Of these, he recognised at least 20 species.*

CONSERVATION GROUPS

These changing attitudes led to the foundation of the first conservation groups. In Britain, the most significant of these were the Royal Society for the Protection of Birds (RSPB) and BirdLife International (formerly the International Council for Bird Preservation).

A NEW THREAT

In the early 1960s, it became clear that we were poisoning our wildlife through the widespread use of non-decomposable pesticides such as DDT. These "miracle" sprays were great for growing insect-free produce but were devastating to "apex" predators (animals and birds at the top of the food chain). For birds such as Ospreys and Peregrine Falcons, the absorption of DDT caused them to lay eggs with shells too thin to incubate or eggs with no shells at all.

HABITAT DESTRUCTION *today threatens many birds, such as the Black-tailed Godwit (left).*

As a result, populations of raptor species plummeted.

By the time Rachel Carson's prophetic *Silent Spring* (see p. 36) alerted politicians and public to the danger, much damage had already been done.

CONTEMPORARY THREATS

There is no question that the most serious contemporary threat to birds is the continuing destruction of habitat. Numbers of many migratory species have dropped dramatically as their habitats in their summer homes in Europe and their winter residences in Africa and southern Asia have been cleared for agriculture and urban development.

Other threats to the survival of native species are also a

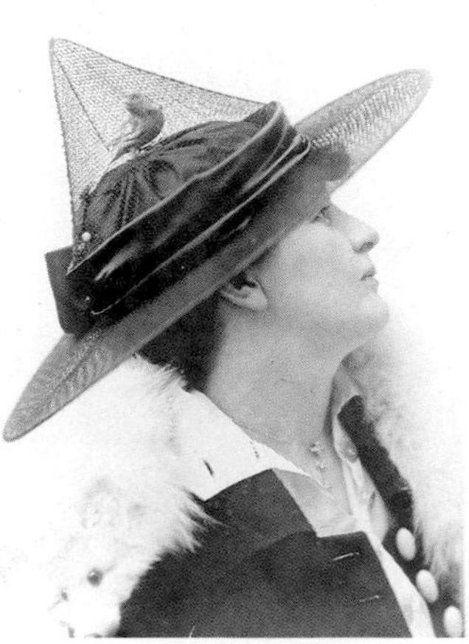

EXTINCT SPECIES IN EUROPE IN 19TH AND 20TH CENTURY

Canary Islands Oystercatcher, Great Auk

SOME ENDANGERED SPECIES IN EUROPE AND NORTH AFRICA

Species	*Range*	*Status*	*Causes*
Zino's Petrel	Madeira	In danger	Lack of safe nesting sites
Dalmatian Pelican	SE Europe/Asia	In danger	Habitat loss; shooting
Bald Ibis	Morocco (extinct Central Europe, Turkey)	In extreme danger	Pesticides; shooting
Lesser White-fronted Goose	Northern Europe	Faltering	Overhunting
Spanish Imperial Eagle	Spain	Faltering	Shooting; habitat loss
Great Bustard	Central Europe	Faltering	Overhunting; habitat loss
Sociable Plover	North Caspian region	Faltering	Habitat loss
Slender-billed Curlew	Mediterranean in winter, Russia in summer	In extreme danger	Shooting; habitat loss
Azores Bullfinch	Sao Miguel, Azores	In danger	Habitat loss

EXTINCT SPECIES IN NORTH AMERICA

Labrador Duck, California Condor (survives in zoo), Eskimo Curlew (probably), Great Auk, Passenger Pigeon, Carolina Parakeet, Ivory-billed Woodpecker, Bachman's Warbler (probably)

UNDER SIEGE *Recent re-introduction projects of Lesser White-fronted Geese (above) appear to be successful, and numbers migrating between Swedish Lapland and the Netherlands have shown a promising increase in the past few years. Nearly all breeding colonies of Bald Ibis (above left) have vanished in recent decades, and only one, south of Agadir, Morocco, is still thriving. The Slender-billed Curlew (top) seems to be on the verge of extinction.*

result of human intervention. The introduction of mammals, such as rats and cats, has wiped out entire bird populations, especially on islands. Human structures, too, have taken their toll: huge numbers of birds die annually as a result of collisions with plate-glass windows (see p. 53).

On the Bright Side

Illegal shooting and trapping is now rare in most parts of Western Europe, and legislation prohibits misuse of pesticides. Many wildlife agencies have implemented local control programs to protect vulnerable species, and many private organisations are buying property to protect habitats and care for animals and birds.

Organisations such as BirdLife International continue to campaign effectively for endangered species and habitats. To counterbalance continuing habitat destruction, it is imperative that these efforts are not only continued but stepped up. If you want to help, you can start by contacting one of these groups or joining a local birdwatching organisation. See p. 277 for a list of addresses.

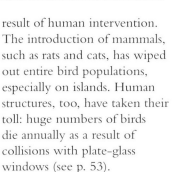

TOP BIRDWATCHING SITES

Europe offers an extraordinary range of habitat types, a superb system of national parks and some of the world's top birdwatching areas.

It is not easy to make a selection of top birdwatching sites because there are so many of them scattered around Europe. Here, however, are ten of our favourites. More information on all of these destinations and many others can be found in the birdfinding guides listed in the Resources Directory on p. 274.

LOCAL LISTS

The following list will give you some idea of the number of species that have been recorded in different countries around Europe.

Great Britain	555
France	470
Germany	465
Spain	465
Sweden	450
Netherlands	445
Morocco	420
Denmark	420
Ireland	415
Greece	390
Switzerland	380
Iceland	325

❶ VARANGERFJORD, FINNMARK, NORWAY ▶ *The spectacular setting and rich birdlife of this northernmost end of the Western European mainland makes the long journey worthwhile. In spring and summer, it is not too cold, and it remains light for 24 hours. There are large flocks of King and Steller's Eiders, Long-tailed Ducks and Kittiwakes (above). Many arctic breeders can be found, including White-billed Diver (rare), Long-tailed Skua and Red-throated Pipit.*

◀ **❸ ISLES OF SCILLY, ENGLAND** *These islands at the extreme southwestern end of England form the birdwatching hot spot for rarities in Europe. It is a great place to see American vagrants. For the chance of seeing vagrants from Siberia, it rivals Fair Isle (Scotland) and Heligoland (Germany). Besides, during October it is also a favourite meeting place for many British birdwatchers.*

❺ TEXEL, NOORD-HOLLAND, THE NETHERLANDS *This is the westernmost in the chain of Dutch, German and Danish islands that fringe the bird-rich tidal mudflats of the Waddensea. This shallow sea is of utmost importance as a feeding area for huge numbers of migrant waders and nesting Eiders, Oystercatchers, gulls (right) and terns. Spoonbill, Avocet, and Black-tailed Godwit are common breeders on Texel.* ▶

❷ FALSTERBO, SKÅNE, SWEDEN *This, the most famous migration spot of Northern Europe, is situated at the southwestern end of the Swedish mainland. In autumn, it rivals Gibraltar and the Bosporus for the numbers of raptors passing through. Migration of waders and passerines is often also spectacular. Öland is a Baltic island not too far—186 miles (300 km)—northeast from Falsterbo. Its southern tip is also famous for rarities in spring and autumn.* ▼

◀ **❹ CAPE CLEAR ISLAND, IRELAND** *At the extreme southern tip of Ireland, Cape Clear is the most famous of many excellent seawatching sites in Ireland. In late summer and autumn, Cory's, Great, Sooty and Manx Shearwaters, Storm and Leach's Petrels, Northern Gannet, skuas and Black Guillemot (left) are often numerous. Chough and migrant passerines can be seen, and rarities turn up regularly.*

▲ **6 LAKE NEUSIEDL, AUSTRIA** *This shallow steppe lake fringed by huge reedbeds offers excellent summer birdwatching, with breeding colonies of Great White Egret and uncommon marsh species. In the plains extending eastwards, Great Bustards and many raptors can be seen, such as this Montagu's Harrier (above). In woodlands, eastern species of woodpeckers, warblers and flycatchers may be found.*

▲ **7 HORTOBÁGY, HUNGARY** *This area of steppe with marshes, grasslands (above) and woods forms an excellent area to see eastern species in summer. Breeding birds include Black Stork, Glossy Ibis, Spoonbill, Red-footed Falcon, Great Bustard, White-winged Black Tern, Aquatic Warbler and, infrequently, Rose-coloured Starling. In the winter season, White-tailed Eagles arrive to feed, along with large numbers of geese.*

▲ **8 DANUBE DELTA, ROMANIA** *This enormous wetland area has few tourist facilities but there are many birds worth travelling to see, especially in summer. Species with more than a thousand breeding pairs include Pygmy Cormorant, White Pelican, Night Heron, Squacco Heron (above), Purple Heron, Glossy Ibis, and Whiskered Tern. Other important breeders are Dalmatian Pelican, White-tailed Eagle, and Saker Falcon. Thousands of Red-breasted Geese winter here.*

▲ **9 CAMARGUE, FRANCE** *Situated between two arms of the river Rhône and the sea, this area is famous for its Greater Flamingo colony (above). Saltpans, rice-fields and reedy lakes are excellent for many herons, Slender-billed Gull, Bee-eater, Roller, and Spectacled Warbler. The stony area of La Crau to the east is a stronghold for Little Bustard and Pin-tailed Sandgrouse. Eagle Owl. Some mountain species can be found in Les Alpilles to the north.*

10 COTO DOÑANA, ANDALUCIA, SPAIN *This vast area at the outlet of the Guadalquivir is seasonally flooded. Greater Flamingo, Spanish Imperial Eagle, Marbled Duck, White-headed Duck, Spoonbill (far right), Purple Gallinule, Audouin's Gull, Red-necked Nightjar and Azure-winged Magpie are among the more interesting species to be seen. There are several other excellent birdwatching areas nearby, including the raptor migration hot spot between Tarifa and Gibraltar.* ▶

It was the nightingale, and not the lark,
That pierc'd the fearful hollow of thine ear;
Nightly she sings on yon pomegranate tree;
Believe me, love, it was the nightingale.

Romeo and Juliet,
WILLIAM SHAKESPEARE (1564–1616), English playwright

Chapter Four
The Habitat Birdfinder

INTRODUCTION

In Europe, there are more than 850 species of bird. How does a beginning birdwatcher get to know them? Our Habitat Birdfinder is the perfect introduction—to all the main bird groups and to more than 200 of the most commonly encountered species.

Getting to grips with the large number of species that may be encountered in Europe can be a daunting task. A good way to start is to learn something about the general characteristics that distinguish groups of related birds.

THE TAXONOMIC APPROACH

In the following pages you will find concise but informative descriptions of the main bird groups in Europe. These include information on shared physical features; behavioural characteristics; differences in plumage between males and females, and from season to season; and the number of species in that group found in Europe compared with the world as a whole.

It may be a little hard to digest all of this information at once, but it is worth persevering as it will give you a good foundation on which you can build.

You will probably be surprised at how much you already know. For example, you probably recognise a duck or an owl when you see one. You may not be able to say exactly what species it is, but you at least can recognise it immediately as a duck or an owl.

Greater familiarity with the shared characteristics of bird groups will help you narrow down the identity of an unknown bird in the field. Knowing how many species there are in a group will mean that you are aware just how many similar birds there are. And an awareness of plumage cycles and differences will mean you are better placed to make a more precise identification. For all these reasons, it makes sense to read this section carefully and return to it again and again.

THE HABITAT APPROACH

Learning about families and other groups will give you a good grounding in European birds, but groups can be large and widespread. Furthermore, you will quickly want to start naming the individual species that you see around you. So how can you predict what species you are likely to see in your area? One answer is to consider birds in relation to their habitats.

FAMILY TRAITS *Most of us recognise an owl—such as this Little Owl (top)—immediately, even though we may not know the exact species. It takes only a little more practice to learn to recognise the family traits of many less familiar birds, such as the Sedge Warbler (right).*

Birds do not occur at random across the landscape. Instead, each species has its own set of environmental requirements and preferences, based on what it eats and where it nests (see p. 30). Most of the species that you find in open country, for instance, do not normally occur in woodlands, and vice versa.

This concept sometimes holds good for entire groups of birds: if you want to look for a duck, for example, you go to a lake or marsh, not to a dry field or a wooded park. But it is generally true at the species level as well: the Short-eared Owl, for example,

START WITH THE HABITAT

Many birds are restricted to an easily recognisable habitat, offering a useful aid to identification. You will normally find Little Grebes, for example, only near a lake, marsh or small river.

lives in open country, while its close relative the Long-eared Owl lives in forests and woodlands.

We have, therefore, arranged our selection of some of the most commonly encountered European birds into six habitat categories: urban areas, woodlands, open country, wetlands, seashores and mountains. These are broad, widespread, familiar environments, and it should be easy for you to relate them to the kind of area you live in. This, in turn, will help you familiarise yourself with the birds you are most likely to see around you.

Pitfalls

The habitat approach is ideal for the beginner; however, it does have its limitations, and to use the approach to best effect it is important to be aware of them.

In the first place, birds don't always relate to their environment in ways that make sense to humans. Some occur in many habitats, while others are found only in very restricted environments. Some dwell in different habitats at different times of the year.

Moreover, the concept of habitat alone may give us an incomplete notion of how the bird relates to its environment, and we need the concept of niche to complete it. For example, both warblers and thrushes occur in woodlands (often the very same patch of woodland), but thrushes can be seen on the ground and in bushes,whereas warblers usually favour the leafy canopies of trees.

To help you deal with this, preferences for particular niches are described where relevant within the species profiles. Furthermore, each habitat is introduced by two sections, the first of which presents a typical scene from that habitat and highlights commonly used niches. The second recommends strategies and equipment that may assist you within a particular environment.

A Two-pronged Approach

Both approaches—the taxonomic and the habitat—have advantages and disadvantages. On the whole, it is best to view them as complementary: by exploiting them both fully you will rapidly improve your knowledge of birds and your identification skills.

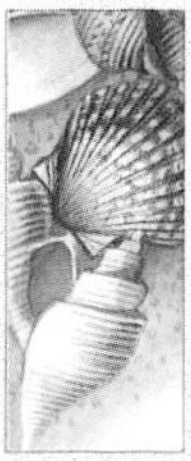

FAMILY GROUPS

All bird species belong to broad family groups. A sound knowledge of these groups and their shared characteristics is a real boon to any birdwatcher.

In taxonomy, bird species are organised into groups at different levels: order, family, subfamily, genus and so on (see p. 20). To most birdwatchers, groups of certain species will be better known at one level than another.

For example, we tend to think of plovers as one group and phalaropes as another, even though the plovers constitute a family while the phalaropes are only a subfamily; we think of owls as one group even though there are two distinct families. It is simply more straightforward and more useful for us to think of the birds in these groups, even if they are not at the same taxonomic level.

We have, therefore, arranged the birds of Europe into the groups that we feel will be most familiar to birdwatchers and most easily grasped by beginners. These groups are listed in traditional taxonomic order.

Each group name in our list is highlighted in bold. Scientific names of families and subfamilies are given. These names can prove useful when consulting other publications.

A useful starting point when considering groups is to think of birds as either passerines (songbirds) or non-passerines, as passerines make up more than half of all species.

Familiarising yourself with the traditional taxonomic sequence will also help you to navigate through other sources of information on birds, as most field guides (including this one), handbooks and bird lists use similar sequences.

NON-PASSERINES

Divers (Gaviidae) are strongly aquatic birds that dive beneath the surface for their food and come ashore only to nest. To some extent, they resemble ducks and cormorants, but they ride low in the water and their bills are pointed and often quite stout.
4/5 ➤232

Grebes (Podicipedidae) resemble small divers and, like them, are strongly aquatic, generally inhabiting wetlands. One distinctive feature is their apparent lack of a tail—their bodies end in a "powder-puff" effect of loose feathers.
5/19 ➤194–196

The three families of seabirds—**albatrosses** (Diomedeidae), **shearwaters and petrels** (Procellariidae), and **storm-petrels** (Hydrobatidae)—are often known as tubenoses because their nostrils are set in tubes on top of their bills. Strictly pelagic, they seldom come within sight of land except when breeding.
10/105 ➤233, 234

KEY TO SYMBOLS

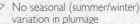

- No difference in plumage between males and females
- Males and females have different plumage
- Plumage difference between sexes in some species but not in others
- No seasonal (summer/winter) variation in plumage
- Seasonal (summer/winter) variation in plumage
- Seasonal (summer/winter) variation in plumage in some species but not in others
- **7/20** Number of species in the group in Europe/the world
- ➤23 Page references for species in the group that feature in The Habitat Birdfinder

Cormorants (Phalacrocoracidae) are mainly black in plumage and their longish bills are distinctly hooked at the tip. They swim low in the water, dive for their food and inhabit fresh and salt water alike. There are two related groups with few species and widely differing appearance: **pelicans** (Pelecanidae) have huge, pouch-like bills; **gannets and boobies** (Sulidae) inhabit coastal waters and dive for fish in spectacular plunges from high above the sea.
6/44 ➤235, 236

Herons, egrets, and bitterns (Ardeidae); **storks** (Ciconiidae); and **ibises and spoonbills** (Threskiornithidae) are all long-legged, long-necked, long-billed and short-tailed birds that wade in shallow water in search of much of their food. Many egrets are entirely white but dull reds and greys are common among herons. Bitterns may be brown and streaked. Ibises have downward-curving bills; spoonbills have the bill shape their name suggests; storks are large, black-and-white birds with bright red bills and legs.
13/108 ➤164, 165, 197, 198-202

Swans, geese and ducks (Anatidae) all have some recognisable variation of the familiar duck bill, which is difficult to describe concisely but is instantly recognisable. Most moult all their flight feathers in one go, so are flightless for a few weeks every year while the new feathers grow. Male ducks often have a striking courtship plumage.
43/151 ➤100, 101, 166-170, 203-208, 237-240

The diurnal **birds of prey** are often known collectively as raptors. Key subgroups include the buzzards, kites and eagles (Accipitridae) and falcons (Falconidae). Raptors are extremely variable in plumage, and in identification subtle details of flight silhouette (length of tail, breadth of wing and so on) are often far more important than colour pattern.
37/211 ➤102, 124-127, 262, 263

Of the **gamebirds** (Phasianidae) the grouse, partridge and Quail are native to Europe, while the pheasant has been introduced. All are chicken-like birds that feed almost exclusively on the ground.
15/265 ➤171

In body form, **crakes, rails, and coots** (Rallidae) look faintly chicken-like, but for the most part inhabit swamps and marshes. Shy and elusive, most are seldom seen by the casual observer. Their tails are frequently cocked high and persistently flicked. Allied to the crakes and rails are the two European cranes (Gruidae), the Common Crane and the Demoiselle Crane.
11/189 ➤103, 104, 172, 212, 213

Closely related are two other small but distinctive groups: **stilts and avocets** (Recurvirostridae) and **oystercatchers** (Haematopodidae). Stilts and avocets occur in coastal wetlands, salt pans and brackish lakes, especially in Southern Europe; they are mainly black and white in plumage, and have very long legs. Oystercatchers live along coastlines and have long, stout, chisel-like beaks.
4/22 ➤241, 242

Top to bottom: Little Bittern (Ardeidae); Moorhen (Rallidae); Black Grouse (Phasianidae); Mallard (Anatidae)

Anyone familiar with the Ringed Plover should have little difficulty recognising any of the other **plovers** (Charadriidae). These are birds of coasts and open country, with long, pointed wings, rather large, dark eyes and a pigeon-like bill. Plovers have a characteristic habit of dashing over sand or mud on twinkling feet, with head held low, then periodically coming to an abrupt halt, as though called smartly to attention.
9/62 ➤173, 174, 243, 244

The **sandpipers** and their relatives (Scolopacidae) mostly inhabit seashores, especially tidal mudflats. Many are strongly migratory, nesting in the high arctic and travelling south in autumn. Most are gregarious and habitually congregate in large, mixed roosting flocks at high tide, scattering to feed over exposed mudflats as the tide recedes. Plumage is mainly dull brown or grey, and many species are extremely difficult to identify. The slender bill ranges from very long to quite short, and may be straight, strongly downcurved or even slightly upcurved. An important first step in identifying shorebirds is to carefully note length and shape of bill; whether there is a white rump or not; and whether there is a white stripe down the length of the upper wing (a wingbar) or not.
30/81 ➤128, 175, 214, 218, 245-248

Right: Black-winged Stilt (Recurvirostridae); below: Sanderlings (Scolopacidae); bottom left: Guillemots (Alcidae).

Almost everyone knows what **gulls** (Laridae) look like, but there are many different species (and some are found nowhere near the sea). Furthermore, most take several years to reach maturity, going through a series of different immature plumages, which makes identification of the species a matter of considerable intricacy. A typical adult gull is white with a grey back and wings, and some have black heads.

Terns (Sternidae) are similar to gulls but usually smaller and slimmer, with long, slender, pointed wings, and most have a black cap. The bill is sharply pointed and the tail is often forked. Generally, gulls are scavengers but most terns feed on small fish captured by splash-diving from a few feet above the surface.

There is one smaller group closely related to gulls but very distinctive in appearance. **Skuas** (Stercorariidae) look rather like dark brown gulls but specialise in piracy, bullying and harassing other seabirds until they abandon their catch.
30/91 ➤105, 219, 249-254

The family Alcidae includes the **guillemots** and **Puffin**. Auks are exclusively marine birds that catch their food under water. Their small wings lend their flight a distinctively "buzzy" appearance, low over the water. Many species congregate in large colonies on seacliffs to nest. They are well represented in the arctic, but several species extend southward, especially along the Atlantic coast and around the North Sea.
6/21 ➤255, 256

Pigeons and doves (Columbidae) come in a range of colours and sizes, but all resemble the ordinary street pigeon (or Feral Rock Dove) closely enough to make confusion unlikely at group level.
5/280 ➤106, 107, 129, 130

The **cuckoos** (Cuculidae) are a worldwide parasitic group with relatively few species in Europe. These are all generally slender, long-tailed birds with slightly decurved bills.
2/127 ➤131

Left: Woodpigeon (Columbidae); above: Bee-eater (Meropidae); below left: Eagle Owl (Strigidae); below right: Great Spotted Woodpecker (Picidae)

Nightjars (Caprimulgidae) are for most people disembodied voices in the night. They catch flying insects at night but spend the rest of the day on the forest or woodland floor, relying entirely on their extraordinarily cryptic coloration to avoid detection.
2/72 ➤133

There are, in fact, two distinct groups of **owls**—barn owls (Tytonidae) and "typical" owls (Strigidae)—but they are so similar in most respects that the distinction is more or less academic. A typical owl is a nocturnal bird of prey with remarkably well-developed night vision and acute hearing, and strong, curved talons. Unlike most other birds, their eyes are forward-facing, like those of humans.
13/126 ➤132, 176–178

Swifts (Apodidae) quite closely resemble swallows in general appearance and behaviour, although they are not related. They spend almost all of their time in the air, feeding on small flying insects. They have compact, cigar-shaped bodies and long, narrow, scythe-like wings. They typically fly much higher than swallows and martins.
4/71 ➤108

Bee-eaters (Meropidae) are unmistakable. No other bird in Europe is so brightly coloured, with long, pointed wings and a fine black bill. Bee-eaters take large insects, in particular bees, while sweeping acrobatically through the air.
1/23 ➤179

The **Hoopoe** (Upupidae) has a black and white wing and tail pattern, can raise its crown feathers to a crest and is the single member of its family.
1/1 ➤180

The vividly blue Kingfisher is the only **kingfisher** (Alcedinidae) that is common and widespread throughout Europe. Kingfishers perch in trees overhanging rivers and streams and catch fish by splash-diving.
1/90 ➤220

A typical **woodpecker** (Picidae) clasps a tree trunk with strong-clawed feet, leans back to throw much of its weight onto its stiffened, spine-tipped tail feathers, and uses this tripod stance as a fulcrum from which to batter away at the bark with its rather heavy, chisel-like bill. Males often have a small patch of red on the head.
10/206 ➤134, 135

Passerines

Larks (Alaudidae) are small, inconspicuous, brownish birds of open country. In spring, most larks sing while hovering high in the air.
9/76 ➤136, 181

Swallows and martins (Hirundinidae) are small, slender birds that catch insects in mid-air, more or less sucking them up as they fly in graceful swoops, flurries and glides, usually at no great height over open ground. When not feeding, they may perch in twittering flocks along telephone lines.
5/74 ➤109, 110, 221

In Europe, there are only two resident but numerous migrating species of **pipits** (Motacillidae), a group that also includes the wagtails and which is otherwise widespread in Eurasia and Africa. These are small, drab, streaked birds resembling larks, except that they have slender bills and frequently wag their tails.
11/54 ➤111, 182, 183, 264, 265

Waxwings (Bombycillidae) are slender, elegant, crested birds with soft, silky plumage and yellow tail-tips. They are gregarious and feed largely on fruit.
1/8

Dippers (Cinclidae) are compact birds with short tails. They live exclusively around fast-flowing rivers.
1/4 ➤266

Wrens (Troglodytidae) are small, drab, brown birds that usually inhabit undergrowth or very low vegetation. They are active and have high-pitched, vigorous songs. There is only one species in Europe, but there are many in the Americas.
1/59 ➤137

Accentors (Prunellidae) are small, ground-dwelling birds with fine bills and brownish-grey plumage inhabiting temperate woodlands and mountains.
3/13 ➤138, 267

Thrushes (Turdidae) are medium-sized songbirds that spend much of their time on the ground in woodlands. They are soberly coloured, and often have strikingly beautiful, evocative songs. They include the familiar Blackbird and Song Thrush.
24/304 ➤112, 113, 139-142, 184, 185, 268

The many European members of the enormous, essentially Old World assemblage of **warblers** (Sylviidae) are very small, energetic birds of forests and woodlands. This group includes Goldcrest and Firecrest, which are tiny birds of coniferous forest, given to dangling and fluttering acrobatically at the very tips of branches, nervously flicking their wings.
39/339 ➤143-145, 186, 223, 224

Flycatchers (Muscicapidae) are small woodland birds with a distinctive habit of perching upright on vantage points and sallying forth to catch flying insects, often with an audible snap of the bill. Many species are brightly coloured and highly migratory.
5/134 ➤146, 147

Babblers (Timaliidae) are small to medium-sized, long-tailed birds that are highly social. In Europe, there is only one representative, the Bearded Tit, which lives exclusively in marshes with reedbeds.
1/250 ➤225

Left to right: Jay (Corvidae); Waxwing (Bombycillidae); Yellow Wagtail (Motacillidae)

Left: Robin (Turdidae); below: Hawfinch (Fringillidae)

The true **tits** (Paridae) and **Long-tailed Tit** (Aegithalidae) are often the most obvious, small songbirds in winter woods across Europe, while the **Penduline Tit** (Remizidae) frequents wetter thickets and reeds. Small, intensely active, acrobatic birds, many share a similar colour pattern consisting of a dark cap, white cheeks, and a small black bib on the throat.
⚥✎ **12/46** ➤148-150

Both **nuthatches** (Sittidae) and **treecreepers** (Certhiidae) are usually instantly recognisable by their behaviour alone: nuthatches are the only birds to creep head-first down tree trunks, and treecreepers are the only small birds that creep up the trunks of trees.
⚥✎ **6/27** ➤151,152, 269

Orioles (Oriolidae) are medium-sized birds, usually bright yellow or green, with strong, slightly hooked bills. Europe's only species is strictly arboreal and builds nests high in the treetops.
⚥✎ **1/28**

The most characteristic feature of the **shrikes** (Laniidae) is that they seem like a songbird version of a falcon: they select the highest perches available in open country as a vantage point from which to look for large insects, mice or small birds.
⚥✎ **5/70**

Jays, **magpies**, **crows**, **nutcrackers and ravens** all belong to the group Corvidae. Jays are often brightly coloured, but crows and ravens are black. Most are big, bold, conspicuous and versatile songbirds, and they appear in most habitats.
⚥✎ **11/103** ➤114, 115, 153, 154, 270

Starlings (Sturnidae) form an Old World group of predominantly small to medium-sized birds with strong bills and legs. Their plumage is variable but usually a more or less iridescent black. Most species occur in open country, are highly gregarious outside the breeding season and often live in close association with humans.
⚥✎ **3/106** ➤116

The Old World **sparrows** (Passeridae) are small birds with thick, conical bills adapted for seed-eating. Most species are highly gregarious throughout the year and occur in a variety of habitats, usually open country, from fields to mountains, and often in close association with humans. Several species have successfully colonised many parts of the world.
⚥✎ **6/34** ➤117

The **finches** (Fringillidae) are very like sparrows in size and appearance but are, on the whole, more brightly coloured and have stout, seed-cracking bills, except for the crossbills, which have peculiar, scissor-shaped bills to extract pine seeds from cones.
⚥✎ **21/125** ➤118, 155-158, 271

Buntings (Emberizidae) are present in a wide variety of habitats from lowland marshes to arctic tundra and alpine meadows. Most females are small, brown and streaked, but the males usually have at least some brighter markings. Most have conical bills.
⚥✎ **13/281** ➤187, 188, 226, 272

USING *the* HABITAT BIRDFINDER

The following pages present 148 of the most commonly encountered European species, arranged according to the habitat they favour. In many cases, similar or related species are also discussed, bringing the total number of birds featured to more than 200. Each page incorporates the features shown here.

A clear photograph of the species in typical plumage and attitude. Captions indicate, where relevant, the sex, age, seasonal plumage and subspecies.

The habitat code indicates which type of environment the bird most often frequents. See the key on page 87.

The name of the group of bird—family or subfamily—that the species belongs to.

The common and scientific names of the species. Within each habitat, the species are arranged in taxonomic order.

The map shows the bird's breeding distribution in yellow and its winter range in blue. Green indicates that the species is present all year.

The text provides important information on where and how you are likely to encounter the bird; its behavioural characteristics, life cycle and migration patterns; and how to identify the species in the field, including how to distinguish it from any similar species.

The calendar bar indicates the months in which the species is most likely to be found in Western Europe.

Rallidae: Rails and Coots

Adult

Corncrake

Crex crex

The Corncrake is a mysterious bird which hides itself in hay meadows and wet grasslands. The dry, rasping song of the male can be heard from May well into July, especially on warm, summer nights.

Corncrakes are long-distance migrants and spend the winter in the savanna of East Africa. Although it is still a common bird along most natural rivers in Eastern Europe, mechanised cutting of hay and crops has eradicated Corncrakes in many parts of Western Europe by destroying nests, eggs and adults. The species still hangs on in remote parts of Ireland and the Hebrides, where—because of the climate—mowing occurs only very late in summer and fewer nests are destroyed.

The Corncrake is a rail by origin but resembles the much smaller Quail (*Coturnix coturnix*; 6½–7" [16–18 cm]) in its preference for long grass and secretive behaviour. Quails are also found in wheat fields and their presence is usually denoted by the song of the male, a repeated *kwik-me-dit*. Their small size and brown, rounded wings distinguish Quails from Corncrakes in flight.

J F M A M J J A S O N D

FIELD NOTES
■ 10½–11½" (27–30 cm)
■ Long, reddish-brown wings
■ Feet dangling in flight
■ Short, pinkish bill
■ Wings with chestnut patches
▲ Quail is smaller and has brown, rounded wings
Hidden in tall grass and lined with dry grass
♪ Call: a monotonously repeated, dry rasping "errp-errp"

172

Accurate, full-colour illustrations show field marks, plumage variations, similar species and subspecies and behavioural characteristics.

Quick-reference Field Notes include:
- ■ *The size of the bird from the bill tip to the end of the tail*
- ■ *Distinctive plumage and behavioural features*
- ▲ *Information on similar species that may cause confusion*
- *Form and location of nest*
- ♪ *Call, song*

Urban Areas

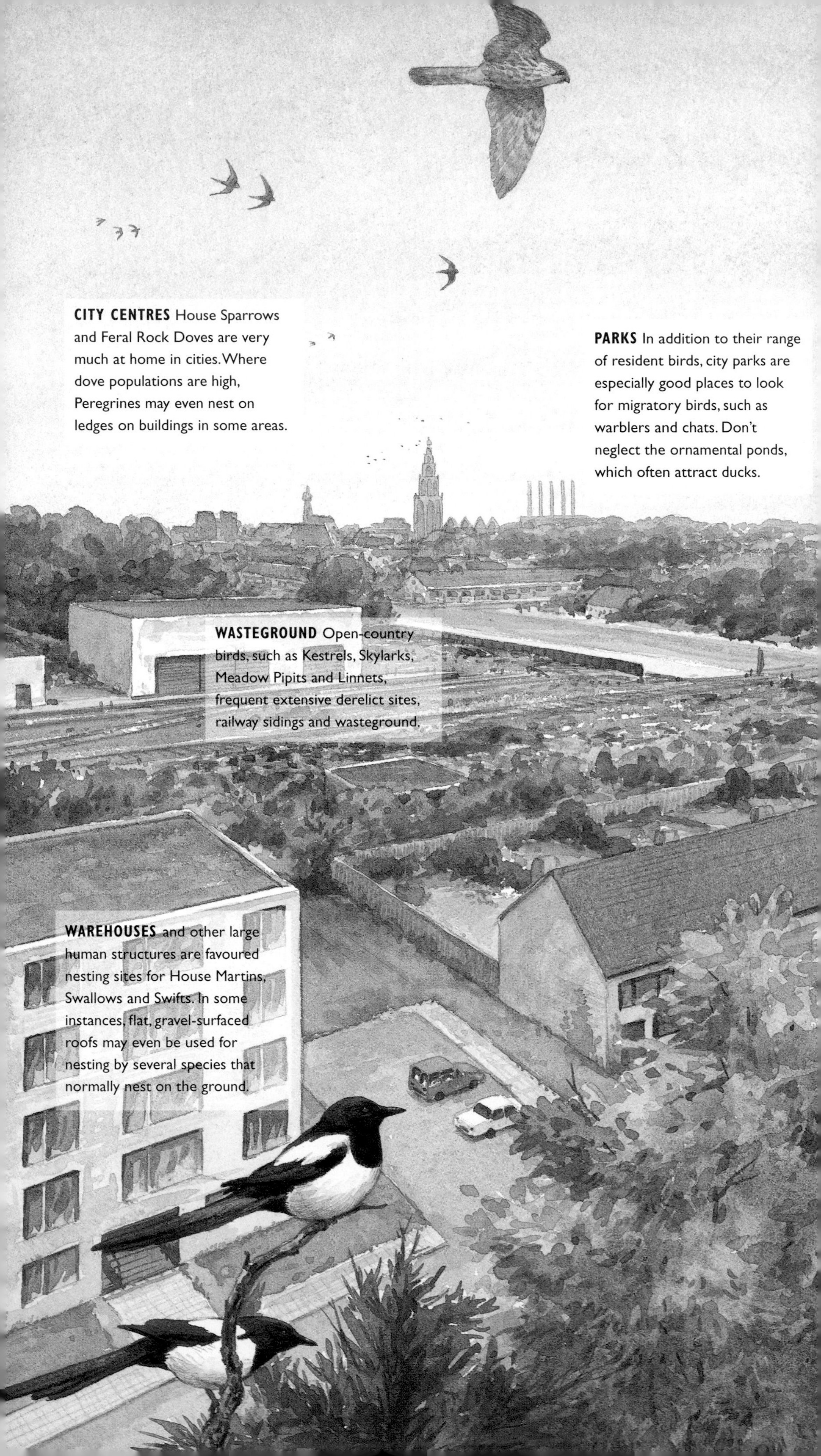

CITY CENTRES House Sparrows and Feral Rock Doves are very much at home in cities. Where dove populations are high, Peregrines may even nest on ledges on buildings in some areas.

PARKS In addition to their range of resident birds, city parks are especially good places to look for migratory birds, such as warblers and chats. Don't neglect the ornamental ponds, which often attract ducks.

WASTEGROUND Open-country birds, such as Kestrels, Skylarks, Meadow Pipits and Linnets, frequent extensive derelict sites, railway sidings and wasteground.

WAREHOUSES and other large human structures are favoured nesting sites for House Martins, Swallows and Swifts. In some instances, flat, gravel-surfaced roofs may even be used for nesting by several species that normally nest on the ground.

URBAN AREAS

City Areas, Parks, Gardens, Derelict Sites

All urban and suburban areas, by their very nature, are characterised by the presence of humans and major alterations to the natural environment. These factors affect bird populations in a variety of ways.

The loss of natural habitat inevitably leads to the elimination of certain species, and many birds are unable to live where they are constantly disturbed and where the air and water are polluted.

On the other hand, some species thrive in urban environments. Birds such as the Feral Rock Dove and the House Sparrow have made themselves entirely at home in cities, to such an extent that they are seldom seen in places that have *not* been disturbed by human activities.

Many woodland birds, too, such as Blackbirds and Chaffinches, have adapted well to the parks and gardens of urban Europe. Gulls scavenging along waterfronts and at rubbish dumps, and ducks bobbing on the waters of local ponds, are further examples of birds that co-exist happily with humans.

For a number of birds, the change to an urban habitat makes little difference to their behaviour or feeding tactics. For example, in many cities around the world, Peregrines live and breed on buildings very much as they have always lived around sea cliffs, hunting pigeons. (Indeed, there are hopes that the Peregrine, almost wiped out in parts of its range a few decades ago, will come to flourish in our cities.) From the Peregrine's perspective, of course, city buildings and sea cliffs are very much alike.

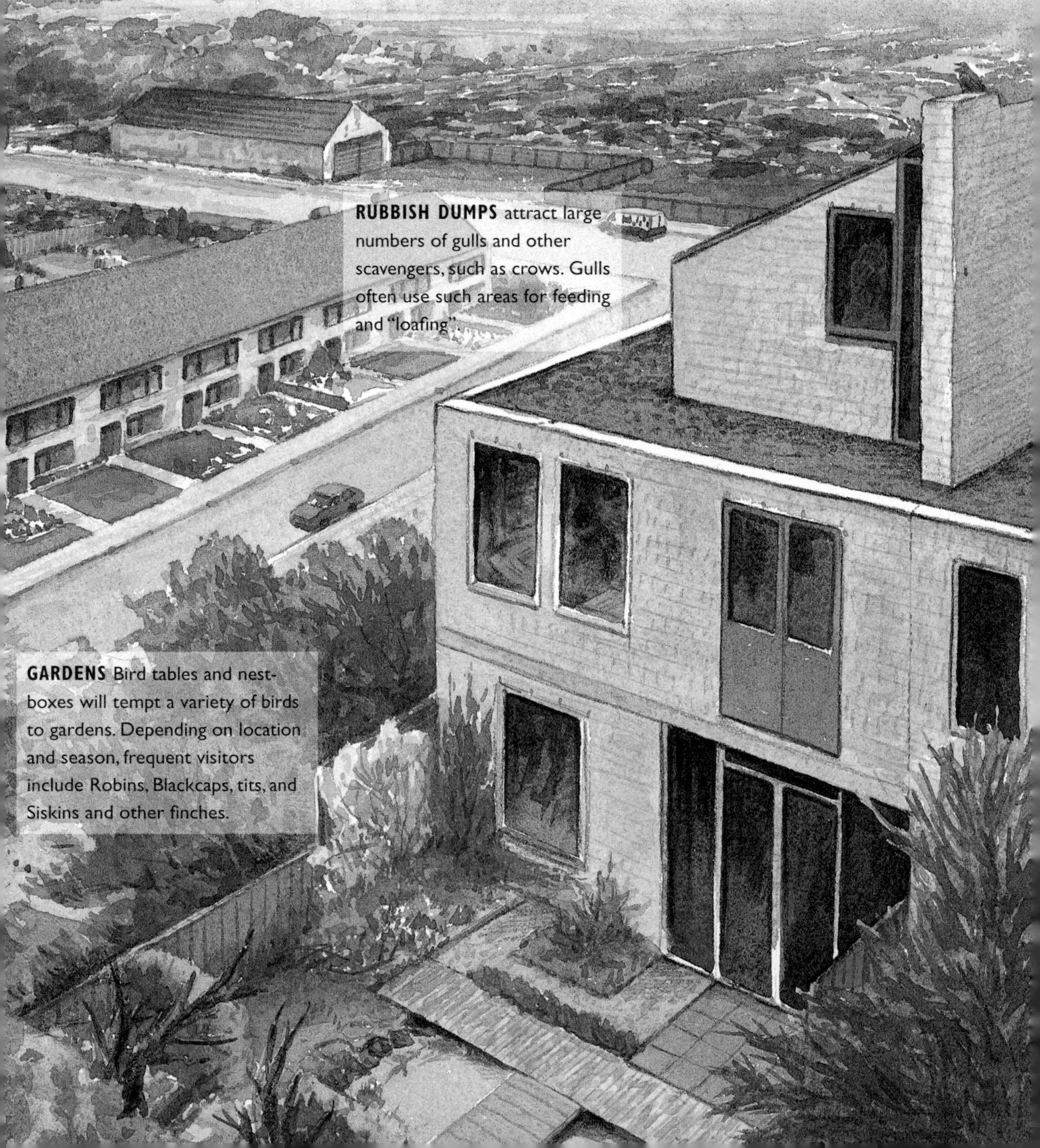

RUBBISH DUMPS attract large numbers of gulls and other scavengers, such as crows. Gulls often use such areas for feeding and "loafing".

GARDENS Bird tables and nest-boxes will tempt a variety of birds to gardens. Depending on location and season, frequent visitors include Robins, Blackcaps, tits, and Siskins and other finches.

BIRDWATCHING *in* URBAN AREAS

From the relatively sterile concrete and glass environment of business districts to the suburbs with their parks and gardens, opportunities for urban birdwatching abound.

It is a mistake to think that if you live in a city there will be few opportunities to observe birds. Urban birdwatching can be extremely rewarding. Even if you live in a block of flats, you will normally not be too far from a park, a formal garden, a reservoir or even some waste ground, all of which attract their share of birdlife.

If you have your own garden, then chances are that you are already aware of various bird residents and visitors, and the information and suggestions in Chapter Two will add greatly to the pleasure of your back garden birdwatching.

YOUR LOCAL PATCH

Learning to recognise and appreciate the variations in common local birds is the first step to becoming a good birdwatcher, and building up a degree of familiarity with one area is the best way to form a reference base to build upon when you visit other habitats and regions. Even in urban areas, if you look carefully around your local district you will find a surprising range of habitats. Corners of your town or city that you may pay little attention to from day to day—a piece of open waste ground, a small ornamental garden—may prove very interesting from a birdwatching point of view.

Once an area becomes your "local patch", you will soon learn when certain species of migrants arrive in the spring and autumn, which birds are most common in winter, which species start to sing when, and so on. With

URBAN SPECIALISTS *Grey Herons (above left), Jackdaws (above) and Mute Swans (left) are among the birds that have thrived in urban areas across much of Europe.*

IN THE CITY *many urban parks (left) attract a host of migrant birds. High on an antenna, a Starling (below) noisily declares its presence. House Sparrows (right) are easily attracted to almost any suburban garden.*

time and patience, you can learn a great deal about bird behaviour and nesting biology right on your own doorstep.

Rare Visitors

While relatively few species of birds live permanently in cities, or are regular visitors, a quite remarkable number of different species have been recorded in towns and cities at one time or another.

This is in part due to the fact that all urban areas are fragmented environments that can contain a broad range of habitat types, and these habitats attract a correspondingly varied range of species. In particular, many migrating and vagrant birds (birds that are lost or off course) will make temporary use of any small pocket of suitable habitat that they can find, even in the centre of a city.

These migrants and vagrants are far more likely to be detected in urban areas than in more remote regions. In cities and suburbs there are often hundreds or thousands of bird-watchers, and there is a better chance of any visiting rarity being noted. Indeed, a number of countries in Europe have well-organised "hotlines" (see p. 279 for numbers in Britain and Ireland) that one can telephone to receive a recorded summary of the rarities "in town tonight". Many a birdwatcher has accumulated a very respectable life list based solely on the species seen in his or her own home town.

LOCAL RESOURCES

For birdwatchers, one great advantage of living in an urban area is that you will almost certainly have access to local resources such as birdwatching clubs and educational institutions that may hold classes or talks relating to birdwatching.

Most of these clubs have the equivalent of an activities officer who organises bird-watching trips and excursions, typically ranging from half-day walks in a local park to two-week expeditions to far-off corners of the continent. Many trips are designed as outings for beginners, and some are bound to fit your own particular circumstances.

With a guidebook such as this one you can identify many species on your own, but nothing equals having an experienced birdwatcher explain to you—on the spot, while the bird is in view—just what you should be looking for.

For details of organisations in your area, see p. 277.

Mute Swan

Cygnus olor

J F M A M J J A S O N D

Mute swans are familiar and graceful residents of our parks, ponds and rivers. With their long necks, they can forage on submerged water plants. Occasionally you can see them with their heads submerged and their tails in the air, paddling with their feet to reach for the deepest plants. This posture is called "up-ending", and can also be observed in several species of dabbling ducks.

Pairs are usually formed for life. If you see a pair, look at the black knob above the bill: the bird with the largest is the male. Mute Swans can raise large families. Their young are dull grey until they moult into the white adult plumage.

In contrast with their slow and graceful movements, the males can fight fiercely in territorial disputes, sometimes until death. During autumn and winter, they gather in large flocks on lakes and rivers. Two smaller species can be found in Britain and Europe in winter: the Whooper Swan and Bewick's Swan (p. 166), both breeding birds of the arctic tundra. Apart from the colour of the bill, Mute Swans can be distinguished from these species by their longer tails and curved necks.

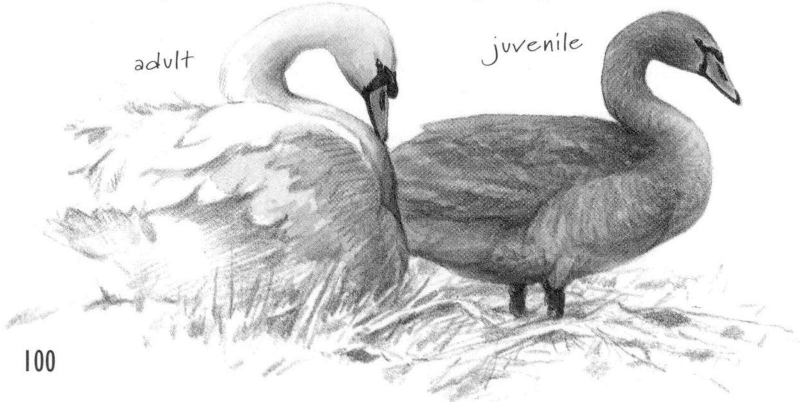

FIELD NOTES

- 57–63" (145–160 cm)
- White
- Orange bill with black knob
- Curved neck
- Huge platform, made of reed stems and dry grass
- ♪ Hissing when aggressive, "whooshing" wings in flight

Adult male

Mallard

Anas platyrhynchos

J F M A M J J A S O N D

The Mallard is the most widespread and familiar duck in the northern hemisphere. As it is often tame and found in city parks, it can provide an excellent opportunity for learning the important basics of duck breeding, biology, plumage and moult—lessons that will serve you well when identifying less familiar species.

Mallards are the ancestors of all breeds of domestic or farmyard ducks, except the Muscovy Duck. Wild and feral birds may interbreed in parks, giving rise to an array of plumages ranging from typical male Mallards, with their green head, white neck band, and mahogany breast, to birds that are mostly white. Females are dull brown and mottled, like most female dabbling ducks.

The young, like all ducks, are precocial (p. 41) and able to feed on their own as soon as they are out of the egg and dry. After breeding, the males concentrate in moulting sites, where they shed their feathers. They even moult all their flight feathers at the same time, rendering them temporarily flightless. During this period, they have a brown, female-like eclipse plumage, which makes them less conspicuous during this vulnerable time.

FIELD NOTES

- *20–24½" (51–62 cm)*
- *Male: glossy green head, mahogany breast, narrow white collar; bill greenish yellow*
- *Female: mottled dull brown; bill orange with brown*
- *Cup of leaves and grass on ground, lined with down*
- *A nasal "quack"*

Adult male

Kestrel

Falco tinnunculus

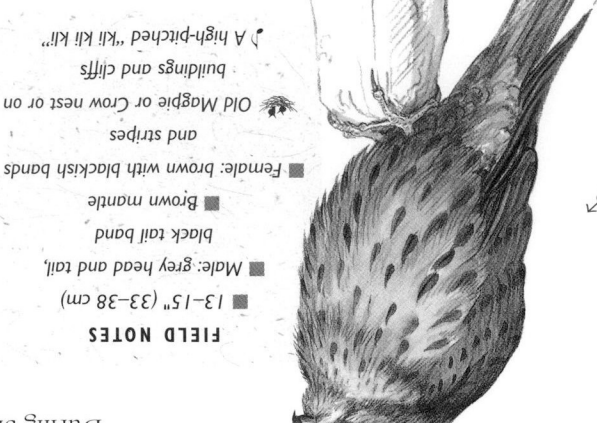

The Kestrel is the most familiar falcon throughout Europe and Asia and large parts of Africa. It is a common sight perched on roadside wires or hunting, with its characteristic hovering flight, over fields and roadside verges. With rapid wing movements Kestrels can hang still in the air, and then plunge down with folded wings like a stone if they spot a mouse or lizard. When hovering, they spread their tail, which reveals whether the bird is an adult male or a female: males have a grey, unbarred tail with a black terminal band, whereas the female's upperparts and tail are a more uniform reddish brown, barred with black.

J F M A M J J A S O N D

The pointed wings of the Kestrel and other falcons distinguish them from buzzards and Sparrowhawks, which have broader and rounded wings. As with many raptors, females are larger than males, and this helps them to stay at the nest for longer periods.

During breeding, the male brings food while the female takes care of the eggs and young. Prey is usually passed from one bird to the other in the air near the nest. Populations fluctuate, depending on food supply. In years when rodents are plentiful, more young survive than in other years.

♂

FIELD NOTES

- *13–15" (33–38 cm)*
- *Male: grey head and tail, black tail band*
- *Brown mantle*
- *Female: brown with blackish bands and stripes*
- *Old Magpie or Crow nest or on buildings and cliffs*
- ♪ *A high-pitched "kli kli kli"*

Moorhen

Gallinula chloropus

JFMAMJJASOND

Almost every kind of freshwater habitat, from small ponds to large lakes and small streams to wide rivers, is home to the Moorhen. It is a highly adaptable species and found in cities, suburbs and almost every park, as long as there is water with some reed vegetation as cover.

When swimming or walking, the tail is held high and jerked incessantly. The white undertail coverts constantly flash white. Moorhens readily walk about in the open on the grass in parks. They are usually solitary, but sometimes form small groups during winter.

Moorhens build nests concealed in dense vegetation. The chicks are sooty black with a bright red bill. They can swim from the first day, but still need to be fed by the parents. Their breeding biology is special in that young birds of earlier broods will help their parents in raising a subsequent brood—this type of behaviour is rare among birds.

The Moorhen is a truly cosmopolitan species, occurring all over the world, except Australia.

FIELD NOTES

- *$12\frac{1}{2}$–$13\frac{3}{4}$" (32–35 cm)*
- *Black, white undertail coverts*
- *Yellow bill with bright red shield*
- *Greenish legs*
- *Just above waterline, reed stems on rotting plant material*
- *♪ A sudden, gurgling "pyurrrrk" or "kurruk" and a sharp "kik ack"*

Coot

Fulica atra

Coots are likely to be found on almost any urban water. These sooty-black birds with their ivory-coloured bills and pure white shields, dive frequently to gather aquatic plants and organisms. But they also love to be fed bread in parks and ponds.

Their downy young are surprisingly brightly coloured, with fiercely red heads, bluish eye patches and a few spiky yellow hairs. While begging for food they constantly utter a penetrating call reminiscent of rusty door hinges.

In winter, Coots flock together on lakes, and during cold spells, some may also move to the coast. They do not fly often and have to run a long distance paddling the water surface before taking off. If they walk on land, see if you can see their lobed toes.

The similar Moorhen (p. 103) is easily distinguished from a Coot by its red-and-yellow bill and the white stripe along its sides. Moorhens skulk more than Coots and are less likely to be seen on open water or in groups.

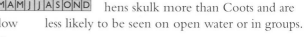

J	F	M	A	M	J	J	A	S	O	N	D

FIELD NOTES

- 14–15" (36–38 cm)
- Sooty black
- Brilliantly white bill and frontal shield
- Greyish legs with lobed toes
- ▲ *Moorhens can be distinguished by their red-and-yellow bill and the white stripe along their side.*
- *Reed stems, among vegetation, sometimes floating*
- ♪ *A repeated "kwok" and explosive, high "pitts"*

Black-headed Gull

Larus ridibundus

J F M A M J J A S O N D

The Black-headed Gull is the most common and widespread gull in Europe and is very well adapted to an urban way of life. It will take almost any type of food and can be found outside the breeding season almost everywhere, including inner cities.

Black-headed Gulls breed in noisy and often very large colonies, always near water and usually on small islands. During this time of the year, they have a chocolate-brown cap with white "eyebrows". As early as summer, the dark feathers begin to be replaced by white winter ones. Young, freshly fledged birds are, surprisingly, dark brown. These juvenile feathers, however, are quickly replaced by grey winter feathers. During winter, young birds still can be recognised from mature birds by browner feathers on the mantle and wing coverts.

Being so well adapted to the human environment, Black-headed Gulls do not usually migrate over large distances. Many birds from the North and East spend the winter in Western Europe due to the mild climate and the extensive urban areas that meet all of their feeding and roosting requirements.

FIELD NOTES

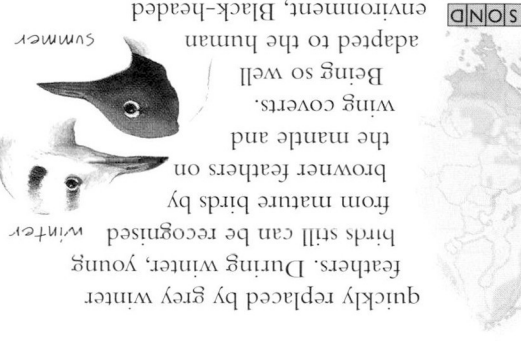

- *15–17¼" (38–44 cm)*
- *Summer: with dark brown hood and grey mantle*
- *Winter: white head with black spot*
- *Red bill and legs*
- *Nests in colonies, a shallow cup, scruffy, dry grass, leaves*
- *♪ A raw "aäarrgghh"*

Feral Rock Dove

Columba livia

Also known as Feral Pigeons, Feral Rock Doves are among the birds most familiar to city dwellers throughout Europe. The natural environments of their wilder cousins are rocky seacoasts and mountainous areas. This is an outstanding example of a bird that was domesticated for showing and racing purposes and which has now successfully colonised the human environment. Healthy populations can be found in most towns and cities across Europe.

Many city dwellers enjoy feeding these birds, so they have become extremely tame and are sometimes quite a nuisance, with large numbers nesting on windows sills and in enclosed areas. However, the Feral Rock Dove's tameness provides many opportunities for observing interesting aspects of bird behaviour (often difficult and time-consuming when watching truly wild birds). These include social hierarchy in feeding groups (individual recognition is made easy by the pigeons' varied plumages), courtship and even their drinking. Pigeons are among the very few birds that drink by sucking up water.

FIELD NOTES

- *12–14" (30.5–35.5 cm)*
- *White rump*
- *Double black wingbar*
- *Plumage highly variable*
- *Shallow saucer of sticks on a ledge*
- *♪ During display flight "kooo-rooo-kooo"*

Collared Dove

Streptopelia decaocto

J F M A M J J A S O N D

Collared Doves are small, pale grey-brown doves with a relatively long tail. A narrow black collar distinguishes the Collared Dove from the similar Turtle Dove (p. 130), which is chestnut brown on the mantle and wings and has a broad, diffuse collar. In spring, the soft songs of Collared Doves can be heard in many gardens and almost every park.

They make a very simple nest from branches high up in trees or in crevices of old buildings. Their food consists of a wide variety of seeds and berries. Less appreciated is their love of seeds provided for hens.

For a species so widespread today, it is difficult to imagine that less than 50 years ago Collared Doves were completely absent from Europe. They colonised North-western Europe in the early 'fifties and established themselves for the first time in Britain in 1955 (in Norfolk). Since then, the species has been incredibly successful and is now one of the commonest and most widespread birds in Europe. In winter, Collared Doves roam the countryside in small flocks, finding food in fields and farmyards.

FIELD NOTES

■ *12¼–13¼" (31–34 cm)*

■ *Pale grey-brown*

■ *Narrow black collar on neck*

■ *Long tail with broad white band*

▲ *Turtle Dove is chestnut brown on the mantle and wings and has a broad, diffuse collar.*

Simple "saucer" of sticks high in the trees

♪ *A repeated "roo-kooo, koo"*

Swift

Apus apus

After wintering in Africa, Swifts return to Britain and Europe at the end of April and during May each year. Look for Swifts over towns, open country and lakes, and listen for their high-pitched screaming calls.

Swifts are supreme flyers, well adapted for life on the wing. In this way they resemble Swallows, but although the two families look alike and are often seen together, they are not closely related. The Swift can be distinguished from the Swallow by its more rapid, stiff wing beats; faster and more direct flight; and overall blackish plumage.

The Swift originally nested in hollow trees, as it still does in Northern Europe, but has readily adapted to nesting under roof tiles or in holes in old buildings.

Swifts feed on aerial insects and spiders by "raking" them in their large gape. The food is stored in the crop as a small ball. During bad weather in spring or summer, they stop feeding the young, which survive for several days by lowering their body temperature (torpor) and becoming lethargic. Males and non-breeding immatures sleep at night high in the air and may fly continuously for many months.

FIELD NOTES

- *$6\frac{1}{4}$–$6\frac{3}{4}$" (16–17 cm)*
- *Sooty black*
- *Scythe-shaped wings*
- *Forked tail*
- *Clumsy heap of grass, feathers, dry leaves glued with saliva*
- ♪ *Shrill, screaming "srreee"*

Swallow

Hirundo rustica

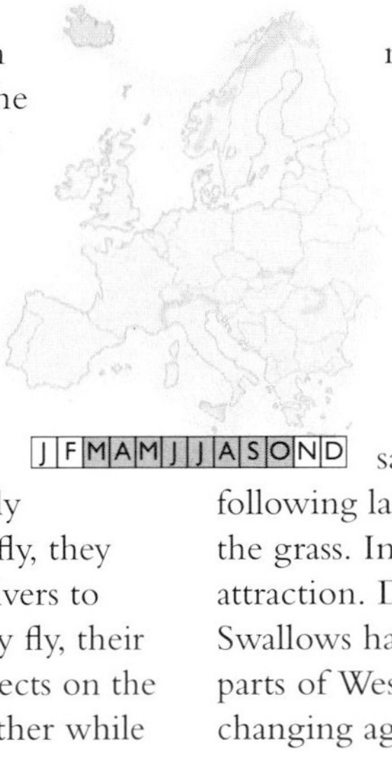

J F M A M J J A S O N D

A familiar summer visitor to urban and rural areas across Europe, the Swallow is often welcomed as a herald of spring. This graceful bird, identified by its long tail streamers (short or lacking in the juvenile), nests singly or in small colonies on or inside buildings, where it builds a cup-like nest of mud.

Swallows are masters of the air, where they swoop and glide, apparently effortlessly, for hours on end. As they fly, they dip down to the surface of lakes and rivers to drink and bathe. They also feed as they fly, their wide gapes enabling them to catch insects on the wing. When forced down by bad weather while migrating, they can be seen in huge numbers feeding on insects over lakes and rivers.

In autumn, they roost in reedbeds, sometimes in flocks of thousands, and at dusk gather and settle swiftly in the reeds before nightfall.

Swallows winter in the African savanna and rural areas, often following large mammals that disturb insects in the grass. In Europe, grazing cattle have the same attraction. Despite their abundance, however, Swallows have decreased in number over large parts of Western Europe, mainly because of changing agricultural practices.

FIELD NOTES

■ *5–5½" (12.5–14 cm)*

■ *Glossy blue above, reddish face*

■ *Deeply forked tail with streamers*

■ *Dark rump*

Mud cup lined with grass and feathers on or inside buildings and barns

♪ *A cheerful "vit" or "vit vit"*

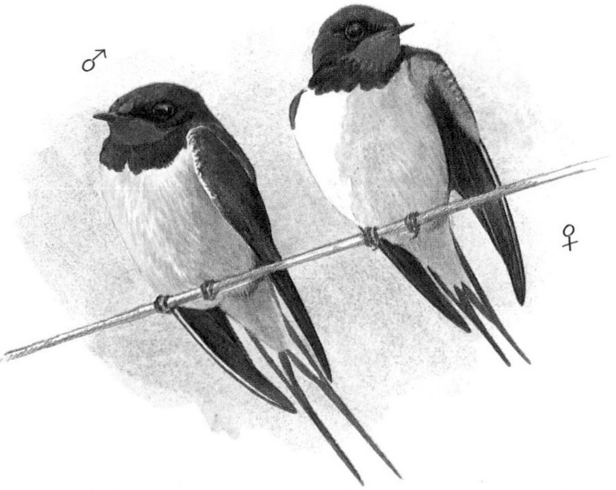

House Martin

Delichon urbica

House Martins can be easily recognised by their white rumps. If you look at them closely, you will see the brilliant glossy blue on their heads and backs.

These handsome birds are highly social and build their nests in small colonies on buildings. The nest is bowl-shaped and made of mud, which the birds collect from the edges of ponds or from small pools of rainwater.

Aerial insects are their main food, which they catch as high as 330 feet (100 m).

J F M A M J J A S O N D

House Martins forage in higher regions than Swallows (p. 109), but still lower than Swifts (p. 108). On summer days, their cheerful call, a babbling twitter, can be heard. In autumn, House Martins leave behind the cold European weather to spend the winter in tropical Africa. On migration, they join other groups of hirundines. In April and May, they return to their northern breeding grounds.

FIELD NOTES

- *5" (12.5 cm)*
- *Blue-glossed black*
- *White rump*
- *White underparts*
- *Bowl-shaped cup of dried mud lined with feathers*
- ♪ *A rasping "prit"; song: a prolonged twitter*

Bowl-shaped nest of mud

Pied Wagtail

Motacilla alba

J F M A M J J A S O N D

Pied Wagtails are lively birds of open fields, farmland and urban areas. Wagtails get their name from their characteristic tail movement: after landing, they pump their tail up and down incessantly. When they spot an insect, they dash over to it with remarkable speed.

These strikingly patterned birds are often, but not always, found along the margins of ponds, rivers and lakes, and announce their presence with a melodious *chizzik* or *tslee-vit*. Small territories are defended against birds of their own species.

Two races occur in Europe, the race *M. a. yarrellii*, almost exclusively in Britain, and the race *M. a. alba*—also known as the White Wagtail—in the rest of the Continent. In most plumages, Pied can be distinguished from White by its black mantle and back and sooty-grey flanks.

Pied Wagtails are usually resident, but White Wagtails move from Northern Europe to winter southward as far as Central Africa. Outside the breeding season, Pied Wagtails roost in groups of hundreds, sometimes thousands, of birds. Just before dusk, they can be seen flying in to gather at their roosting sites, which are usually reedbeds but sometimes greenhouses and even city buildings.

FIELD NOTES

■ 6¾–7" (17–18 cm)

■ Black crown and back, white mask, sooty-grey flanks

■ Long black-and-white tail

▲ White Wagtail has a grey back and white flanks and are common in Europe in March–October

Cup of grass lined with hair and feathers

♪ A melodious "chizzik" or "tslee-vit"

Black Redstart

Phoenicurus ochruros

Although they originate from mountainous regions in Southern Europe, Black Redstarts have successfully adapted to city life. Their melancholy song, a Wren-like *swee-swee-swee-swee,* can be heard coming from high perches on residential or industrial buildings. They can be difficult to spot, but if you find one, perhaps on a church tower or chimney, look out for its tail. It is reddish and quivers every time the bird moves or dashes for insects. Black Redstarts typically hover and flutter along the walls of houses when searching for food.

In Britain, the species is an uncommon breeding bird or passing migrant. On the Continent, birds are present in spring and autumn but few stay for winter. More widespread is its close relative the Redstart (*P. phoenicurus*; 5½" [14 cm]). The male Redstart (see p. 131) is easily distinguished from the male Black Redstart by its red breast and belly and white forehead. It also lacks the white wing patch found on the male Black Redstart. Females are rather similar, but the female Redstart has a pale throat and buffish belly. This species is a long-distance migrant to Africa, south of the Sahara. Droughts in the Sahel have caused a decrease in numbers throughout Europe.

FIELD NOTES

- *5½" (14 cm)*
- *Male: dark grey; black throat, red outer tail feathers and rump, white wing patch*
- *Female: grey-brown, except for reddish tail and rump*

▲ *Female Redstart is similar, except for the pale throat and buffish belly*

Cup of dry vegetation lined with wool and feathers

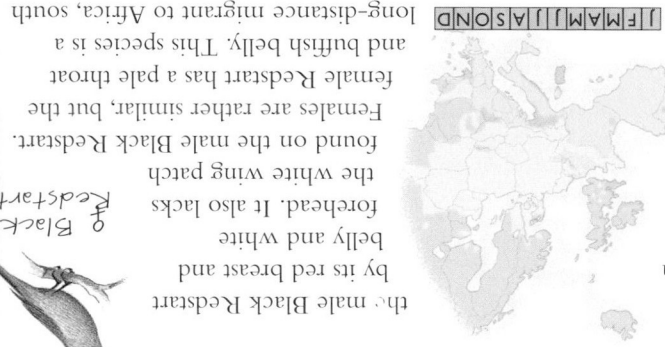

♪ *Call: "tseep", sometimes followed by "tak-tak-tak"; song: "swee-swee-swee"*

Blackbird

Turdus merula

The Blackbird is one of the most familiar birds of gardens and parks. Throughout the year, Blackbirds can be seen stalking on lawns while looking for earthworms. Young birds and females are earth brown, a perfect camouflage for their typical environment amid the leaf litter and the dark soil of woodlands and parks. Adult males are entirely black, except for a bright orange-yellow bill and ring around the eye.

Like many thrushes, Blackbirds spend much time on the ground. In autumn and winter, when earthworms and insects are difficult to find, they switch to fruit and berries. If disturbed, they will fly directly into cover uttering a penetrating and repeated *chak*. Blackbirds have a pleasant song with slow, flute-like notes, which they deliver in a rather lazy and relaxed manner.

Some Blackbirds migrate south for the winter, while others stay in Britain. This phenomenon is called partial migration. In late autumn, large numbers of birds arrive in Britain from Scandinavia. These northern migrants are somewhat larger than the resident birds, and return to their breeding grounds in early spring.

FIELD NOTES

- *9½–9¾" (24–25 cm)*
- *Male: black; yellow bill*
- *Female: dark brown; pale brown throat and breast*
- *Compact cup of dry plants strengthened with soil, lined with fine grass*
- ♪ *A tongue-clicking "chak", also a thin "tseeh"*

Magpie

Pica pica

The raucous call of the Magpie is a common sound in much of the British countryside, from farmland and woods to urban areas. They are watchful birds and will give noisy alarm calls if cats or birds of prey are near. Magpies build bulky nests, which are used year after year and are conspicuous features of the landscape.

J F M A M J J A S O N D

From a distance Magpies look black and white, but a closer view reveals green, purple and blue in the gloss of the black feathers. Males are slightly larger than females, and pairs are usually formed for life. Birds with short tails are lowest in rank. Juvenile birds without a territory often form loose flocks, especially in winter. In spring, large aggregations of more than one hundred birds are occasionally observed. It is thought that pair-bonding takes place in these so-called "arenas".

Magpies are omnivores and are infamous for their occasional interest in the eggs and young of other birds.

FIELD NOTES

- *17¼–18¾" (44–48 cm)*
- *Glossy black with white*
- *Long black tail*
- *White wing patches*
- *Bulky, dome-shaped structure of branches, inside neatly lined with fine branches and roots*
- *♪ Hoarse, croaking call*

Jackdaw

Corvus monedula

The Jackdaw is one of the most social and intelligent of birds. Jackdaws breed in colonies in towns and villages, often in or near church towers or in holes in old trees. Pairs stay together for life, and are usually seen flying or foraging together, except when they are raising young.

J F M A M J J A S O N D

Jackdaws are omnivores and feed in fields, farmland, parks and gardens. In winter, they flock together with other corvids, particularly Rooks. Then they can be recognised by their smaller size and quicker movements.

In autumn and winter, migrants from Northern and Eastern Europe reinforce the resident stocks in Western Europe. These northern birds of the race *C. m. monedula* can sometimes be distinguished from the resident race *C. m. spermologus* by their light grey necks with a whitish crescent on the sides.

Outside the breeding season, Jackdaws roost communally in large flocks. You can often see them in the evening performing acrobatic manoeuvres on air currents, before settling into trees to sleep.

"Northern" Jackdaw

FIELD NOTES

- *13" (33 cm)*
- *Black; grey nape*
- *Pale grey eye*
- *Short bill*

▲ *"Northern" Jackdaws have a light grey neck with whitish crescent on the sides*

Bulky cup of branches in hollows or trees, lined with hairs and feathers

♪ *Metallic "kya" or short, high-pitched "chak"*

Jackdaw

Starling

Sturnus vulgaris

J F M A M J J A S O N D

Whether feeding and squabbling in city parks or flying in vast swarms to roost in the warmth of town centres, Starlings are a familiar sight in cities across Britain and Europe.

These birds are easy to watch and provide a good opportunity to observe how summer and winter plumages can vary. Most songbirds moult twice a year, but the Starling has a single moult in late summer (after breeding), when the glossy adult and the dull grey juvenile acquire new blackish feathers marked profusely with pale spots. The spots then wear off through the winter, to be replaced by the purple and green sheens of summer plumage. The bird's bill is darker in winter and changes to a bright yellow in breeding birds.

Starlings are masterly mimics, copying not only songs and calls of birds but also mechanical sounds. Melodious song elements are alternated with characteristic whistles, chirps and twitters. Starlings are also very vocal when flocking together before roosting.

Most Starlings in Western Europe migrate southwest in autumn, to be replaced by huge flocks from Northern and Eastern Europe and Western Asia.

winter plumage

FIELD NOTES

- 8–9" (20.5–23 cm)
- Stocky, stub-tailed bird
- Glossy black plumage
- Winter: speckled plumage, dark bill
- Cup of grass and twigs in cavity
- ♪ Clicks, chirps, twitters and clear whistles, also mimicry

summer plumage

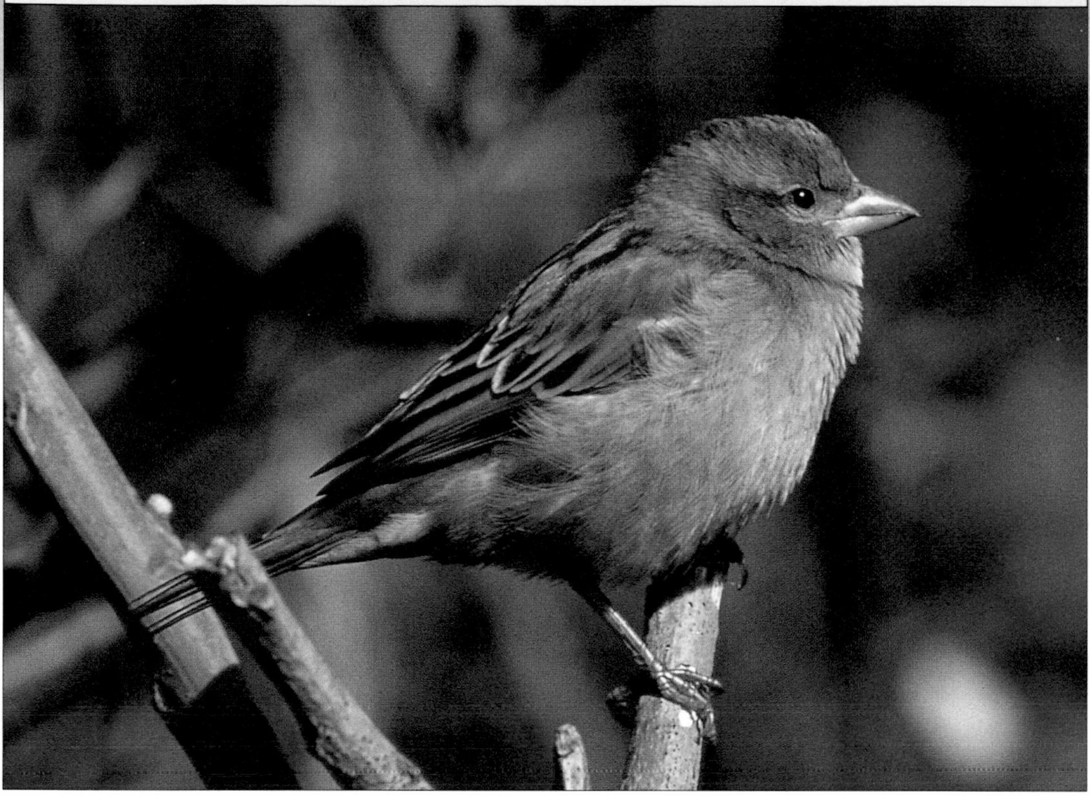

House Sparrow

Passer domesticus

J F M A M J J A S O N D

House Sparrows like to live near humans and, along with the Feral Rock Dove (Feral Pigeon), they are perhaps the bird most familiar to city dwellers. Their chirps and chatters may be heard all over town, from the inner city to wooded parks and gardens in the suburbs.

The male is quite handsome, with chestnut-coloured head stripes and a black bib. In winter, his bill is dusky palish brown, but in summer, it becomes blacker. Males with larger bibs are dominant over small-bibbed males. During fights among them, these bibs are shown off by pushing the chin and breast forward. If you want to practise taking notes and sketching birds in the field, the female House Sparrow is a good subject to start with, providing an excellent introduction to bird anatomy and the subtleties of plumage. This superficially nondescript bird can puzzle even experienced birdwatchers when they encounter it out of context.

House Sparrows eat a variety of food including seeds and insects. They nest in cavities and beneath roof tiles. Although still very common, they have decreased somewhat in number due to changes in agriculture and the loss of nesting sites as a result of improved roof insulation.

FIELD NOTES

- ■ *5½–6" (14–15 cm)*
- ■ *Male: grey crown, grey rump*
- ■ *Female and juvenile: brownish*
- ▲ *Tree Sparrow: sexes similar, chestnut crown and black ear spot*
- *Bulky dome of grass and straw in a cavity or dense foliage*
- ♪ *Call: a chatty "chilp" or "cheerp"*

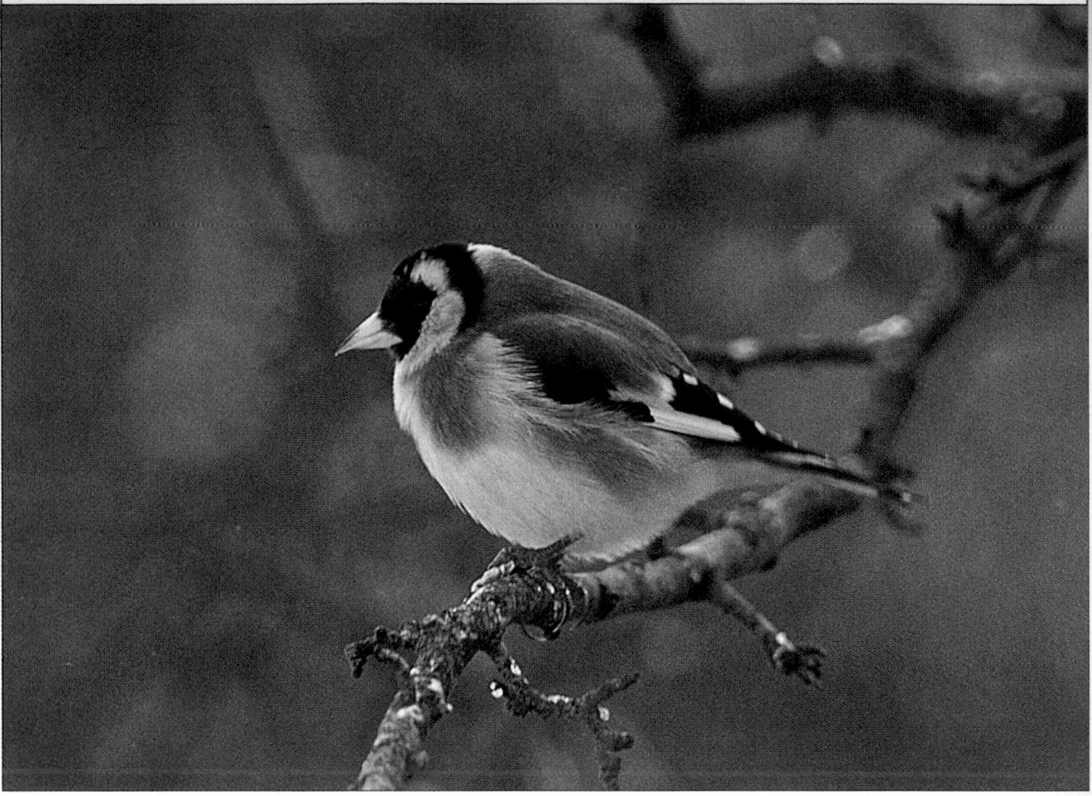

Goldfinch

Carduelis carduelis

The Goldfinch is one of the most colourful birds in Britain and Europe. Its golden-yellow wing patches are particularly conspicuous in flight, when the white rump and black-and-white tail also show well. Juvenile birds lack the red face, which is acquired by a moult in autumn.

With their long, pointed bills, Goldfinches are well adapted to take the deep-seated seeds of thistles on which they prefer to feed. Look for these plants, or teasels and burdocks, in autumn, and you will often find a flock of Goldfinches feeding on them. Young birds are fed almost exclusively with insects.

Some of the British breeding population migrates south in autumn and returns in spring. Goldfinches can be found in open cultivated country with hedgerows, in woodland edges and gardens in suburbs. Goldfinches have a characteristic call, a soft and tinkling *stikelitt* or a simple *stik*.

Goldfinch on a thistle

FIELD NOTES

- *5½" (14 cm)*
- *Black-and-white head with red face*
- *Black wing with yellow patch*
- *Pointed beak*
- *Strongly braided cup of grass, moss and poplar fluff high in a tree, lined with hair and wool*
- *♪ Soft, tinkling "stik" or "stikelitt"*

Woodlands

CANOPY Warblers and flycatchers are typical of a number of songbirds that spend much of their time high in the canopy.

CONIFEROUS FOREST is favoured by a number of species. Listen for the high-pitched song of Goldcrests, and watch out for Coal Tits and crossbills.

MIDDLE LEVEL Thrushes, nuthatches, tits and most woodpeckers are among those birds most commonly seen in the middle foliage layers of the forest.

WOODLANDS

Forests, Clearings and Heaths, Riverside Vegetation, Woodland Edge, Thickets

Many centuries ago, before it became so widely settled, much of Europe was heavily forested. Except in areas such as the drier Mediterranean regions and the northern tundra, forests of differing character covered the continent and reflected profound differences in climate and landscape.

Dense coniferous forests characterised the colder northern countries, with the Caledonian forest of Scotland serving as a western outpost of the vast tracts of pine, spruce and larch that extended east of Scandinavia to the taiga zones of Russia and Siberia. Eastern Europe contained extensive belts of primaeval woodland, a few relict areas of which still remain in Poland today. Much of Britain and Western Europe was covered in deciduous and mixed forest, while farther south were woodlands of different species, such as cork oaks in Spain and poplars in Italy. All these forests supported a different community of birds.

Some original areas of tree cover still remain, but huge expanses were cleared to make way for farmland and human settlement. Plantations of conifers, poplars and other species that have been established in some areas now provide a range of habitats for birds. When the timber is harvested, clearings are created that provide short-term habitat for heathland species. After this, second-growth woodland—forest at an intermediate stage of regrowth—becomes established.

During regrowth, forests go through a series of distinct stages, each with its own plant community. Many birds are characteristic of a specific stage in this process, rather than of a particular area.

Without further setbacks, second-growth woodland will grow to maturity. Forests that have reached equilibrium with their environment are described as climax forests.

In general, deciduous trees lose their leaves in winter, while conifers do not. A forest canopy is described as closed if the trees' foliage overlaps; if it does not, it is said to be open.

While the terms "forest" and "woodland" are generally interchangeable, the former is often used to imply a closed canopy, whereas the latter often suggests an open canopy.

FOREST EDGE Birds along forest edges may be of the same species as those within the forest, but are much easier to observe.

CLEARINGS AND HEATHS are attractive to many birds that use woodland for nesting and roosting but prefer to feed in the open. Other birds, such as the Woodlark and Dartford Warbler, only occur in heathland areas and forest clearings.

UNDERSTOREY Some woodland birds, such as Dunnocks, Wrens and Nightingales, spend almost all of their time on or near the ground. Depending on locality, grouse, Woodcocks and Nightjars may also be found at this level.

BIRDWATCHING *in* WOODLANDS

European woodlands contain a wealth of birdlife. However, dense foliage can make it difficult to locate many species, so you may be able to identify some only by their calls. Moreover, what you hear and see will depend very much on the time of year.

In winter, the Northern European woods are home only to those birds that eat foods which last through cold weather, such as seeds, and insects that shelter under tree bark. These birds often congregate in wandering, mixed feeding parties of several species—woodpeckers, nuthatches, treecreepers, tits, and others—all moving through the woods together in search of food. You might walk for an hour or more through a forest that seems to be entirely empty of birdlife, then suddenly encounter such a flock. For a few moments only, the trees will be crowded with birds, but the birds keep moving along and soon their soft calls will die away in the distance and the woods will become silent again.

In the warmer climates of Southern and Western Europe, you may find more species in winter, perhaps including a few warblers such as Goldcrest and Firecrest.

In spring and summer, there is food for many more birds, and Nightingales, Redstarts, warblers, flycatchers and a host of other birds return from their winter homes in sub-Saharan Africa to nest. The spring and autumn migration periods (mainly April to May and August to October) are therefore the best times to see the most species, particularly if you live in Southern Europe.

WOODLAND WATCHERS *A group of birdwatchers takes a close look at a woodland bird. Stiff necks are an occupational hazard of forest birdwatching, as so many of the birds are situated directly above you.*

HABITAT PREFERENCES *Some species frequent only one type of forest—either deciduous or coniferous. Crested Tits (right) prefer conifers; Hawfinches (above right) favour deciduous woods.*

WOODLAND BIRDS *may live mostly on the ground, as the Woodcock (above) does; in the middle layers of foliage, as in the case of the Coal Tit (left); or high in the canopy, like the Wood Warbler (below left).*

Knowing the Habitat

In woodlands, perhaps more than in other habitats, it pays to learn something about the details of the environment, in particular the names of the trees and other plants that you will see around you.

Many bird species are closely associated with specific trees and bushes. If you take time to learn the names of these plants and note which birds you see on or near them, you will soon be able to predict, just by studying the surrounding flora, which birds are likely to inhabit a particular area of forest.

In the text of The Habitat Birdfinder we indicate, where relevant, which trees and plants each species is most closely associated with.

Tracking by Ear

Unlike marshlands and open country, where birds can be readily seen, woodlands may at first seem less rich in birdlife, since birds can easily remain out of sight in the foliage. In these conditions, your hearing becomes an important aspect of birdwatching.

It takes practice to learn the songs and calls of different species (see p. 72). A useful way to start is to listen to recordings of songs and calls at home.

When in your local woods, try tracking down the sources of songs and calls for yourself. At first, identifying the bird by sight will be easier than by its call, but as you match the most common songs and calls with the species that make them, you will soon be able to identify those birds as soon as you hear them. In turn, you will be able to distinguish the songs of species that are new to you.

Learning something of the meaning or context of bird calls in woods can also be useful. For example, small woodland birds have a characteristic alarm note they use if a bird of prey is in the area, and the scolding notes they make on discovering an owl at its daytime roost can often lead you to the owl itself.

STEALTH AND STRATEGY

You need to move quietly in woodlands, not so much for fear of scaring birds away as for your own ability to concentrate on what you can hear. The denser the forest, the truer this is, tropical rainforests being the extreme case. Look for a trail or some little-used country track to wander along, rather than crashing through the understorey. Remember to keep scanning all levels of the forest. Some species are birds of the treetops and seldom come low. Others prefer the middle levels, and quite a few species are almost always found in the understorey or on the ground.

Woodland birds vary widely in their response to a human observer. Some are extremely wary, while a few are inquisitive and may even follow you as you go. If you are patient and move carefully or, better yet, sit still for a while, many woodland birds will accept your presence. The trick is not to crowd the bird, or trigger its "startle"

response. Once startled into flight, the bird is unlikely to allow you within range again.

Red Kite

Milvus milvus

J F M A M J J A S O N D

With its rusty-red colour and white wing patches, slender wings and forked tail, the Red Kite is one of the most elegant and handsome raptors in Europe.

When flying, the long, forked tail is constantly tilted at different angles to help steer the bird's flight, a behaviour typical for most kite species.

A close relative is the Black Kite (*M. migrans*; 21½–23½" [55–60 cm]), which shares the typical kite silhouette and flight action, but is smaller, more uniformly coloured and has a shallowly forked tail. It is a common and widespread bird in Continental Europe, migrating to Africa to winter, but is only rarely seen in Britain. The Red Kite, however, is mainly resident, though young birds may wander.

The Red Kite is a true European endemic bird species, with an isolated population in Wales. It has been heavily persecuted in the past and much action has been taken to protect this species, including recent reintroduction programmes in parts of England and Scotland. It lives on small rodents and birds and large insects, but also takes carrion.

FIELD NOTES

■ 24–26" (61–66 cm)

■ Deeply forked tail, rusty-red body

■ Underwing with white wing patches

▲ Black Kite is dark brown and has a shallowly forked tail

Stick platform at mid to upper levels in tree

♪ Near nest: "hee-hee-hee-heeagh"

Adult male

Sparrowhawk

Accipiter nisus

The Sparrowhawk is the most common small woodland raptor in Europe. Like other accipiters (from the genus name), it preys mainly on small birds, and may visit gardens to take sparrows and other species, as its name suggests. Even birds at feeders are taken—a spectacular sight to witness.

J F M A M J J A S O N D

To tell the Sparrowhawk from small falcons such as the Kestrel (p. 102), note the broad, rounded wings and its flight style—bursts of quick flapping followed by a glide. Adult males are slaty grey above and barred orange-red below. Adult females are larger, brownish grey above and barred brown below. Females can be confused with the much larger Goshawk (*A. gentilis*; 19–23½" [48–60 cm]). In this latter species, females are clearly larger still—the size of a Common Buzzard (p. 126). Look for the shape of the wings: the basal part of the wing, called the "arm", is broader and the tip, known as the hand, is narrower than in a Sparrowhawk.

FIELD NOTES

- *11–15" (28–38 cm)*
- *Long tail and blunt wings*
- *Females: clearly larger than males*
- ▲ *Goshawk is much larger with longer wings*
- *Stick platform at mid to upper levels in tree*
- ♪ *In breeding season "kyi-kyi-kyi"*

Common Buzzard

Buteo buteo

This buteo is the most widespread and familiar buzzard species in Europe. It is found in woodland, farmland and even wooded urban areas. As well as hunting from perches, such as roadside telegraph poles, Common Buzzards often hunt while flying. At times, they can hang, or even hover, in the wind like a giant Kestrel, and then drop down on their prey, usually a rodent.

This hunting behaviour is more typical of the Rough-legged Buzzard (*B. lagopus*; 19½–23½" [50–60 cm]), a breeding bird of the northern tundra, which winters at more southerly latitudes. It can be distinguished by its white tail with a distinct brown terminal band.

J F M A M J J A S O N D

Care should be taken in identification as Common Buzzards are highly variable. Other good markers are the dark carpal patches and dark belly in the Rough-legged Buzzard.

Another similar species, particularly in flight, is the Honey Buzzard (*Pernis apivorus*; 20½–23½" [52–60 cm]). Its long, banded tail and protruding head are important features in distinguishing it from the others. This intriguing species specialises in eating wasp larvae and migrates to tropical Africa in winter.

FIELD NOTES

- ■ 20–22½" (51–57 cm)
- ■ Broad, rounded wings, short tail
- ■ Highly variable; often pale V-mark on breast
- ▲ Rough-legged Buzzard has longer wings and tail, and the tail has a broad black band at the tip
- ▲ Honey Buzzard has a long tail with three dark bands
- Stick platform at mid to upper levels
- ♪ A crying "pieee-lu"

Common Buzzard immature

Hobby

Falco subbuteo

If, on a summer evening, you spot a small falcon capturing dragonflies or other insects and eating them while flying, it will almost certainly be a Hobby. Its slender, pointed wings and short tail often suggest a giant Swift, especially when it is chasing small birds.

Its larger relative, the Peregrine Falcon (*F. peregrinus;* 15¼–19½" [39–50 cm]), specialises in taking medium-size birds, such as waders and small waterbirds, which are also taken in the air. It differs by its larger size, broader wing base and broad moustache-like stripes. Adult Peregrines are finely barred grey-brown below, while juveniles are darker brown above with heavily streaked dark brown underparts. While Peregrines favour open areas, rocky cliffs and the coast, Hobbies prefer open woodland, farmland and marshes. Juvenile birds lack red "trousers" and vent, and are much browner above than adults. In autumn, Hobbies follow their favourite prey, Swallows, to tropical wintering areas in Africa.

J F M A M J J A S O N D

FIELD NOTES

- 11–13¾" (28–35 cm)
- Long, pointed wings, short tail
- Dark grey-brown above, white cheeks
- Reddish "trousers"
- ▲ Peregrine has broad-based, pointed wings and is larger
- Old crow nest
- ♪ In breeding season: "ki-ki-ki-ki..."

Woodcock

Scolopax rusticola

J F M A M J J A S O N D

Few European birds mingle so perfectly into the background of their habitat as the Woodcock. They rely heavily on this camouflage and are usually flushed out only when the unwary observer almost treads on them.

The best time to look for Woodcocks is in spring, when the males perform their territorial display known as "roding"—they fly along a particular route with measured wing beats uttering strange calls: loud squeaks alternating with low grunts.

With its long bill the Woodcock probes for worms and insect larvae among the leaves on the forest floor. Like most waders, it lays four eggs in a shallow cup, which hardly deserves to be called a nest. If disturbed while on the nest, the adult will take one chick between its legs to safety. The young can fly when not more than ten days old.

British birds are predominantly resident, but northerly breeders migrate a short distance to the milder climate in Britain and Western Europe.

FIELD NOTES

- *13–13¼" (33–35 cm)*
- *Large with broad, rounded wings*
- *Plumage patterned like dry leaves*
- *Shallow cup in the ground with some leaves*
- *Males: during territorial display a highly pitched, explosive "pseep" followed by a grunting "orr-orr"*

Woodpigeon

Columba palumbus

This large, stocky pigeon is a common and widespread bird in woodlands, farmland and parks. In autumn and winter, large flocks can be found in fields, often near woodland, and ever vigilant for their eternal enemy, the Goshawk (p. 125).

In autumn, juveniles are easily recognised by the absence of the white collar and greenish gloss to the neck, which is so prominent in adults.

J F M A M J J A S O N D

Another pigeon commonly found along with Woodpigeons in open farmland is the Stock Dove (*C. oenas*; 12½–13" [32–34 cm]). It is clearly smaller and appears almost uniformly grey but for a greenish neck patch. Unlike Woodpigeons, Stock Doves breed in holes in trees made by woodpeckers, in rabbit burrows or in nestboxes.

Both species have a vegetarian diet consisting of beech nuts, acorns, seeds and berries. In Britain and Western Europe both species are resident, but migratory in the North and East.

FIELD NOTES

■ *15¼–16½" (39–42 cm)*

■ *Adult: slaty grey; breast purple-red; white neck patch*

■ *Juvenile: neck without white patch and greenish gloss*

▲ *Stock Dove is smaller and more uniformly grey with no white wingbars*

A very simple platform of sticks

♪ *Display call: a soft "roo-coo-coo coo-coo"*

Turtle Dove

Streptopelia turtur

J F M A M J J A S O N D

On a warm, summer day as you walk along a woodland edge, a purring sound indicates the presence of the Turtle Dove. This small, handsome dove is common in open deciduous woodland and groves in parks and countryside. Turtle Doves are not particularly easy to see, but with some luck you might find one perched in a tree or foraging in a field or meadow.

This species can be distinguished from Collared Doves (p. 107) by its smaller size and reddish-brown, patterned upperparts. The neck patch is broader and striped black and white. When you see a Turtle Dove in flight, which is fast and straight, the dark underwings and white tail markings are distinctive.

Juveniles are more grey-brown above and the mantle and wing coverts lack dark centres; in this plumage they also lack the neck patch of adults. Turtle Doves are highly migratory and winter in tropical Africa; they are still heavily hunted in the Mediterranean as they pass through.

FIELD NOTES

- *10¼–11½" (26–29 cm)*
- *Reddish-brown upperparts*
- *Blue-grey rump*
- *Distinctive white tail patches*
- ▲ *Collared Dove is bigger and has no reddish-brown, patterned upperparts.*
- *Small platform of sticks*
- ♪ *A low, purring "toorrr toorr roorr"*

Cuckoo

Cuculus canorus

Cuckoos announce their presence in spring simply by calling their name. Less well known are the vocal expressions of agitated males, typically a chuckling *kju-kju-kju-kju,* when encountering a rival.

Cuckoos are infamous for their parasitic nesting habits. A female will find a nest of a small songbird and, if it is unattended, lay an egg. Some Cuckoos are uniquely adapted to their host species by producing an egg similar in size and coloration.

J F M A M J J A S O N D

The young Cuckoo throws out other young birds in the nest and grows until it is several times the size of its host parents. It has an insatiable appetite, and the host species, unable to resist the deep red mouth of the young Cuckoo, continues to feed it. The high, penetrating, begging call of a Cuckoo fledgling can sometimes lead you to the pitiful sight of a small bird feeding an enormous chick while standing on the chick's head!

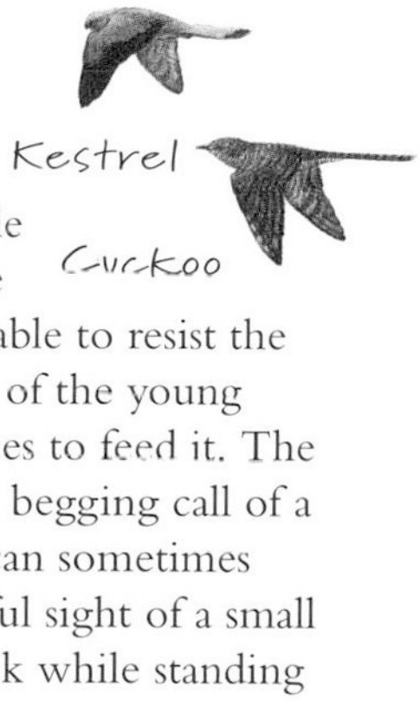

Cuckoos are particularly fond of hairy caterpillars, which are despised by most other birds. Dependent on insects for food, they have to spend the winter in tropical Africa.

FIELD NOTES

- *12½–13¼" (32–34 cm)*
- *In flight resembling Kestrel by pointed wings and long tail*
- *Grey or grey-brown upperparts*
- *Barred below like Sparrowhawk*
- *Lays eggs in nests of songbirds*
- ♪ *In spring: the familiar "hoo-cooh"*

Tawny Owl

Strix aluco

The presence of a sleeping owl is often betrayed by a flock of anxious woodland birds—in particular tits—flying around and mobbing it. If its head is rounded and its eyes are dark, you will have encountered a Tawny Owl.

Another typical woodland owl is the Long-eared Owl (*Asio otus*; 13¾–14½" [35–37 cm]), with orange-red eyes and long eartufts.

J F M A M J J A S O N D

When faced with danger, both owls try to hide by stretching their bodies along the tree trunk and merging into the background. Both species are relatively common and widespread across Britain and Europe in mixed and deciduous forests.

Tawny Owls build their nests in tree holes, but also use old crow or raptor nests. They are strictly nocturnal in foraging habits and take a wide variety of prey, although rodents are preferred.

FIELD NOTES

- *14½–15¾" (37–40 cm)*
- *Dark eyes; reddish-brown plumage*
- *Rounded head without eartufts*
- ▲ *Long-eared Owl has long eartufts and orange-red eyes*
- *Large tree holes or old crow or raptor nests*
- ♪ *Territorial call of male: a melancholy "hoo-hooo"; also a sharp "ki-wik"*

Nightjar

Caprimulgus europaeus

Nightjars are among the most fascinating creatures of the night. Their flight is silent like a falcon's, and they feed on large moths, which they catch mid-flight in their huge gapes. Only at dusk might you catch a glimpse of them over a heathland or open woodland, preferably with young stands of pine.

The male has prominent white patches on the wing and tail. At night his song fills the air with a purring sound varying between two pitches, and occasionally interrupted by a loud *che-wik*.

During short breaks from singing and feeding, the bird often perches on an exposed branch and then may be visible as a silhouette against the fading light.

In the daytime, Nightjars sit on the ground or a branch, made almost invisible by their perfect, cryptic coloration. As might be expected from their strictly insectivorous diet, they leave Europe between August and September for the African savanna, only to return in May.

J F M A M J J A S O N D

FIELD NOTES

- 10¼–11" (26–28 cm)
- *In flight resembles Cuckoo; grey-brown barred*
- *Male: white wing patches*
- *Female: no wing patches*
- *Lays egg on bare ground*
- *Nocturnal song of male: alternating "orrrrrr....errrrrr....orrrrr"*

Green Woodpecker

Picus viridis

J F M A M J J A S O N D

If you hear a loud, laughing call in the woods, you might have disturbed a Green Woodpecker at one of its favourite activities: digging in an ant hill for ants and their nutritious larvae. If you see the bird in flight, look at the rump: bright yellow indicates a male, dull yellow a female. Closer observation will reveal more subtle differences: males also have a red moustache in the black facial mask.

In Continental Europe, a closely related species is the Grey-headed Woodpecker (*P. canus;* 9¾–10¼" [25–26 cm]). This species is smaller and much greyer on the head and underparts than the Green Woodpecker, and lacks its black mask. Only the male Grey-headed has a little red on the forehead. Both species of woodpecker are resident.

Unfortunately, numbers of Green Woodpeckers have decreased somewhat in Continental Europe, as acid rain has made their staple food—ants—more scarce.

FIELD NOTES

- *11¾–13" (30–33 cm)*
- *Green plumage, yellow rump*
- *Red cap and black mask in both sexes*
- ▲ *Grey-headed Woodpecker is greyer on head and below; only male has a little red on crown*
- *Hole dug into trees*
- ♪ *A loud "kjuu-kjuu-kjuu-kjuu"*

Great Spotted Woodpecker

Dendrocopos major

The Great Spotted Woodpecker is the most common and widespread woodpecker in Britain and Europe. It is found in woodlands, parks and even gardens, and provides ample opportunity to get to know the habits and adaptations of woodpeckers in general.

Woodpeckers search for insects and their larvae in and under the bark of trees. With their massive bills they can hammer out deeply buried prey or reach them with their very long tongues. In winter, they become more dependent on seeds, in particular those from conifers.

Much smaller is the Lesser Spotted Woodpecker (*D. minor*; 5½–6" [14–15.5 cm])—in fact the smallest woodpecker in Europe. It looks more uniformly black and white, as only the male has some pinkish red on the crown.

In spring, males choose a dead branch or hollow tree to drum out an acoustic territorial "song". Every species of woodpecker drums in its own specific way, and the Great Spotted can be recognised by its very fast drumming, about 10 to 15 beats per second.

J F M A M J J A S O N D

FIELD NOTES

- *8½–9½" (22–24 cm)*
- *Black and white, reddish undertail coverts*
- *Male: red on nape*
- ▲ *Lesser Spotted Woodpecker is the size of a House Sparrow; lacks red on vent*
- *Hole dug into deciduous trees and conifers*
- ♪ *A loud, explosive "chik"; repeated when alarmed*

Woodlark

Lullula arborea

J F M A M J J A S O N D

Larks are small, ground-dwelling songbirds of open country, grasslands and desert. They are generally streaked brown, have stubby, pointed bills and forage exclusively on the ground.

The Woodlark can be found near woodlands in heathland, or in open country with scattered trees. If you are lucky enough to see one singing high up in the air, you might note its short tail and broad wings that give it a bat-like silhouette. It performs a sweet, melancholy song at night and in the morning.

On the ground, look at the Woodlark's head pattern: the well-defined white supercilium meets on the nape and distinguishes it from all other European larks. However, it is the small black-and-white mark on the leading edge of the wing that is diagnostic.

In Britain, Woodlarks have become rare and now breed locally only on heathlands in the south. Like other lark species, they form flocks on migration.

Woodlark on heathland

FIELD NOTES

- *5¾–6¼" (14.5–16 cm)*
- *Broad wings; short tail*
- *Clear, whitish supercilium*
- *Black-and-white mark on wing*
- *Small cup of grass on the ground*
- ♪ *Call: a clear, fluting "djuoo loo-ueet"*

Wren

Troglodytes troglodytes

J F M A M J J A S O N D

The English translation of the Wren's scientific name—"cave-dweller"—refers to its habit of building dome-shaped nests with a side-entrance, in cavities, nestboxes or dense scrub. The male makes several dummy nests for the female to choose from, then lines the chosen one with feathers ready for egg-laying.

The Wren can be a difficult species to see as it slips in and out of thickets and brush piles. A lively, chortling song or scolding chatter often calls attention to this small, fairly drab-looking brown bird with its slender bill, short, cocked tail and dark barring on the wings, tail and flanks.

Wrens are abundant in places with good undergrowth or shrubbery, such as gardens, parks, woodland and farmland. They are common and widespread in Britain and Europe, from Iceland to Northern Africa. In Britain, they are resident, but migratory in Northern Europe. Several populations in isolated places such as Fair Isle and the Faeroes have evolved subtle differences in plumage.

FIELD NOTES

- 3½–4" (9–10 cm)
- *Reddish brown, whitish supercilium*
- *Short, cocked tail*
- *Dome-shaped nest of moss, leaves and grass lined with feathers*
- ♪ *A loud, dry rattling song; also "trrrrt", "chik" or "chet chet"*

Dunnock

Prunella modularis

The Dunnock is an inconspicuous, common bird of woodlands, parks and gardens that likes areas with undergrowth, shrubs and thickets. In habits it resembles a bunting, but its fine bill suggests a diet of insects.

Its head and breast are slaty grey; its upperparts and flanks streaked warm brown. The overall appearance is quite dark and, because of their skulking behaviour, Dunnocks are not always easy to observe. The male, however, delivers its song from the top of a low bush or tree, usually at dawn. The clear jingle is Wren-like, but slower and varied around one pitch.

In contrast to its rather unremarkable appearance, the Dunnock engages in a highly complex social life during the breeding season. Although they form breeding pairs, many females raise their young with the help of two males. While either male could have fathered her brood, one is usually dominant over the other. Some of these habits may be revealed when studying the Dunnocks in your back garden.

FIELD NOTES
- *5½–6" (14–15 cm)*
- *Streaked, rusty brown above*
- *Greyish on head and below*
- *Thin, black bill*
- *Small cup of moss, grass and sticks in dense shrub*
- *Call: a shrill "pseeeh"*

Nightingale

Luscinia megarhynchos

Nightingales are famous for their vocal abilities. The song of the male is a loud, beautiful warble, usually performed at night and early morning, but also during the day. A characteristic phrase is a crescendo of whistled notes *lu-lu-lu-lee-leee.*

As do most other small thrushes, Nightingales frequently forage on the ground, but are difficult to observe, as they prefer dense thickets and damp undergrowth in woodlands and parks. If you are lucky enough to see one, you might notice its slightly cocked tail, which is reddish brown.

The Thrush Nightingale (*L. luscinia;* 6¼–6½" [16–17 cm]) breeds in Eastern Europe and is very difficult to distinguish from the Nightingale in the field. It is a "colder" brown and lacks the reddish tone in its plumage. Its characteristic song is much louder than the Nightingale's, often audible several hundred yards away. Slower in tempo, most phrases are repeated only two or three times. Both species are highly migratory and leave Europe as early as August, to return in April or May from tropical winter quarters in Africa.

J F M A M J J A S O N D

FIELD NOTES

■ *6¼–6½" (16–17 cm)*

■ *Brown with reddish tail*

■ *Dark eyes*

▲ *Thrush Nightingale is very similar, but "colder" grey-brown and mottled on the breast*

Cup of dry leaves lined with grass on the ground

♪ *Calls: "chak chak", "hueet" or a low "coo-orrr"; song is rich and varied*

Robin

Erithacus rubecula

The rusty-orange breast and forehead, bordered with grey, gives the Robin an unmistakable appearance. It is a familiar bird of woodland, parks, gardens and hedgerows. In Northern Europe, it also occurs in luxuriant coniferous forest. Like other small thrushes it hops on the ground with an upright posture. It is not shy but always keeps close to cover, in particular during the breeding season.

A repeated *tic-tic-ic-ic*, like the winding of an old clock, reveals its presence. In winter, both sexes sing a territorial song, and use their orange-red breasts to warn others from their area. Robins can easily be lured into battle with a reflection or a "mimic".

Freshly fledged juveniles, still lacking the orange breast feathers, look surprisingly different. They are brown with dense yellowish-brown spotting above and below, giving them a scaly appearance. Juveniles moult in late summer into adult plumage, but a small buffish wingbar still apparent in autumn marks their age.

British Robins are sedentary, but nocturnal migrants from Northern Europe arrive in September to October and leave in early spring.

FIELD NOTES

- *5¼–5¾" (13.5–14.5 cm)*
- *Adult: brown, with orange-red breast and face*
- *Juvenile: without orange breast; buffish spots*
- *Ground nest of leaves and grass lined with dry roots*
- *Calls: a sharp "tic-tic-tic" or a thin "tseeeh"; song is a clear, relaxed series of whistling notes*

Fieldfare

Turdus pilaris

J F M A M J J A S O N D

Redwing

Fieldfares have characteristics typical of thrushes, being medium-sized ground-dwelling birds, with slender but strong bills and fairly long tails. The same size as Blackbirds (p. 113) they are chestnut-brown above with grey head and rump, and spotted with arrowheads below. The white underwings are a useful marker in flight.

Fieldfares are common autumn and winter visitors from Scandinavia. They form flocks of up to hundreds of birds, usually mixed with other species, such as Redwings (*T. iliacus*; 7¾–8½" [20–22 cm]), another migrant from Northern European forests. Redwings are smaller and easily recognised by their conspicuous pale stripe over the eye (supercilium), rusty-red flanks and underwings.

During a clear October night, as they migrate south, you can hear Redwings call, a thin *tseeeh* or *tsreeeh*, or watch them crossing a full moon.

The winter season is the time to look for Fieldfares and Redwings in fields and open woodland, but also in parks and gardens. Both are fond of rowan trees. The Fieldfare is a rare and localised breeder in Britain; the Redwing is a rare breeding bird in Scottish woodlands. Both are common throughout Northern European forests.

FIELD NOTES

- *9½–10½" (24–27 cm)*
- *Grey head and rump*
- *Chestnut mantle, yellowish throat and breast*
- *Boldly marked with arrow-like spots below*
- ▲ *Redwing has white or buffish supercilium; rusty-red underwings and flanks*
- *Compact cup of dry grass in a tree or shrub*
- ♪ *A loud "chack-chack-chack"*

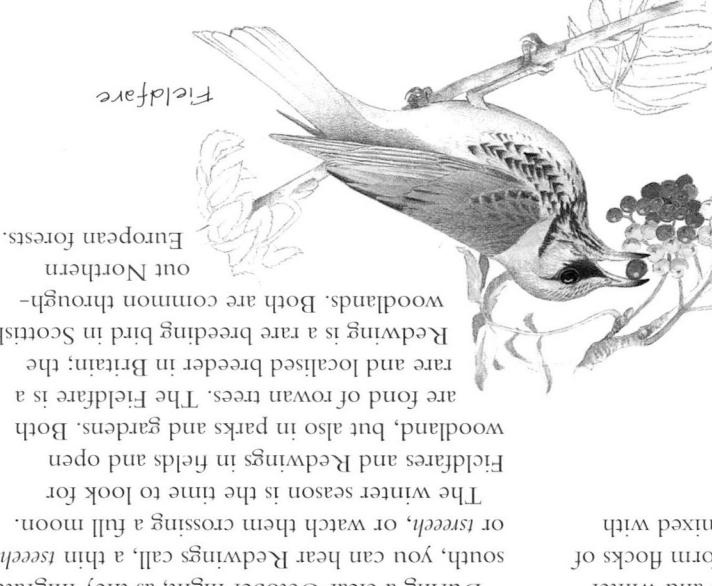

Fieldfare

Song Thrush

Turdus philomelos

J F M A M J J A S O N D

All over Europe, in gardens, parks and many woodlands with rich undergrowth, you will find the Song Thrush. In flight it is similar to the Redwing (p. 141), with rusty-buff underwings, but can be distinguished by its flight call—a short, sharp *tsip*. When seen feeding on a lawn, the plain brown upperparts and head, and the neat brown spots below are clearly visible.

The Mistle Thrush (*T. viscivorus;* 10¼–11" [26–28 cm]) is larger, greyer brown above, and has pale fringes to the wing feathers. Look for the white tips of the tail feathers on closer viewings. The clearly undulating flight and a rattling *rrrrr* immediately identify it. Like the Song Thrush, it is common and widespread in Britain, particularly in larger stands of woodland with extensive grassy areas.

Although Song Thrushes have a varied diet, they are particularly fond of snails. They select a large stone as an anvil on which to smash the shells.

FIELD NOTES

- 8½–9½" (22–24 cm)
- Brown upperparts
- Dark brown spots on underparts
- ▲ *Mistle Thrush is a larger bird with a longer tail and a distinctive rattling flight call: "rrrrr"*
- *Solid cup of grass and sticks lined with mud*
- ♪ *Flight call: "tsip"; alarm call: "chuck"; song: a series of soft fluted notes and mimicry*

Blackcap

Sylvia atricapilla

The Blackcap is a large, greyish warbler easily identified by its cap, which is black in the male, and rusty brown in the female and juvenile. In spring, it is often detected by its beautiful song, which starts as a rippling babble to burst out into a few clear and powerful fluted notes.

The Garden Warbler (*S. borin;* 5¼–5¾" [13.5–14.5 cm]) is similar in size and colour but lacks the distinctive cap. In fact, it is the general lack of any obvious markings that positively identifies it. Note the rounded, rather plain head and the short, grey bill. Its song is very like Blackcap's but longer and deeper pitched.

Both species are well known migrants. In autumn, they feast on berries and brambles to build up energy stores. Garden Warblers migrate to tropical Africa. Blackcaps from Western Europe winter in West Africa, while the East European breeders spend the winter in East Africa. Studies in Germany have shown that Central European populations have evolved a new migratory route to Britain, as winters have become milder and the prevalence of birdfeeders has soared.

FIELD NOTES

- 5¼–5¾" (13.5–14.5 cm)
- Brown-grey
- Male: black cap
- Female and juvenile: brown cap
- ▲ Garden Warbler is unmarked grey-brown
- Loose cup of grass lined with hair
- ♪ Call: a loud "chek"

Chiffchaff

Phylloscopus collybita

This rather plain warbler is a common breeding species in Britain and Europe. It favours deciduous and mixed woodland. The Chiffchaff's song is simply a repetition of its name: a chatting *chiff chaff, chiff chiff chaff* in an irregular rhythm. Chiffchaffs are small and brown, with a weak supercilium, dark legs and a fine bill.

Birdwatchers always find it challenging trying to tell it apart from its sibling species, the Willow Warbler (*P. trochilus*; 4¼–4½" [11–11.5 cm]), especially when the birds are on migration or when they are not singing. Willow Warblers are generally greener, and yellower on the throat and breast, especially the juveniles. The supercilium is more pronounced and the wings are slightly longer. But the best marker to look for is the leg colour: usually pale brown, often even yellow, in Willow Warblers, but black in Chiffchaffs. The song is completely different: it is a slightly melancholy series of notes in a descending scale that ends in a soft flourish.

FIELD NOTES

■ *4–4¼" (10.5–11 cm)*

■ *Brown; weak supercilium*

■ *Dark legs*

▲ *Willow Warbler is very similar, but has pale legs, is greener above and has more yellow on throat*

Dome-shaped groundnest of grass and moss lined with feathers

♪ *Call: "weet"*

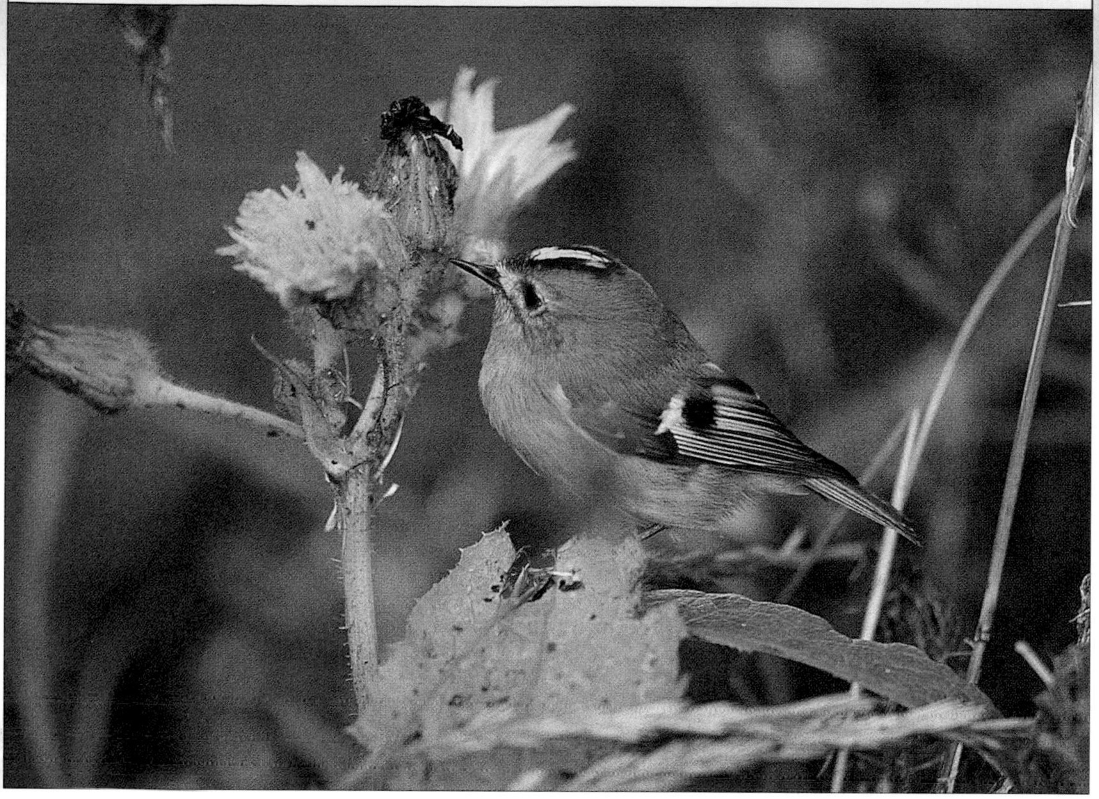

Goldcrest

Regulus regulus

Goldcrests, among the smallest birds in Europe, are olive-green above and paler below, with two white wingbars. They have a pale area around the eye, which gives them a "sad" look. The crown in the female is yellow bordered with black markings, and orange in the male, and visible only when the crown feathers are raised.

J F M A M J J A S O N D

Goldcrests frequent coniferous or mixed forests in summer, while in winter they often join mixed-species feeding flocks of tits. Listen for the very high-pitched, trisyllabic *see-see-see* and look for a tiny, active bird that often hovers briefly while picking at twigs and leaves for food.

In the same habitats you might also find the Firecrest (*R. ignicapillus*; 3¼–3½" [8.5–9 cm]). It has a beautiful bronze tinge to the shoulders; broader, black crown stripes; a white supercilium; and dark eyestripes. It is a rare breeding bird in southern England and a rare visitor from the Continent in autumn and winter.

FIELD NOTES

■ *3¼–3½" (8.5–9 cm)*

■ *Green; white wingbar; pale "spectacles"*

■ *Male: orange crown stripe*

■ *Female: yellow crown stripe*

▲ *Firecrest has bronze shoulders; white supercilium and dark eyestripe giving "mean" facial expression*

Pouch of moss and spider's silk at upper levels in spruce trees

♪ *A very high-pitched "see-see-see"*

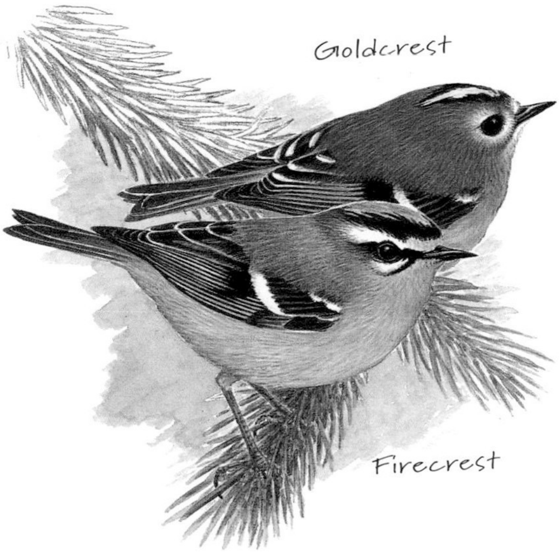

Spotted Flycatcher

Muscicapa striata

Like all flycatchers in Britain and Europe, the Spotted Flycatcher is present here only in summer. It is common in woodlands and woodland edges, but also in well-vegetated residential areas. From an exposed perch it catches flying insects, and the clicking sound of its broad mandibles snapping at a fly can often be heard during the day. This behaviour, in combination with the grey-brown plumage, streaked breast and crown, and very long wings, makes it easy to identify. As with most other flycatchers the legs and feet are relatively small and weak. Its call is a sharp, thin *tsee* or *tsree*. The song is very simple and consists of nothing more than three to four call-like notes.

J F M A M J J A S O N D

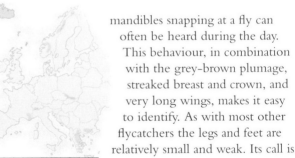

FIELD NOTES

■ *5¼–5¾" (13.5–14.5 cm)*

■ *Brown; streaked breast and crown*

■ *Long wings, relatively short tail*

Small cup of grass on a sheltered ledge in a variety of places

♪ *Call: a thin, high-pitched "tsee"; song: a series of very soft call-like notes*

♂ and ♀ Spotted Flycatcher at nestbox

Pied Flycatcher

Ficedula hypoleuca

The Pied Flycatcher nests commonly in woodlands with deciduous trees, but also in parks and large, old gardens. It arrives from its winter quarters in tropical Africa in April and leaves again in August. In typical flycatcher manner, it sallies forth after insects in the air from a perch in a tree.

The male is usually sooty black above and white below, especially the breeding birds from Northern Europe, but in some populations the males are often dull dark brown. Males also have a white area on the wings, much larger than in the females and juveniles.

J F M A M J J A S O N D

After moulting in July or August both sexes become grey-brown above and are virtually indistinguishable from juveniles. After a moult of body feathers in the winter quarters, males regain their black-and-white plumage.

FIELD NOTES

- 4¾–5" (12–13 cm)
- Male: black above, white below; white wing patch
- Female: greyish brown above; smaller wing patch
- Autumn: both sexes greyish brown above
- Cavity in tree, nestbox
- ♪ Call: a sharp "beet" or "twit"; song: a short sequence of clear notes

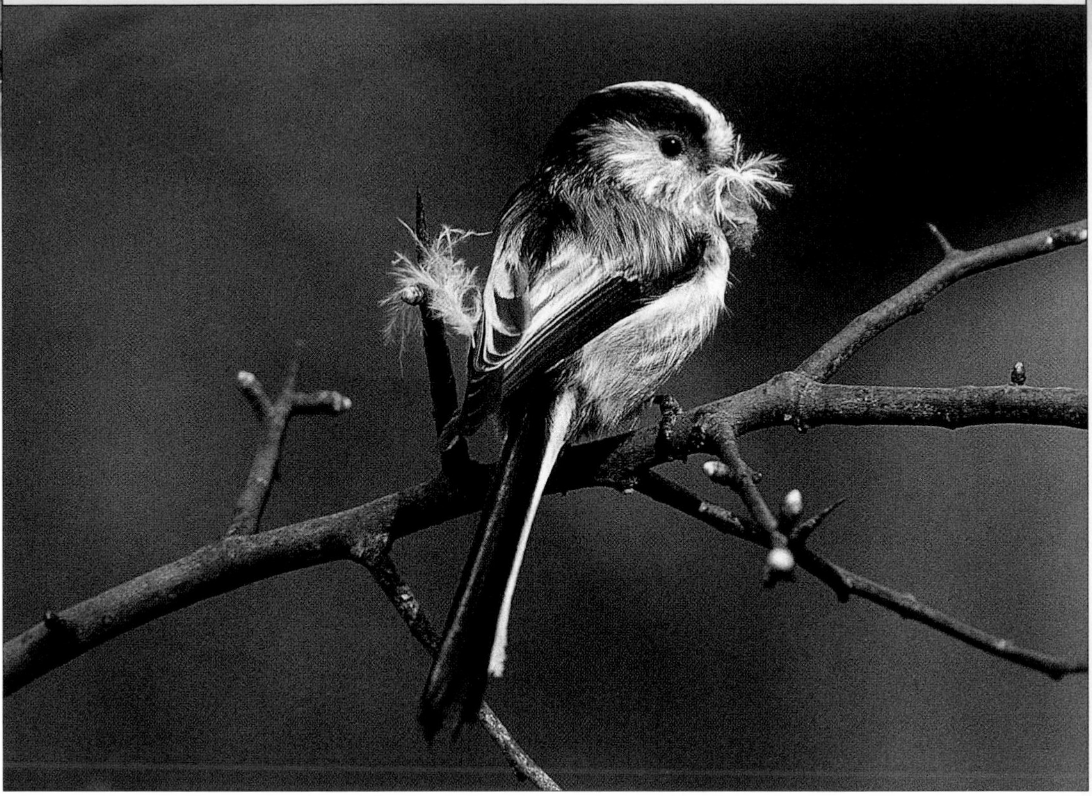

Long-tailed Tit

Aegithalos caudatus

Although not belonging to the family of true tits—the Paridae—Long-tailed Tits are similar in build and behaviour. Most striking is their long, black tail with white markings. The mantle is black with pinkish-brown feathers on the shoulders. A clear pinkish tone to the plumage is also present on the flanks, rump and vent. The British race (*A. c. rosaceus*) and populations in Western Europe have a dirty-white head with a broad, black stripe above the eye. Adults of the Northern and Eastern European populations (*A. c. caudatus*) have an all-white head and more white on the wings.

The nest is a beautiful construction of moss and spider's silk decorated with lichen.

After the breeding season, families stay together in closely knit parties, often mixing with other tits. You can pick them out in these flocks by their characteristic call, a churring *tserrr*.

FIELD NOTES

- *$4\frac{3}{4}$ – $5\frac{1}{2}$" (12–14 cm)*
- *Long tail, short bill*
- *Black above, pinkish brown on shoulders, rump and below*
- *Head pattern variable in different populations*

▲ *British race has a dirty-white head with a broad, black stripe above the eye*

Pouch of moss, lichen and spider's silk

♪ *Song: a high-pitched "tssirrp" or "see-see-see"; call: a churring "tserrr"*

Blue Tit

Parus caeruleus

J F M A M J J A S O N D

Tits of the Paridae family are small, agile birds with short bills. Most species are confined to woodlands and are usually sedentary, but a well-known member of this group is the Blue Tit—a common and widespread breeding bird of deciduous and mixed woodland, gardens and parks. It is a readily identifiable, familiar visitor to birdfeeders. If Blue Tits are regular winter visitors to your garden, you may be able to persuade them to stay all year by erecting a suitable nestbox.

Blue Tits have blue on the crown, wings and tail. The mantle is green, the underparts are yellow and the head is white with bluish-black markings.

In summer, juveniles have yellow cheeks and a greyish-green cap. The song is cheerful and starts with two thin, drawn-out notes followed by a clear trill *seeh seeh zirrrr.*

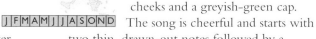

FIELD NOTES

- *$4\frac{1}{4}$–$4\frac{3}{4}$" (11–12 cm)*
- *Blue crown, wing and tail*
- *Green mantle*
- *Yellow below; head white with blue crown and black markings*
- *Cavities in trees, nestboxes*
- *Song: a cheerful "seeh seeh zirrrr"; calls: "tjerr err err err", "tjie die die die" or "psie"*

Great Tit

Parus major

The Great Tit is one of our most common birds in woodlands, parks and gardens. The head is sooty black, with pure white cheeks. The wings and tail are greyish blue, the underparts yellow with a black stripe from breast to belly. Adult males are more intensely coloured than the females, and their black breast band is broader, especially on the belly. Among a roaming family party in summer you may notice the drab-coloured juveniles, with a little black on the breast and yellowish cheeks.

Great Tits breed in tree cavities, but are easily attracted to nestboxes, which may also be used in winter for roosting. Their song is a characteristic *tee-time tee-time tee-time* or *free-kick free-kick*.

Coniferous stands are the domain of Coal Tits (*P. ater*; 4–4½" [10.5–11.5 cm]), a smaller relative, without any yellow in the plumage, but with a diagnostic white nape patch. When spruce-cone seeds are in short supply, Northern European populations may irrupt into the South in autumn.

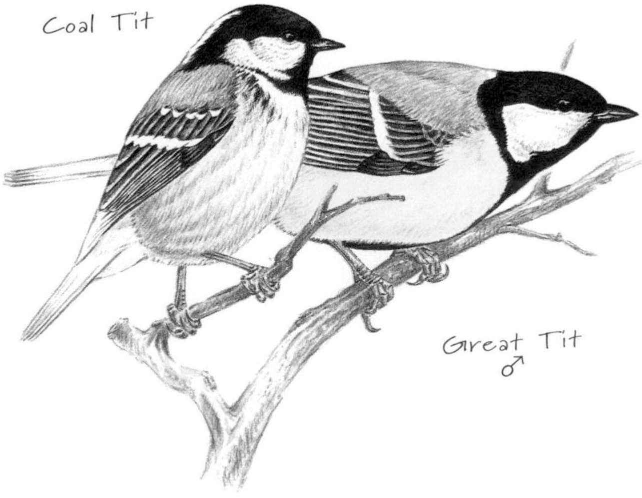

FIELD NOTES

- *5¼–5¾" (13.5–14.5 cm)*
- *Black head, white cheeks, bluish green above*
- *Yellow below with black breast band*
- ▲ *Coal Tit has a white nape patch and is greyish above and flesh-coloured below*
- *Cavities in trees, nestboxes*
- ♪ *A variety of calls, including chaffinch-like "pienk pienk"*

Nuthatch

Sitta europaea

J F M A M J J A S O N D

A loud and repeated *twit twit twit* is often the first clue that a Nuthatch is close by. These small, lively birds creep along trunks and branches, both head-up and head-down, as they forage under loose bark and in tree crevices. Often, they accompany mixed-species flocks of tits in woodlands in winter; they will also visit birdfeeders.

The Nuthatch is a common breeding bird of deciduous forests, in particular, with old oaks. As usual with sedentary bird species with a wide distribution, there is considerable variation in plumage. The British and Western European race is rusty buff on breast and belly, whereas populations in Northern Europe are white. Males are vivid rusty buff on the flanks, the females duller.

Nuthatches nest in tree cavities, and if the nest entrance is too wide, they plaster it with mud to fit them exactly. The powerful bill is also used to hammer at nuts to get the kernel inside.

FIELD NOTES

- *5¼–5¾" (13.5–14.5 cm)*
- *Grey above, black eyestripe*
- *Rusty buff on breast and belly*
- *Long bill*
- *Cavities in trees, plasters mud on nest entrance*
- ♪ *Call: an explosive "twit twit twit"; song: a penetrating "piuu piuu" or "vivivivi"*

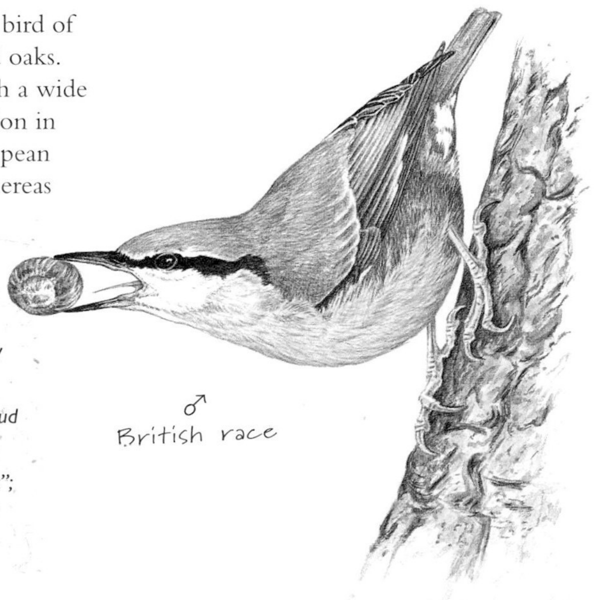

Common Treecreeper

Certhia familiaris

When you see a bird climbing up tree trunks and branches, and probing the bark with a fine, curved bill for insects and their larvae, you have most likely encountered a Common Treecreeper. To give them more support while climbing trees in this manner, Common Treecreepers have developed stiff, pointed tail feathers like the woodpeckers.

Two species occur in Continental Europe, and these are so similar that they are regarded as sibling species. The Common Treecreeper is found only in Britain, while on the Continent the Short-toed Treecreeper (*C. brachydactyla*; 4¾–5" [12–13 cm]) occurs as well. In plumage, they are almost impossible to tell apart; both are streaked brown above, dingy white below and have buffish markings on the wing. Common Treecreepers are pure white below, while Short-toed Treecreepers are usually buffish on the flanks.

Common Treecreepers are widespread in older, deciduous woodlands and parks. Outside the breeding season, they will often join roving flocks of tits. In winter, small numbers might roost together in a cavity for warmth on cold nights.

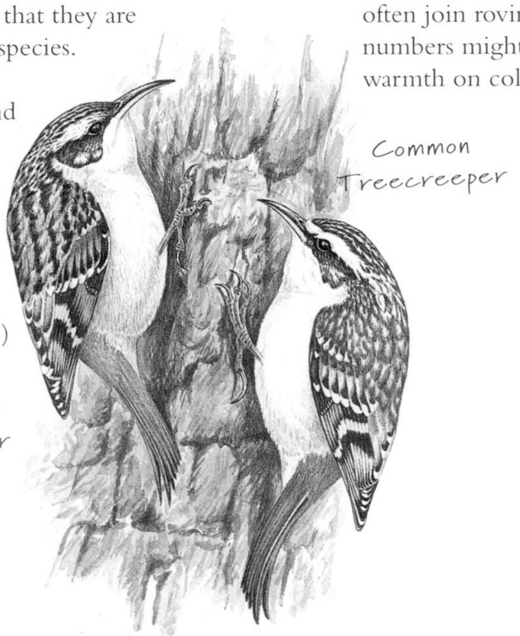

FIELD NOTES

■ *4¾–5" (12–13 cm)*

■ *Streaked brown above, white below*

■ *Fine, curved bill*

■ *Pointed tail feathers*

▲ *Short-toed Treecreeper is buffish-brown on flank and vent; its call is a clear "teet teet"*

In crevices, bark of old trees or nestboxes

♪ *A high-pitched, piercing "tsreeht" or "tseeit"*

Jay

Garrulus glandarius

J F M A M J J A S O N D

Jays are fairly shy but common woodland birds of unmistakable appearance: pale blue and white wing patches; black tail; white rump; and pale brown plumage above and below. In flight, which is slow and fluttering, the white rump and wing patches are striking features. It is a typical woodland bird and never found very far from trees, both deciduous and coniferous. In suburban areas with old parks and gardens, Jays successfully exploit new environments and may also visit bird tables.

Jays are well known for their habit of burying acorns in autumn, and retrieving them in times of shortage during winter.

In contrast to their usual loud and raucous calls, Jays can sing a very pleasing song in spring. Outside the breeding season, birds may remain for some time together in small, noisy family groups.

Northern European birds may disperse southward in autumn and even cross the North Sea to reach the British Isles.

FIELD NOTES

- *13–14" (33–36 cm)*
- *Unmistakable: blue, white and black wing markings; pale brown above*
- *Rounded wings, white rump in flight*
- *Medium-sized cup of sticks*
- ♪ *A scraping "kraah" or barking "kah"*

Rook

Corvus frugilegus

J F M A M J J A S O N D

The Rook is often seen foraging in fields and pastures in open cultivated country. Although it feeds on worms and insects, it is less appreciated by farmers for its appetite for freshly sown seeds. Rooks are social birds, especially in winter when feeding and roosting flocks may number hundreds. Rooks nest in colonies known as rookeries, and may use the same sites for many years in succession.

Adult birds are easily recognisable by their bare, grey bill base. Immature birds, however, with the bases of their bills still feathered, are almost impossible to tell from Carrion Crows (*C. corone corone;* 17¾–19¼" [45–49 cm]). Carrion Crows are also common and widespread birds of open country, but breed in isolated pairs rather than colonies. In Scotland, Scandinavia and Eastern Europe, the Carrion Crow is replaced by another race, the Hooded Crow (*C. corone cornix;* 17¾–19¼" [45–49 cm]), which is grey on the mantle, nape and below. In a narrow hybridisation zone "intermediate" birds can also be found.

FIELD NOTES

- *17¾–18½" (45–47 cm)*
- *Glossy black, pointed bill*
- *Adult: base of bill grey*
- *Juvenile: base of bill feathered and very similar to Carrion Crow*
- ▲ *Carrion Crow has a black bill base*
- ▲ *Hooded Crow has a grey mantle, belly and vent*
- *Large platform of sticks and branches; nests in colonies*
- ♪ *A raucous "kaah"*

Chaffinch

Fringilla coelebs

J F M A M J J A S O N D

The Chaffinch is one of the most frequently seen birds in Britain and Europe in woodland, open country with trees, parks and gardens. In spring and summer, the male is brightly coloured: pinkish below, chestnut-brown above, with a grey head, green rump and white on the wing and the shoulder. In late summer, birds moult all their feathers, after which males look more like females, being dull greyish brown above and below. Broad fringes on the body feathers of males hide the bright colour, which gradually reappears when the fringes wear away during the winter.

Bramblings (*F. montifringilla;* 5¾–6¼" [14.5–16 cm]) are common autumn and winter visitors from Scandinavia, and often form mixed flocks with Chaffinches. They can easily be distinguished by their pure white rumps and orange breasts. As with the Chaffinch, the beautiful summer plumage of the males becomes apparent in late winter and spring as the feathers rub off revealing blackish brown on the head and mantle, and bright orange on the breast and shoulder.

FIELD NOTES

■ *5¾–6¼" (14.5–16 cm)*

■ *Male in spring: grey head, pinkish red below, brown above, white wingbars*

■ *Female and male in autumn: brown above, greyish head, green rump*

▲ *Brambling has a rusty-orange breast and white rump in autumn*

Cup of grass and moss lined with hair and feathers

♪ *A high "pink pink" or soft "tyup"*

Greenfinch

Carduelis chloris

J F M A M J J A S O N D

In Britain and Europe, the Greenfinch is the largest yellow-green finch. It has a big, conical bill, greyish-green plumage and yellow markings on the wing. As with most finches, the males are more brightly coloured than the females, especially in spring. The juveniles resemble females and are lightly streaked on the back and below.

Greenfinches are resident birds in Britain and occur commonly in parks, gardens and farmland with hedgerows. While singing in spring, the male may engage in a butterfly-like display flight, during which the yellow wing and tail markings appear particularly striking.

In winter, Greenfinches are readily attracted to birdfeeders. With their short, thick bills, they can take large seeds, such as hemp and sunflower. In this season, you may also notice red-orange patches around the bill, the remains of a recent feast of rose-hips.

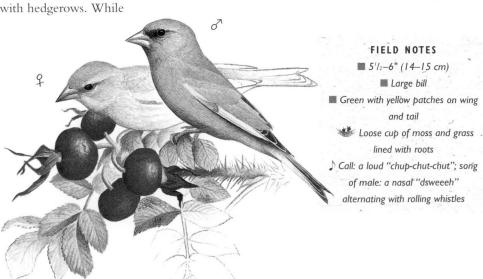

FIELD NOTES

- 5½–6" (14–15 cm)
- Large bill
- Green with yellow patches on wing and tail
- Loose cup of moss and grass lined with roots
- ♪ Call: a loud "chup-chut-chut"; song of male: a nasal "dsweeeh" alternating with rolling whistles

Common Crossbill

Loxia curvirostra

J F M A M J J A S O N D

Crossbills are large, bulky finches with mandibles that cross at the tip—a unique adaptation to take seeds out of spruce cones. The male plumage is highly variable and can range from greenish yellow with a few reddish feathers to entirely red. Females are brownish green with a yellowish rump. Juveniles are greyish brown, often with prominent pale brown wingbars.

The breeding season coincides with the ripening of spruce cones and can start as early as February. In areas Common Crossbills are known to inhabit, try looking for ponds used as drinking sites, where you can study them when they come to the ground in the open. Like most birds with a diet exclusively of seeds, they have to drink regularly.

During irruption years, when a large number leaves Scandinavia for Western and Eastern Europe, you should also look out for Parrot Crossbills (*L. pytyopsittacus*; 6½–7" [16.5–17.5 cm]), a larger relative with a massive and more rectangular head, and uniformly thick bill. It feeds mainly on pine seeds and, like a parrot, breaks a cone with its beak, then holds it with one leg to empty the contents.

FIELD NOTES

■ 6¼–6¾" (16–17 cm)

■ Crossed mandibles

■ *Male: variable, from red to greenish with yellowish rump*

■ *Female: greenish, yellowish-green rump*

▲ *Parrot Crossbill has a huge head and a thick bill*

Cup of twigs, bark and moss lined with dry grass

♪ *Flight call: "keep keep kip-kip"*

Bullfinch

Pyrrhula pyrrhula

J F M A M J J A S O N D

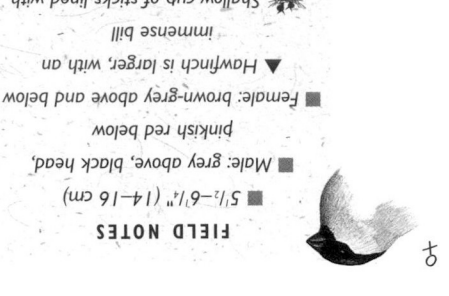

When you see a bird with a thick, black bill, grey back, and pink breast, it's unmistakably a male Bullfinch. The female is dull grey-brown above and below, but can be still identified by the black cap and black wings with a broad, white wingbar. Juveniles are similar to females but lack the black in the head.

The Bullfinch is a fairly common breeding bird of gardens, orchards, woodlands and forest edges. It feeds on berries, seeds and flowerbuds. In size it is surpassed by the Hawfinch (*Coccothraustes coccothraustes*; 6¾–7" [17–18 cm]), the largest British finch. Its immense bill is steel-grey in summer and yellowish in winter. The male is chestnut-brown above and pale brown below, with a conspicuous white wingbar. The female is similar but duller, and with pale grey markings on the wing. With its powerful bill, the Hawfinch can even crack open cherry seeds. Both of these finches are resident in Britain but Northeastern European populations migrate to the Southwest in late autumn and winter.

FIELD NOTES

■ *5½–6¼" (14–16 cm)*

■ *Male: grey above, black head, pinkish red below*

■ *Female: brown-grey above and below*

▲ *Hawfinch is larger, with an immense bill*

Shallow cup of sticks lined with roots and hair

♪ *Call: a soft and low "pju"; song: a soft chattering mixed with soft whistles*

Open Country

HEDGES allow a wider range of woodland birds to penetrate open areas. Little Owls, Tree Pipits, Tree Sparrows, Yellowhammers and a variety of warblers are all species to look out for.

GRASSLANDS may provide important feeding areas for a range of birds, including such diverse species as White Storks, Barnacle Geese and Short-eared Owls.

PASTURE Only a few species favour open pasture and similar grasslands, but these include Black-tailed Godwits and Skylarks.

ROADSIDE VEGETATION Some species, including Turtle Doves, like to forage in these areas, and even bathe in roadside puddles and gather grit along verges.

Open Country

Meadows, Downs, Fields and Farmland, Moorland

The term "open country" encompasses a broad range of habitats with a correspondingly diverse array of birds. These habitats share many common elements, however, and across Europe similarities can be seen between the different representatives of bird families that depend on them.

In Britain, the description "open country" can be applied to every habitat type from lowland meadows and agricultural land to rolling downland and even upland moors. In such landscapes, what little cover there is may at best be restricted to hedgerows, low roadside scrub and isolated trees. These small but important zones of vegetation often support many of the relatively small number of songbirds found in open country. Other passerines, such as Skylarks, and Yellow Wagtails, are at home in featureless expanses of meadow or field.

Elsewhere in Europe, the same type of habitat may support different species. In the Netherlands, for example, damp, low-lying grassland holds large numbers of breeding Black-tailed Godwits and Ruffs, and in the warmer climates of Europe, colourful species such as the Hoopoe and Bee-eater add to the great diversity of birdlife.

In all types of open country, the effect of humans has often been harmful and led to declining bird populations, through intensive agriculture, clearing of hedgerows and scrub, and the use of pesticides. The Corncrake, for example, has suffered drastically in Britain through mechanisation of grass-mowing techniques. For a few species, however, human influence has been more beneficial. Gulls, for example, have learned to follow the plough for food, and many species, such as Skylarks and Corn Buntings, have come to rely on overhead wires and fences as important song perches or lookout posts.

PLOUGHED FIELDS attract gulls, Lapwings, Stock Doves and corvids. In winter or spring, they may also attract flocks of Golden Plover or a variety of finches and buntings.

FENCES A broad range of birds, from small species such as Swallows and Corn Buntings to larger birds such as breeding waders, will perch on fences and wires to rest, sunbathe, or just look around.

BIRDWATCHING *in* OPEN COUNTRY

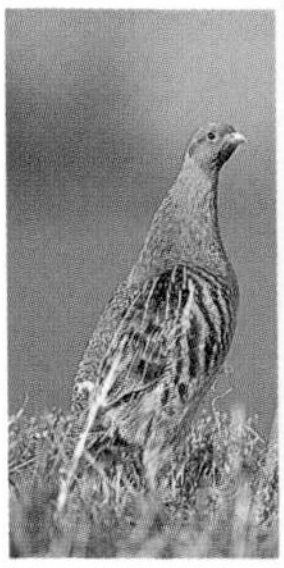

Open expanses of countryside allow easy observation of numerous birds, from birds of prey perched on overhead wires to larks foraging in farmland. Other species, however, require a more cautious approach.

An excellent way to go birdwatching in open country is by car. Many species are conspicuous along roadsides, and the car acts as a hide, from which you can watch birds more closely than if you were on foot. Driving is also often the best way to spot species that occur in low densities or that have large hunting territories, as is the case with raptors in winter.

However you get around, it is always good birdwatching policy to keep an eye on overhead wires, poles and fences as these all provide perches for many species of birds. For example, in summer the best place to spot Corn Buntings is usually on roadside wires, while in winter, poles and pylons are favoured roosting and even hunting perches for many raptors. In some areas, Ravens nest readily on pylons—tree substitutes in a wide open environment.

It pays to stop and scan any freshly ploughed field you may pass. Ploughing, of course, brings to the surface many insects, grubs, worms,

OUT IN THE OPEN *Mist gradually clears over a meadow, home to many open-country species such as the Lapwing (above right). This bird is especially attracted to rough pasture and wasteground, where weeds such as thistles abound. Tall grass shelters many birds, like the Grey Partridge (top). A group of birdwatchers (above) explores one of the richest of all open-country habitats—the arctic tundra.*

and similar subsurface fauna. These quickly attract birds, ranging from gulls to larks and pipits. Depending on the season, there are several species (some plovers and buntings, for example) that prefer ploughed fields to grasslands.

Do not assume that all the birds in a group are of one species. Many open-country birds are gregarious outside the breeding season, and any rare vagrant that happens to be in the area is quite likely to attach itself to a group of some common local species.

Note that the presence of hedges and scattered trees will greatly increase the diversity of birds you might find.

Seasonal Changes

In autumn and winter, fields provide food for many species that migrate to open country after nesting in other habitats. If you pass through an area of open grassland or farmland regularly, from late summer through to the end of the winter, you'll see a greater variety of species than at other times of the year, in particular, more raptors, larks, pipits, finches and buntings. These numbers reflect both the population increase following the nesting season, and the migration of other species into a habitat that is good for feeding but would not be a suitable nesting habitat.

Tactics in the Field

Grasslands, with their unrestricted views, provide certain obvious advantages over woods and forests. However, these advantages do not apply to all birds all year round. In spring and summer, the males of most open-country species sing and are therefore fairly easy to find and identify, but during other seasons some birds, such as pipits and buntings, can be hard enough to see well, let alone identify.

If you are walking with a friend and flush a pipit or bunting from cover, watch where it comes down. One of you can then keep an eye on the spot while the other walks part of the distance toward it. If the walker then stops and relocates the spot, the watcher can catch up. In this way you can walk up on the bird without ever losing sight of it, or at least where it landed.

Using Cover

When you are out in open country with hedges, or with a bordering wood, walking along the hedge or beside the trees will make you less conspicuous. Furthermore, such areas are rich in birdlife.

Equipment

Little is required in the way of specialised equipment for birdwatching in open country—just an efficient pair of binoculars. Telescopes do, however, come in handy in open areas where you may be some distance from a bird. Special mounts are available that enable you to clamp your 'scope to the glass of a half-open car window, making it easier for you to use the telescope from your mobile hide. (See p. 62-5 for information on binoculars and telescopes.)

IN OPEN COUNTRY *(left), many species are easy to spot but hard to get close to. The Skylark (above) is one of many birds that perch on fence posts. A typical alpine meadow (top) supports high-country specialist birds.*

Cattle Egret

Bubulcus ibis

J F M A M J J A S O N D

This small heron is identified by its stocky shape and its habit of following cattle to feed on insects and small animals they disturb. Flocks have learned to accompany tractors for the same reason. In the morning and evening, they fly to and from roost sites in small, disorderly flocks.

For most of the year, Cattle Egrets are wholly white with dark legs and yellow bills. At the start of the breeding season they attain golden-yellow plumes on the head, chest, and back; the bill becomes reddish and the legs become orange.

Cattle Egrets are famous for their expansion into the New World from Africa, which started at the end of the last century. Today, they are common in large parts of North and South America. In the Old World, the species is expanding slowly northwards, and has become locally common in Iberia and southern France. Adult Cattle Egrets are resident, but immatures disperse in autumn far from their breeding sites and may turn up as vagrants in the British Isles.

FIELD NOTES

- *17¾–21¼" (45–54 cm)*
- *Small and stocky*
- *Distinctive "heavy-jowled" look*
- *Summer plumage: golden-buff wash on crown, lower breast and back*
- *Platform of sticks in tree or reedbed, often with other herons*
- *A short, low-pitched "arg"*

White Stork

Ciconia ciconia

Probably the most widely known bird in Europe, the White Stork is regarded everywhere as a bringer of fertility and prosperity. It is a typical bird of river meadows and wet grasslands in Continental Europe, North Africa and Asia Minor. Along Europe's more undisturbed rivers the stately White Stork hunts in meadows for large insects, voles and frogs. The huge nests White Storks build on farm buildings and churches are re-used, often over many years.

In Western Europe, the White Stork has fared less well than its symbolic meaning would lead us to hope, and it no longer breeds in several countries, including Britain. It is threatened in many other parts of Europe by the intensification of farming and agricultural practices.

The Black Stork (*C. nigra;* 37½–39½" [95–100 cm]) is glossy black above and white underneath. It is a shy bird of riverine woodlands and marshes in Continental Europe and is slowly spreading west.

When summer nears its end, storks soar high up in the air on warm upward currents and migrate southwards to Africa. In early autumn, they concentrate in Gibraltar and the Bosporus in flocks of thousands, constituting one of the great wonders of nature.

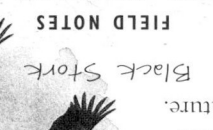

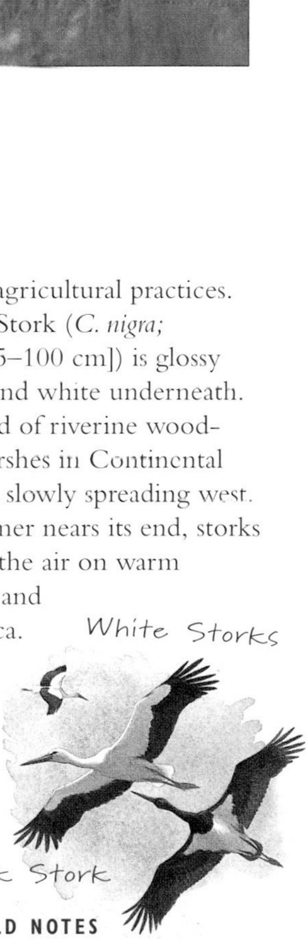

FIELD NOTES

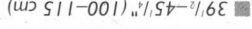

- ■ *39½–45¼" (100–115 cm)*
- ■ *White with black flight feathers*
- ▲ *Black Stork is glossy black above and white underneath*
- *Huge pile of branches on rooftops*
- ♪ *Clappering with bill*

Whooper Swan

Cygnus cygnus

J F M A M J J A S O N D

The loud, trumpeting calls from Whooper Swans, flying southwards in a V-formation, are one of the signs that winter is on its way. In late autumn, they arrive from the arctic tundra to spend the winter in Britain and Western Europe on meadows, pastures and arable fields, often along rivers. Whooper Swans are about the size of Mute Swans (p. 100), but their bills are black with a large area of yellow at the base.

When studying a flock of Whooper Swans, you may notice small groups comprising families of two adults with several immatures; the latter are easily recognised by their uniformly grey-brown plumage and pinkish bills.

Bewick's Swans (*C. columbianus*; 45½–50¼" [116–128 cm]) winter in Britain, in river meadows and lakes, and at traditional sites in a few other areas of Continental Europe. They are smaller, with shorter necks and less yellow at the base of the bill. Individual birds can be recognised by their bill pattern, which is as unique as a fingerprint. Bewick's are frequently found together with Whoopers grazing in pastures or feeding in fields of stubble.

FIELD NOTES

- *57–63" (145–160 cm)*
- *Large, long neck, elongated head shape*
- *Adult: white, bill black with yellow*
- *Juvenile: pale grey-brown, pink bill*
- ▲ *Bewick's: smaller, shorter neck, more black on shorter bill*
- *Platform of reeds in shallow water or on island*
- ♪ *A trumpeting "hwong-hwong"*

Pink-footed Goose

Anser brachyrhynchus

The Pink-footed Goose has a rather limited world distribution, and Britain is one of the few places where you can see this species in winter. Virtually all breeding birds from Greenland and Iceland spend the winter in Britain. Numbers of Pink-footed Geese wintering in Britain have steadily increased in the past few decades as a result of reduced hunting and improved feeding conditions. The smaller Svalbard population migrates to Denmark and the Netherlands.

J F M A M J J A S O N D

Pink-footed Geese use arable fields and pastures to feed on crop shoots and grass. They are grey-brown with darker heads, and have a small amount of pink near their bill tips and pink legs. Immatures are still recognisable in early autumn by their browner plumage and buffish legs. This difference disappears after a moult in late autumn.

In England, small numbers of the Bean Goose (*A. fabalis*; 27½–35" [70–89 cm]) can be seen, mainly in East Anglia. There are two races of Bean Goose: the tundra form, with less orange than black on the bill, and the taiga form. They can be distinguished from Pink-footed Geese by their larger size, orange legs and orange bill patch. In flight, Pink-footed Geese can be distinguished from Bean Geese by their pale grey forewings.

FIELD NOTES

- ■ *24–30" (61–76 cm)*
- ■ *Medium size; grey-brown, pink legs*
- ■ *Dark brown head and neck*
- ■ *Small pink area on bill*
- ▲ *Taiga Bean Goose: large size; large, orange patch on bill, orange legs*
- *Depression in tundra lined with down*
- ♪ *A high, barking "wink-wing"*

White-fronted Goose

Anser albifrons

Thousands of geese taking to the air or alighting in a field make a spectacular sight on the winter landscape. The White-fronted Goose is one the most common species of geese in Britain and Continental Europe and is easily identified by the white forehead and dark belly markings of the adults. Juveniles lack the white around the bill and the distinctive bars below. Two races occur in the British Isles: in Scotland, Wales and Ireland, orange-billed birds from Greenland; and pink-billed birds from Siberia that winter around the North Sea.

J F M A M J J A S O N D

The obvious difference between adults and juveniles makes it possible to observe the social interactions within and between families. The larger males spend much time looking around for predators and chasing away other family groups. A head-down posture in the male signals to neighbours to keep some distance. Families gradually break up during winter.

White-fronted Geese numbers have risen dramatically in areas where hunting restrictions or total bans have been imposed, such as in the Netherlands, Flanders and parts of Germany. The numbers wintering in Britain have remained stable. Like other geese, White-fronts often fly in a distinctive V-formation that aids streamlining.

FIELD NOTES

- *25½–30¼" (65–77 cm)*
- *Grey-brown, pink bill, white forehead*
- *Adult: grey-brown with blackish bands on belly*
- *Juvenile: lacking white on forehead and bands below*
- *Depression in tundra lined with down*
- ♪ *A high-pitched "lyo-lyok" and "kow-lyoo"*

Barnacle Goose

Branta leucopsis

The Barnacle Goose, a small, black-and-white goose from the high arctic, winters exclusively around the North Sea. Like other arctic breeding geese, each population has a different traditional wintering site. The Greenland breeding birds winter in Ireland and Scotland; the Svalbard breeding birds in Scotland and northern England; and the Siberian birds mainly in the Netherlands.

The Barnacle Goose differs from the similar Brent Goose (p. 237) by its white face, the clear contrast between its black breast and pale grey belly, and its underwings. It is highly gregarious and dense flocks of grazing birds can be found in grassy areas along the coast as well as inland.

Most geese species have a regular daily activity pattern: they roost in or near water during the night and fly by dawn to the feeding areas. For Barnacle Geese, however, the grazing activity depends on the moon: during periods with little moonlight, Barnacles forage exclusively during the day, but switch to night foraging when the moon is nearly full.

FIELD NOTES

- *22¼–27¼" (58–69 cm)*
- *Small size*
- *Black neck and breast, white face*
- *Pale grey below, grey barred black above*
- *Depression in ground lined with down on rocky cliffs*
- *♪ A yelping "rak-rak"*

Wigeon

Anas penelope

J F M A M J J A S O N D

Flocks of Wigeon are a familiar sight on grasslands near lowland lakes, in river meadows and particularly on salt marshes in coastal estuaries. In closely packed gatherings, like miniature geese, they graze on shoreline vegetation with their suitably short, stubby bills, but also feed by dabbling in shallow water.

Migrants arrive from September onwards, and groups are composed of juveniles and adults in different stages of eclipse plumage. During this period of body moult, you may notice a startling variety of plumages. The adult males can always be distinguished by the large, white wing panel on the wing coverts. In eclipse plumage they are closer to the females, but during the autumn moult, the bright summer plumage gradually re-appears. In full summer plumage, the brown head with yellowish crown and black-and-white vent are very striking in the field. Females and juveniles are reddish to grey-brown all over and best distinguished from other ducks by the short, grey bill with a black tip and dark shadow around the eye. When disturbed, Wigeon flocks rise suddenly but easily and the white forewings of the males are very striking.

FIELD NOTES

- *17¼–19¼" (44–49 cm)*
- *Male: grey above and below, chestnut head, yellowish crown and forehead, white forewing, black-and-white vent*
- *Female: uniform reddish brown or greyish brown all over*
- *Depression in ground lined with grass*
- *Male: a whistling "wheeh-wheeh"; female: "karr, karr"*

Grey Partridge

Perdix perdix

Grey Partridges occur in coveys of up to 25 birds—usually a family group—for much of the year. In spring, they break up into territorial pairs. They are common in farmland and can be found along hedgerows, edges of arable fields, and meadows with plenty of weeds such as *Polygonum* and *Silene*.

Like other gamebirds, they are particularly fond of "dust bathing" to get rid of parasites such as feather lice. When startled, the whole group will first squat firmly, then rise suddenly into the air with a loud whirring of wings and fly a short distance out of sight. If disturbed, they usually run away with surprising speed into cover, where their grey-brown plumage blends well with the background. The black belly mark is a useful identifying feature, especially in birds standing "on guard".

The Red-legged Partridge (*Alectoris rufa;* 13–13¾" [33–35 cm]) was introduced into Britain from Southern Europe as a gamebird. It is not difficult to tell apart from the Grey Partridge: the back is grey-brown, and the head is well marked, with a white throat bordered with black. The flanks are barred brown and white. In its original distribution range, France and Iberia, it is a common bird of open cultivated country, but also heathland and rocky areas.

FIELD NOTES

- *11½–12¼" (29–31 cm)*
- *Brown above, grey below*
- *Red-orange face, grey bill*
- *Black patch on belly*
- ▲ *Red-legged Partridge: grey above, pink legs, red bill, barred brown and white on flanks*
- *Scrape in ground*
- ♪ *A repeated, crowing "krik-krik-kri-kri krikri"*

Corncrake

Crex crex

The Corncrake is a mysterious bird which hides itself in hay meadows and wet grasslands. The dry, rasping song of the male can be heard from May well into July, especially on warm, summer nights.

Corncrakes are long-distance migrants and spend the winter in the savanna of East Africa. Although it is still a common bird along most natural rivers in Eastern Europe, mechanised cutting of hay and crops has eradicated Corncrakes in many parts of Western Europe by destroying nests, eggs and adults. The species still hangs on in remote parts of Ireland and the Hebrides, where—because of the climate—mowing occurs only very late in summer and fewer nests are destroyed.

The Corncrake is a rail by origin but resembles the much smaller Quail (*Coturnix coturnix;* 6¼–7" [16–18 cm]) in its preference for long grass and secretive behaviour. Quails are also found in wheat fields and their presence is usually denoted by the song of the male, a repeated *kwik-me-dit*. Their small size and brown, rounded wings distinguish Quails from Corncrakes in flight.

FIELD NOTES

- *10¾–11¾" (27–30 cm)*
- *Long, reddish-brown wings*
- *Feet dangling in flight*
- *Short, pinkish bill*
- *Wings with chestnut patches*
- ▲ *Quail is smaller and has brown, rounded wings*
- *Hidden in tall grass and lined with dry grass*
- ♪ *Call: a monotonously repeated, dry rasping "errp-errp"*

Golden Plover

Pluvialis apricaria

The first flocks of Golden Plovers from arctic breeding grounds arrive in Europe in August. They are golden brown above, black below, with a white band from head to vent. The autumn moult replaces the black feathers with white ones. Golden Plovers can be confused with juvenile Grey Plovers (p. 244), which are often yellowish brown above, but the latter can be distinguished in flight by their black armpits and their white rumps.

J F M A M J J A S O N D

Like other plovers, "Goldies" feed with a distinctive stop–start action: standing still, then running and picking at the ground, then standing still again. Winter flocks of Golden Plovers are usually accompanied by Black-headed Gulls (p. 105). Prolonged observation will reveal their aim: every time a Golden Plover finds an earthworm, a gull will dash forward and try to steal it. This klepto-parasitic behaviour can be successfully countered by the plovers only if they fly away or hastily swallow their prey.

Golden Plovers are common winter visitors in grasslands and coastal areas in Britain and Continental Europe. In Britain, they breed locally in moors and upland bogs, and disperse to lower areas in winter.

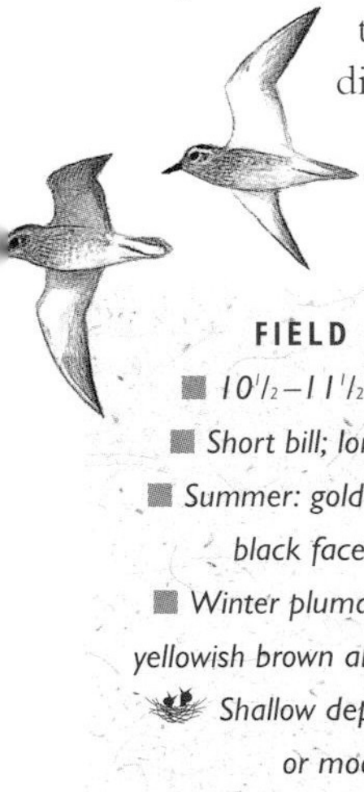

FIELD NOTES

- *10½–11½" (27–29 cm)*
- *Short bill; long, greyish legs*
- *Summer: golden brown above, black face and belly*
- *Winter plumage and juvenile: yellowish brown above, white below*
- *Shallow depression in tundra or moorland*
- ♪ *A melodious and melancholy "pyuu" or "pyee"*

Lapwing

Vanellus vanellus

Lapwings are common and widespread across Britain and Europe, and are characteristic birds of meadows, coastal pastures and arable fields. The striking crest and glossy green back is unique among European waders. They prefer areas of short grass, in which they start breeding very early in spring. The male performs conspicuous display flights, and acrobatically tumbles from high up in the air while the wings make a low humming sound.

As early as June, the young of the first broods begin to congregate in fields with failed breeders. During periods of ice and snow in winter, when earthworms become inaccessible, large flocks move about. Most Lapwings will move southwards until they reach frost-free areas. In winter, Lapwing flocks are often followed by Common Gulls (p. 249), which are always on the lookout to steal an earthworm from an unwary Lapwing.

In autumn, Lapwings moult into winter plumage, which is characterised by brown edges to the feathers on the back and wings and pale edges to the throat. These fringes will wear away during winter, revealing more and more beautiful green glossy plumage as spring approaches.

FIELD NOTES

- *11½–12¼" (29–31 cm)*
- *Glossy green above, white below, long crest, chestnut vent*
- *Male: long crest in summer, black throat*
- *Female: shorter crest, pale throat*
- *Shallow depression lined with grass*
- *♪ A shrill "kee-wit"*

Adult (summer plumage)

Black-tailed Godwit

Limosa limosa

J F M A M J J A S O N D

In Britain, Black-tailed Godwits are usually passage or wintering birds found in estuaries, wet meadows and marshes. In a flock of waders, they stand out with their long, black legs and long, straight bills. In summer plumage, the head is orange-brown and the belly and flanks densely barred dark brown. The winter plumage is rather dull: uniform grey above and below.

When feeding, Black-tailed Godwits are often difficult to tell from Bar-tailed Godwits (*L. lapponica*; 13¼–16" [34–41 cm]), a closely related species from the arctic tundra, also common passage migrant and winter visitors to British coastal estuaries. The best distinguishing features are the shorter legs and shorter, slightly upturned bill. In flight, the bold black-and-white markings on the wing and tail of the Black-tailed will easily distinguish it from the Bar-tailed.

The Black-tailed Godwit is a rare breeding bird in Britain and confined to coastal pastures. If you are lucky enough to observe a pair in courtship in spring, look out for the spectacular display flights of the male, as it dives with incredible speed and calls loudly *kee-wee-wee-wee-wee* and a repeated *kruveet-toh*.

FIELD NOTES

- *14½–17¼" (37–44 cm)*
- *Long legs; straight, long bill; white rump and wingbars*
- *Summer: variable amount of orange-brown on neck and below*
- *Winter: grey above, white below*
- ▲ *Bar-tailed Godwit: shorter bill and legs, barred rump, no wingbars*
- *Cup of grass on ground*
- ♪ *During display flight a repeated "kruveet-toh"*

Barn Owl

Tyto alba

J F M A M J J A S O N D

One of the most widespread birds in the world, the Barn Owl occurs in open cultivated country in rural areas throughout Britain and Europe. It is most frequently seen hunting at dusk or at night along motorways, where the grassy verges are home to its main prey, rodents. Lit up by headlights, the Barn Owl's white underparts combined with its silent, hovering flight, give it an almost ghost-like appearance.

Sadly, a combination of traffic casualties and the loss of trees and old buildings where the owls nest and roost has caused a decline in Barn Owl numbers in many countries. However, the use of nestboxes in some areas has helped maintain or even increase other populations of this beautiful species.

Barn Owls belong to the family Tytonidae, which is distinct from all other owl families in Europe. One peculiar feature of this family is that the downy young moult directly into adult-like plumage. Another feature is their pectinate, or comb-like, central toe-nail, which is used for preening. The Barn Owl has one of the most blood-curdling calls of any European bird: a loud, shrill shriek, often given in flight.

FIELD NOTES

■ *13–14½" (33–37 cm)*

■ *Mottled tan above, white below*

■ *Pale, heart-shaped face, dark eyes*

Cavities in trees, barns and lofts

♪ *A variety of eerie sounds, including a shriek-like "kee-yak"*

Little Owl

Athene noctua

The ancient Greeks dedicated the Little Owl to the goddess of fertility, Pallas Athene. As she was also identified with the moon, this probably explains why the Little Owl, a creature of the night, was chosen as her symbol. Nowadays, the Little Owl is one of the most widely known owl species in Europe. Towards dusk, it can often be seen on a telegraph pole, barn roof or fence. If agitated, it will bob like a small thrush or adopt an upright posture and glare at the intruder with its penetrating, large, yellow eyes.

J F M A M J J A S O N D

Britain, where it was introduced, represents the northwestern edge of the Little Owl's distribution range. It is pre-eminently a resident species and rarely moves more than a few miles from its place of birth. This habit makes it vulnerable in severe winters with heavy snow, when its prey of worms, insects and small rodents becomes scarce or inaccessible. As a result, Little Owl numbers fluctuate considerably. You will find Little Owls everywhere in open cultivated country, if enough hollow trees or old buildings are around to provide cavities for nesting.

Little Owl at nest

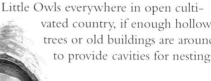

FIELD NOTES

- *8¼–9" (21–23 cm)*
- *Small size, short tail*
- *Grey-brown with white spotting*
- *Large, yellow eyes*
- *In tree holes, buildings*
- *A lamenting, but shrill "kiuw"*

Short-eared Owl

Asio flammeus

The Short-eared Owl is one of the most diurnally active owl species in Britain, and can often be seen hunting in the early morning or late afternoon over open areas such as moorland, meadows and arable fields. Their flight action is very characteristic: a jerky beating of the long, stiff wings alternated with elegant glides and circles. The short tail and rounded head are also striking features, as are the white underwing and dark carpal patches on the upperwing.

J F M A M J J A S O N D

When perched, the yellow eyes contrasting with the black surrounds of the eye give the bird an unforgettable, "fiendish" expression.

In Britain, the Short-eared Owl is a localised breeding bird of moors, marshes and heathland. It is the only European owl that makes a real nest, usually well hidden among grass or shrubs on the ground.

Short-eared Owls feed mainly on small rodents, and their numbers and breeding success depend highly on the abundance of their preferred prey. Winter is the best season to see the species, as many Scandinavian birds migrate southwards. Occasionally they concentrate in areas with abundant food, such as abandoned fields with high densities of voles.

FIELD NOTES

- 13¾–16" (35–41 cm)
- Streaked brown
- Yellow eyes
- White underwings, dark carpal patch on upperwings
- Loose structure of dry plants on ground
- ♪ Male during display flight: "boo-boo-boo-boo"

Bee-eater

Merops apiaster

The Bee-eater is an unmistakable sight: the combination of blue, green, yellow and brown is unique in Europe. It is the only representative of the family of Bee-eaters, Meropidae, in the Continent. The nearest breeding areas to Britain are in France, but occasionally breeding has taken place farther north, even in Britain. Bee-eaters breed communally in excavated holes in the ground or sandbanks.

J F M A M J J A S O N D

Bee-eaters are attracted to beehives, which makes them unpopular with local beekeepers. When a bee is captured, after a graceful pursuit flight, it will be smashed against a branch to get rid of the sting.

Bee-eaters stay in families for much of their life, including during their long-distance migrations to tropical Africa. Their frequent calls, a loud and rolling *pruuh-pruuh*, probably help to keep the clan together. Bee-eaters are famous for using "helpers" during breeding, with some birds assisting their parents or other close relatives in raising a brood. How they recognise their family members still remains a mystery.

FIELD NOTES

- *10½–11½" (27–29 cm)*
- *Brilliantly coloured*
- *Blue below, yellow throat, chestnut-brown crown and shoulders, elongated central tail feathers*
- *Juvenile: green above*
- *Excavated holes in the ground or sandbanks*
- ♪ *A loud, rolling "pruuh pruuh"*

Hoopoe

Upupa epops

The first impression of a Hoopoe in flight, bouncing and flapping with its rounded, black-and-white wings, is often of a giant butterfly. Once on the ground, however, it is often surprisingly difficult to relocate, as it probes with its long, decurved bill for insects and larvae in soft earth or cattle dung. The crest is rarely erected, usually only when the bird is agitated.

It is a common and widespread bird of open cultivated areas in Southern and Eastern Europe. Despite its seemingly erratic flight pattern it is a long-distance migrant to sub-Saharan Africa. Most Hoopoes reaching Britain in spring are stragglers that have overshot the nearby breeding areas.

Hoopoes get their name from the territorial call of the male, a far-carrying *poo-poo-poo-poo*, usually produced out of sight in the canopy of a tree. Cavities, such as hollow trees, crevices, walls or sandbanks, are used for nesting, and the entrance is often clearly marked white with droppings. The female does all of the incubating and is fed by the male until the eggs hatch.

Hoopoe with crest erect

Hoopoe with young in nest

FIELD NOTES

- *10¼–11" (26–28 cm)*
- *Unmistakable black-and-white wings and tail*
- *Buffish head, breast and mantle*
- *Large buffish crest with black markings*
- *Cavities in trees or old buildings*
- *♪ Male territorial call: "poo-poo-poo..."*

Skylark

Alauda arvensis

Male Skylarks draw attention to themselves with their high-pitched singing as they perch on the ground or fly overhead in prolonged song. At other times, both males and females tend to be inconspicuous, blending well with their background and running away or crouching quietly when disturbed. If alarmed, they take off in a low, undulating flight, usually giving a few loud, chirruping call notes as they go.

Skylarks are common in many open habitats, from arctic tundra to southern steppes, and from ploughed fields to wet meadows. You can tell Skylarks in flight from Woodlarks (p. 136), which are similar in size, by the white trailing edge of the wing and longer tail.

Skylark singing

Being both numerous and small, Skylarks are a favourite quarry of falcons and Sparrowhawks. One way for them to escape these predators is to flock together. In a group, birds can forage more safely and for longer periods because there are more vigilant eyes to spot an approaching raptor and, for each individual bird, less chance of being the one attacked. For this reason, small birds, such as Skylarks, gather in flocks of up to hundreds of birds in winter.

feeding party in autumn

FIELD NOTES

- *6¾–7¼" (17–18.5 cm)*
- *Short bill is pointed and stubby*
- *Streaked brown above and on breast*
- *Broad wings in flight*
- *Cup of grass on ground*
- *Call in flight: a loud "chirrup" or "trruee"; song: a constant flood of trills, jubilant sounds and mimicry*

Meadow Pipit

Anthus pratensis

The most widespread member of the pipits in Britain and Europe is the Meadow Pipit, a common bird in all types of meadows and pastures, but also on upland moor and heathland. It is streaked brown above, with a fine bill, slender posture and a relatively long tail with white outer tail feathers.

When a Meadow Pipit is perched on a fence, you may notice that the streaking on the breast merges into a dark spot, a characteristic not found in most other pipits.

It is difficult to distinguish the Tree Pipit (*A. trivialis*; 5¾–6¼" [14.5–16 cm]) from the Meadow Pipit outside the breeding season, but the call is very different, a buzzing *bizzzt*. It breeds commonly in all types of forest and woodlands with clearings.

The Rock Pipit (*A. petrosus*; 6–6½" [15–16.5 cm]) is slightly larger, darker and with dark brown or black legs. It breeds on rocky shores, and in winter it is found almost exclusively on salt marshes and rocky coasts, where it searches for insects and small snails among seaweed.

FIELD NOTES

■ *5½–6" (14–15 cm)*
■ *Small; streaked brown above, white outer tail feathers*
■ *Fine bill, reddish legs*
■ *Streaked breast and flanks*
▲ *Tree Pipit: very similar; different call, a buzzing "bizzzt"*
▲ *Rock Pipit: dark grey-brown, dark legs, different call*
Cup of grass on ground
♪ *A sharp "pseet, pseet, pseet"*

Yellow Wagtail

Motacilla flava

Yellow Wagtails are familiar and conspicuous songbirds of meadows in summer. They are often found close to grazing cattle, feeding on insects disturbed in the grass. They incessantly "pump" their tails up and down in typical wagtail-like manner.

Like many birds with a large geographical distribution, the Yellow Wagtail's plumage varies considerably from place to place. Several races occur in Europe, of which at least three occur in Britain.

J F M A M J J A S O N D

Throughout their range, males are deep sulphur yellow below, greenish above, with a long, brown tail with white outer feathers, but with very different head patterns. Males of the British race (*M. f. flavissima*) have yellow heads, males of the Continental race (*M. f. flava*) have blue-grey heads with a white supercilium, and males of the Scandinavian race (*M. f. thunbergi*) have dark grey heads with dull black sides. The females of all forms look very similar, being much duller and lacking any grey on the head.

Yellow Wagtails migrate long distances to the savanna regions in Africa.

FIELD NOTES

■ *6¼–6¾" (16–17 cm)*

■ *Male British race: bright yellow head and underparts*

■ *Females of all races: yellow below, yellowish brown above*

■ *Immatures: yellowish brown below, olive-brown above*

▲ *Continental races: males with varying amounts of grey and black*

Cup of grass and leaves on ground

♪ *A melodious "sweee" or "tsreee"; song: a chirping repetition of calls*

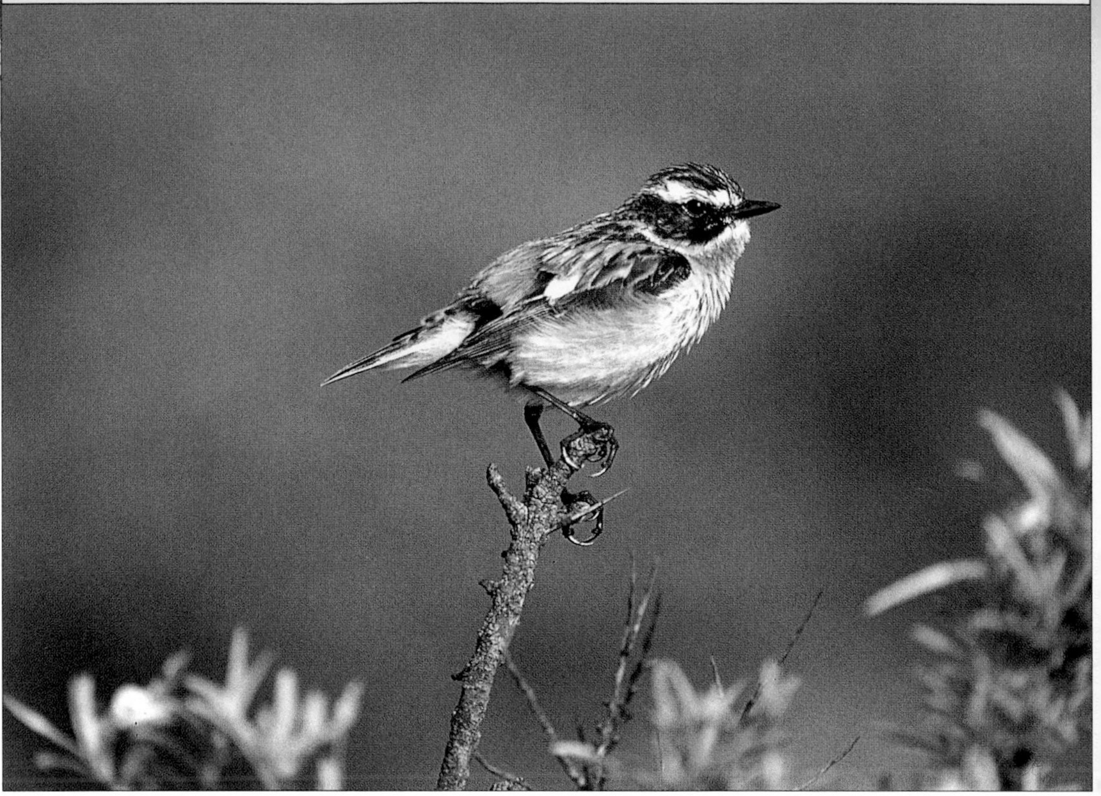

Whinchat

Saxicola rubetra

Whinchats are summer migrants that spend the winter south of the Sahara. On their return in spring, males announce their arrival by singing from the top of small bushes. Whinchats belong to a group of small thrushes known as chats, which have small, fine bills, relatively short tails and an upright posture, whether on the ground or perched on a bush.

The male Whinchat has a bright orange breast and marked dark brown-and-white head. Females and juveniles are less brightly coloured. The white markings in the tail are visible only in flight.

A similar orange-breasted species is the Stonechat (*S. torquata*; 4¾–5" [12–13 cm]), males of which have a blackish throat contrasting with a white neck patch; they also lack the white supercilium.

Stonechats prefer drier habitats such as heathland and commons with gorse, particularly near the coast. Unlike Whinchats, most Stonechats spend the winter in Britain and Europe.

Because of changes in agricultural practices and land use, Whinchat numbers have decreased much in Britain and parts of Europe.

FIELD NOTES

■ *4¾–5" (12–13 cm)*

■ *Summer male: orange breast, striking head pattern, dark brown above*

■ *Summer female: orange-buff breast, pale supercilium, streaked brown above*

■ *Autumn: both sexes like summer female*

▲ *Stonechat has uniform head pattern; summer male: white neck patch*

Cup of grass on ground

♪ *Alarm call: "wee-tek-tek"; song: a grating chatter mixed with mimicry*

Northern Wheatear

Oenanthe oenanthe

♀

The Northern Wheatear is the only representative in Western Europe of the wheatear group, small chat-like thrushes, which all have a conspicuous black-and-white tail pattern. A white patch moving fast in undulating flight low over the ground is usually the first impression of a wheatear. The male has a pure grey mantle and crown, buffish breast and a black mask. After a moult in late summer, both adults and juveniles are very similar to the breeding female, being dull greyish-brown above and with no black mask.

Northern Wheatears perform one of the most amazing migrations known among birds. Twice yearly, breeding birds from east Canada to Greenland cross icy mountains and the Atlantic ocean, travelling to and from their winter quarters in the African savanna. There they meet other wheatears which have travelled from Alaska and eastern Siberia. They are one of the earliest tropical migrants to arrive in spring, reaching Britain as early as the first week of March.

♂ in front of nest in rabbit hole

FIELD NOTES

- 5½–6¼" (14–16 cm)
- *Large white rump in flight*
- *Summer male: grey crown and mantle, black mask, buffish breast*
- *Female: greyish brown above, no mask*
- *Winter: sexes similar*
- *Cavity in rock or stone walls, rabbit holes*
- *Alarm call: a simple "chak"; song: a rapid series of grating notes*

Whitethroat

Sylvia communis

The Whitethroat belongs to the prolific Sylviidae family, also known as the Old World warblers. These small, insectivorous birds are found in a wide range of habitats and are best known for their distinctive songs and well-developed migratory habits.

Male Whitethroats have a greyish head, reddish-brown wing coverts and a pure white throat, often contrasting with a pinkish breast. When singing, the throat feathers often bulge forward, making the white patch visible even from a long distance. The females and juveniles are duller, but always distinguishable by their reddish-brown wings.

J F M A M J J A S O N D

Whitethroats can be found in rough open areas with bushes, hedgerows and weedy thickets, often with long grass. The Lesser Whitethroat (*S. curruca*; 5–5½" [13–14 cm]) prefers areas with higher bushes and deciduous trees and is often found in gardens and parks. Both species, however, may occur in the same area and are then best distinguished by their characteristic songs, a dry, one-note rattle in Lesser Whitethroats and a short, sprightly warble in Whitethroats.

FIELD NOTES

- *5–6" (13–15 cm)*
- *Red-brown wings, white in tail*
- *Summer male: white throat, grey-brown head*
- *Female and autumn plumage: reddish-brown wings, grey-brown above*
- ▲ *Lesser Whitethroat: greyish plumage, dark legs*
- *Cup of grass in undergrowth such as brambles*
- ♪ *Call: a sharp "tek tek" or nasal "ved, ved, vid"*

Yellowhammer

Emberiza citrinella

Yellowhammers are often first noticed by their lazy song, usually given from a telegraph pole or wire: six high chirping notes followed by a lower, melancholy final note, rendered as *tsi-tsi-tsi-tsi-tsi-tsi tsuuh* (or *"a little bit of bread and no cheese"*). In both sexes, the rusty-red rump is a useful marker throughout the year. In summer, the male is easily identified by its yellow head and chestnut markings on the sides of the breast.

Equally distinctive is the male Cirl Bunting (*E. cirlus*; 6–6½" [15.5–16.5 cm]), which has a striking head pattern and black throat.

Telling female Cirl Buntings and Yellowhammers apart is a challenge even for experts, but the rump colour, grey-brown in Cirl Bunting, is a safe distinguishing feature.

The Cirl Bunting is a common breeding bird in Southern Europe and replaces the Yellowhammer in the Mediterranean. It is a rare and localised breeding bird of coastal valleys in southwest England. The Yellowhammer has a more northerly distribution and is widespread and common throughout Britain and Europe. They are typical birds of the woodland edge, but also occur in open country, especially in winter, when flocks roam around in fields of stubble.

FIELD NOTES

■ *6¼–6¾" (16–17 cm)*

■ *Reddish-brown rump*

■ *Summer male: yellow head and belly*

■ *Summer female: duller yellow*

▲ *Cirl Bunting: grey-brown rump; summer male with black throat; female very similar to female Yellowhammer*

Clumsy cup of dry plants in thickets

♪ *Call: a metallic "tsik" or drawn-out "tscheet"*

Corn Bunting

Miliaria calandra

The Corn Bunting is the largest bunting around Britain. Although similar to larks in plumage colouring, the heavy bill and lack of white in the tail, unique among European buntings, are good identification features.

As with many birds of open country and grasslands, the song is highly pitched and often performed in flight. It starts with a few, slow, chipping notes to end in a fast jingle, not unlike the jangling of a bunch of keys. When it flies with shallow wing beats from one songpost to another, often roadside fences or telephone wires, it usually keeps its legs dangling.

J F M A M J J A S O N D

When flushed it often calls as it flies off, giving a low but loud *tik* or a creaky *tsek*.

Male Corn Buntings frequently mate with more than one female, a habit known as polygamy, and it implies that many males remain unmated. Therefore, a lone, singing male is not always an indication of a breeding pair. In Britain, Corn Buntings breed locally in extensively managed farmland and meadows. A large decline in numbers has been noted across much of Northern Europe in recent decades, coinciding with widespread changes in agricultural practices.

♂ Corn Bunting singing

FIELD NOTES

- *6¾–7" (17–18 cm)*
- *Large size*
- *Powerful bill, lack of white in tail*
- *Streaked brown above and below*
- *In spring, only the males perform songs*
- *Cup of plant material on ground*
- *Call: a hard "tik" or "tsek"*

W e t l a n d s

OVERHEAD There is always a good deal of traffic between wetlands areas, so watch out for passing flocks of birds such as Black Terns, or geese flying in their distinctive V-formations.

DEEP WATER Several species of duck that dive for their food, such as Tufted Ducks and Pochards, tend to form rafts in deep water well away from the shore. Divers and grebes are generally found in deep water.

SHALLOWS Depending on the locality, look here for Spoonbills, Avocets and a variety of other birds that gather food while wading in shallow water.

REEDBEDS Water Rails and bitterns generally hide deep in reedbeds, but may forage along their margins when undisturbed. Reedbeds are also home to some songbirds, such as Reed and Sedge Warblers, and may provide nesting and roosting sites for a wide range of different birds.

MUDFLATS Many birds like to forage on mudflats. Some waders, such as Common Sandpipers and Temminck's Stints, actually prefer freshwater to coastal environments.

WETLANDS

Lakes, Marshes, Reservoirs, Rivers, Fens

Ranging from small local reservoirs and ponds in city parks to major rivers, lakes and marshes, wetlands are a prominent feature of the European landscape. The term "wetlands" is generally taken to refer to bodies of freshwater only, but with bird habitats it is hard to make a firm distinction between these areas and saltmarshes, river estuaries and similar coastal environments.

Within each wetland environment, birds can gather their food in a remarkable range of ways, so wetlands are home to a notably broad spectrum of species. The bird population of a cold, deep, Northern European lake, for example, will be very different from that of a damp marshy fen in lowland England, or the riverine forests of Central Europe.

In general, Northern European wetlands tend to be rich in species of duck, whereas Southern European wetlands are favoured by a variety of herons, storks, and similar large wading birds.

From the birdwatcher's perspective, wetlands tend to be characterised by their margins, the bird diversity they support increasing more or less in proportion with the extent of mud, reedbeds, and water shallow enough to wade in.

Unfortunately, humans have tended to regard wetlands as wastelands rather than vital components of a healthy ecosystem, and short-sighted drainage and land reclamation have led to drastic reductions in the numbers of some wetland birds.

More recently, however, the surge in environmental awareness in much of Europe has resulted in a growth in the conservation of wetland areas, and many are now protected as reserves and sanctuaries.

Birdwatching *in* Wetlands

Clearly delineated habitats and a diversity of highly visible species make wetland environments ideal places to study the social behaviour of birds, their feeding tactics and annual migration cycles.

Wetlands provide some of the most exciting habitats for birdwatching because they contain all sorts of spectacular and easily observed species, such as grebes, herons, egrets, geese, ducks, Ospreys and waders. Another appealing aspect of birdwatching in an area of water is that it is a finite region, distinct from the surrounding land, enabling you to keep track of day-to-day changes in the diversity and numbers of birds present.

On a walk in the woods or fields you may see more warblers or finches one day than another, but you will be unable to tell whether there are really more birds because at any one time many birds may be hidden from view. In contrast, if you see 20 ducks and 10 Coots on a lake one day, and 50 ducks and no Coots the next, you can be fairly certain that the variation is real rather than apparent.

Passing Through

Many wetlands are wintering areas or transit points for vast numbers of ducks and shorebirds that nest in the Russian arctic and Siberia.

Southbound migrant waders appear as early as late June, heralding a stream of avian traffic that extends well into November. Some remain for the winter, others continue southward into Southern Europe or Africa. In spring, some birds begin moving north again as soon as ice-free conditions permit, while many others are still moving north as late as early June.

It can be fascinating to note these day-to-day changes in your notebook, and over the years to compare arrival and departure dates for various species. You may also come to see how day-to-day changes relate to weather factors and thus learn how to predict which days are best for birdwatching.

Coexistence

The self-contained nature of many wetland habitats will also allow you to observe the intricacy with which the total resources of a habitat are parcelled out to different kinds of birds.

There is almost sure to be at least one small, short-legged species that forages over the muddy margins but does not actually wade (a sandpiper, perhaps).

WILDLIFE REFUGES *A huge range of highly visible birds can be observed in wetlands, from these ducks "dabbling" for food (below) to a group of roosting Tufted Ducks (right).*

BIRD SPECTACULARS *Wetlands are the stage for many of the most spectacular sights in nature. Events such as Common Cranes in flight (right) attract birdwatchers around the country (above).*

Then there will be a slightly longer-legged species that can cover a wider area because it can wade in shallow water (a Redshank, for example). And there will also be longer-legged birds that can reach deeper water to take full advantage of an even larger percentage of the wetland's total area (Avocets or herons). Other birds—terns, for example—can cover the total surface area, but only at the cost of staying airborne for long periods. Some ducks habitually feed in the shallows, others "up-end" in somewhat deeper water, while still others dive for food, exploiting resources that cannot be reached by other birds. Birds such as the Water Rail have narrow bodies that enable them to slip easily among stems in reedbeds on the margins of the wetland.

More than other habitats, wetlands illustrate that, far from being distributed haphazardly, birds live in clearly structured communities. It can be absorbing to work out the way wetland birds are distributed and how they operate.

Getting Around

Some wetland areas can be difficult to reach. Power-boats, of course, involve far too much noise to be of any use to the birdwatcher but—depending on the kind of wetland—pottering about quietly in a canoe or rowing boat can be a wonderful way of observing waterbirds at close range without disturbing them unduly.

Alternatively, you may be able to find a causeway or dyke to use as a vantage point to scan the wetland with your binoculars or spotting scope. Otherwise, wading may be the only way of exploring the marsh, but this often results in wet feet.

You can, of course, wear rubber boots or waders, but a little-known corollary of Murphy's Law states that the depth of the water you want to wade across is always one inch higher than the top of your boots. That's why experienced birdwatchers often keep a spare pair of shoes and a towel in their car.

One final suggestion for wetland birdwatching: don't forget the insect repellent.

WETLAND RESERVES *are so popular with visitors that boardwalks (left) and blinds have become necessary controls in their management. Visitors are also able to make excursions by boat through these areas.*

Little Grebe

Tachybaptus ruficollis

The Little Grebe, also known as Dabchick, is Europe's smallest grebe and often difficult to observe, because of its small size and habit of diving frequently. In the breeding season, Little Grebes frequent small lakes and shallow ponds with densely vegetated shores, and their presence is usually only signalled by their vocal courtship, a loud duet of high-pitched trills.

Little Grebes carry young chicks on their backs, but less often than, for instance, the Great Crested Grebe (p. 195) does, and instead, the nest, a floating platform of waterplants, is often used as a resting site.

Unlike other grebes, Little Grebes feed primarily on invertebrates, such as insects and their larvae, molluscs and crustaceans, and occasionally on small fish. In autumn, they disperse to larger lakes and channels where they are easier to observe. In Britain, numbers of this common resident breeding bird are swelled in winter by migrant birds from Continental Europe.

FIELD NOTES

- *9¾–11½" (25–29 cm)*
- *Dumpy, short-necked, often fluffing up pale stern*
- *Summer: chestnut throat, cheeks and foreneck*
- *Winter: grey-brown*
- *Floating platform of aquatic plants anchored to submerged vegetation*
- *Display call is a vibrating trill, often in duet*

Great Crested Grebe

Podiceps cristatus

J F M A M J J A S O N D

Great Crested Grebes are elegant birds with a slender neck and a long thin bill, which is a perfect adaptation for catching fish with great speed. The chicks have a striped head and upper neck and are often carried on the back of a parent to rest and to receive food.

An interesting aspect of grebe biology is that these birds consume many feathers, which are thought to form soft balls that protect the stomach against damage from sharp fish bones.

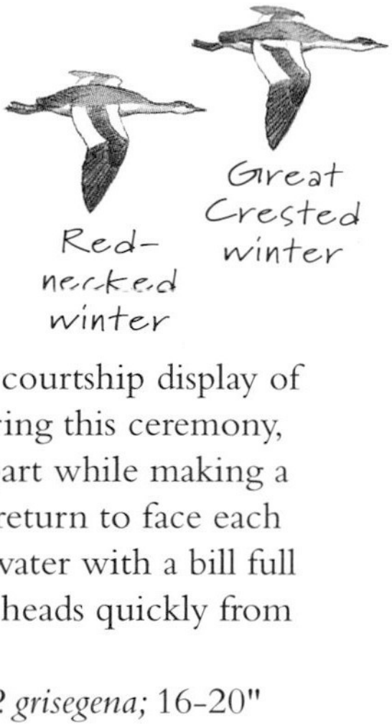

If you watch nesting birds long enough, you may be fortunate enough to see the spectacular courtship display of this species. During this ceremony, the birds swim apart while making a contact call, then return to face each other, sitting upright in the water with a bill full of waterplants, rocking their heads quickly from side to side.

The Red-necked Grebe (*P. grisegena;* 16–20" [40–50 cm]) is similar in size. It winters in Britain in small numbers along the coasts and infrequently inland on large lakes.

FIELD NOTES

- *18–24" (46–61 cm)*
- *Summer: black head tufts, rufous chestnut at base*
- *Winter: whiter on flanks and lacks tufts*
- ▲ *Red-necked Grebe: grey cheeks, rust-brown neck, bill dark with yellow base*
- *Floating platform of aquatic plants, anchored to vegetation*
- ♪ *Various grating and loud calls*

Black-necked Grebe

Podiceps nigricollis

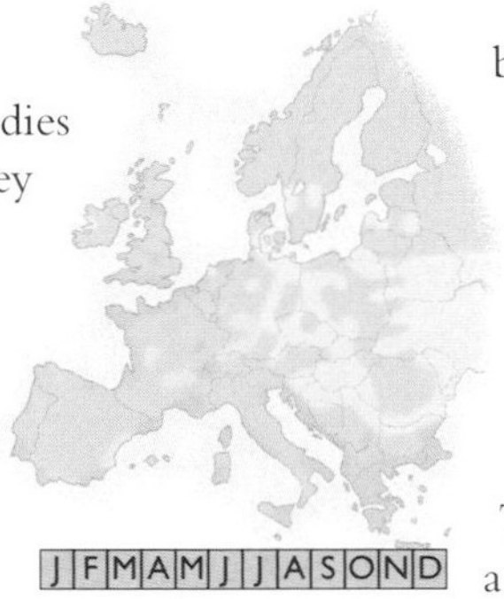

Black-necked Grebes breed in shallow, nutrient-rich water bodies with lush vegetation, where they form small colonies, often associated with gull or tern colonies. Like other grebes, the Black-necked has an elaborate courtship display in which a pair performs a dance on the water, while making short whistles and trills.

During the breeding season Black-necked Grebes feed mostly by diving for insects, but flying insects and items from the water's surface are also taken, an activity for which the rather thin and up-tilted bill is very well suited.

After the breeding season, they move to open standing, generally saline waters, where Slavonian Grebes (*P. auritus*; 12¼–15" [31–38 cm]) can also be found. These smaller grebes are very similar to Black-necked Grebes, but can be distinguished in winter plumage by the pure white cheek and foreneck, with a straight division between black crown and white cheeks, and by a straight, heavier bill. The Slavonian has a more northerly distribution than the Black-necked, and can be found more often at sea and in estuaries in winter.

FIELD NOTES

■ *11–13¼" (28–34 cm)*

■ *Yellow tufts, black head and neck*

■ *Thin and up-tilted bill*

■ *Winter: grey and white, without tufts*

▲ *Slavonian: straight bill, chestnut neck in summer*

Floating platform of plants anchored to submerged vegetation

♪ *A plain "yoorr-eep", short, whistling "peep" or "psheep-chee", or a trill*

Bittern

Botaurus stellaris

The Bittern is a mysterious bird of dense reed beds, and a master of disguise. If you are lucky enough to encounter one closely along the edge of a marsh, it will try to make itself "invisible" by stretching its neck, pointing its bill upwards, and swaying with the movement of the reeds, its eyes swivelled forward to keep track of the intruder.

In spring, the male "booms" like a foghorn, audible at a distance of more than 3 miles (5 km), mostly between dusk and dawn. Males are often polygamous and may mate with up to five females.

The Little Bittern (*Ixobrychus minutus*; 10½–14¼" [27–36 cm]) is also found in marshes. The females and juveniles resemble a miniature Bittern. The male, however, is a very striking combination of dark brown above with pale buffish wing coverts. Little Bitterns climb up reed stems rather than walk along the floor of the reedbed. They migrate to Africa and spend the winter south of the Sahara. In Britain, only odd birds turn up during migration. In most European countries, a serious decline in breeding numbers has occurred in recent decades, probably as a result of a long-lasting drought in the Sahelian winter quarters of the species.

FIELD NOTES

- 25¼–31½" (64–80 cm)
- *Golden brown with blackish stripes and bars*
- *Bill yellowish, legs green*
- ▲ *Little Bittern: small size, with buff wing panels*
- *Platform of dead reeds*
- ♪ *A foghorn-like boom: "uh-woomp", audible at great distances*

Night Heron

Nycticorax nycticorax

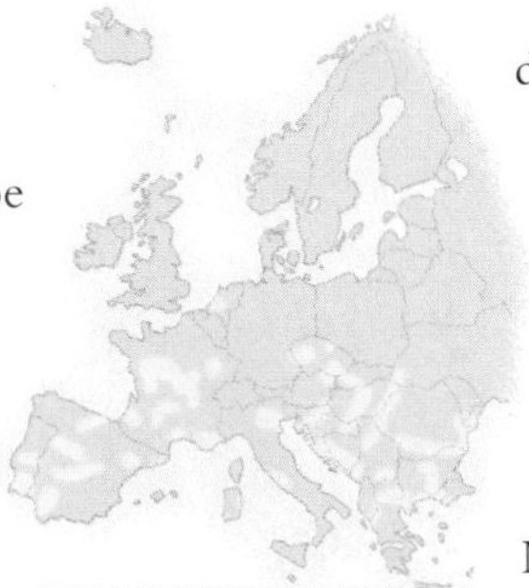

As its name suggests, the Night Heron is a bird of nocturnal habits, although it can often be seen during the day, feeding along the edges of lakes or coastal lagoons, or roosting in trees near water. A barking *kwark* frequently draws attention to birds as they leave their roost at dusk and set out to hunt for food at a time when most other herons are heading in the opposite direction, back to their roosts. By feeding at night, Night Herons avoid competition with diurnal heron species.

Unlike many other herons, the Night Heron's bill is very thick, wide and rather short. This is related to its opportunistic feeding habits, and its varied diet includes fish, frogs, insects and even chicks of marsh birds.

Just after the breeding season, and before the true migration to the winter quarters in Africa takes place, Night Herons, especially juveniles, disperse in all directions. These movements take the birds far north of their breeding range and stragglers may even reach Britain.

FIELD NOTES

■ *22–25½" (56–65 cm)*

■ *Adult: grey wings and tail, black cap and back, grey below*

■ *Summer: white lanceolated plumes on the head*

■ *Juvenile: dull brown, spotted and streaked brown, greyish buff and whitish*

Platform of sticks and reeds in trees, bushes or reedbeds

♪ *A Raven-like "kwark"*

Little Egret

Egretta garzetta

J F M A M J J A S O N D

The Little Egret is the most widespread white heron in Europe. In their Mediterranean range, they can be found along lakes, lagoons, rivers and coastal areas. They nest in mixed colonies with other species of herons.

The Great White Egret (*E. alba*; 33½–41" [85–104 cm]) can be distinguished from the Little Egret by its yellow bill and yellowish legs, as well as by its larger size. However, in the breeding season the adult bird acquires a black bill and darker legs.

In summer plumage, both species have elongated aigrette feathers on the mantle and scapulars, and the Little Egret also has two long head plumes. The large-scale trade of these feathers in the second half of the nineteenth century resulted in a dramatic decline in the population of egrets but protective legislation has since helped egret populations to recover.

In Britain, both egret species are rare migrants, but are being recorded in increasing numbers.

FIELD NOTES

■ 21½–25½" (55–65 cm)
■ All-white plumage
■ Legs black, yellow feet
■ Thin neck; slender, black bill
■ Summer plumage: long aigrette feathers on back
▲ Great White Egret: much larger; outside breeding season, has yellowish legs and stout, yellowish bill
Platform of sticks and reeds in reedbeds, bushes or trees
♪ A nasal "kseeh", grunting "raahk" or "owk"

Grey Heron

Ardea cinerea

J F M A M J J A S O N D

The Grey Heron is the most common and widespread heron in Europe and is found in any kind of shallow water, whether fresh, brackish or saline, standing or flowing. It feeds passively, waiting patiently and motionless for its prey, not infrequently close to an angler.

Grey Herons breed colonially in tall trees, often in parks of towns and cities. Breeding starts early, with the nests occupied from February onwards, so that the first chicks may be born as early as the second half of March.

The populations breeding in Britain and Ireland are mainly sedentary. In Europe, the tendency to migrate increases towards the north and east, though some individuals may winter close to the breeding grounds. Harsh winters, however, will take a heavy toll of the resident birds.

Purple Herons (*A. purpurea*; 30¾–35½" [78–90 cm]) always winter in tropical Africa. They are slightly smaller, look much darker and have dull reddish to purple-brown wing coverts. They prefer reeds and other dense vegetation in which to forage. The species breeds in Western and Southern Europe and migrants are regularly observed in southern and southeastern Britain.

FIELD NOTES

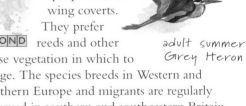

- ■ *35½–38½" (90–98 cm)*
- ■ *Adult: blue-grey body, white face and neck, black crest*
- ■ *Flies with retracted neck and bowed wings*
- ■ *Juvenile: brownish grey*
- ▲ *Purple Heron: darker, slender head and neck with black streaking*
- *Platform of sticks, often in trees*
- ♪ *A raucous "krowrnk"*

Spoonbill

Platalea leucorodia

This exotic-looking bird is the only representative in Europe of a group of specialised species with spoon-shaped bills. Their bill is a unique adaptation to fishing by touch in shallow water. Spoonbills are specialised in catching small freshwater fish, such as sticklebacks and shrimps, in tidal wetlands.

J F M A M J J A S O N D

Alone or in small groups, they forage in creeks and ditches with their bills sweeping from side to side, regularly tossing their catch in the air to swallow it swiftly. The breeding colonies in large marshes are very sensitive to disturbance and are found only in strictly protected areas.

The best time to look for Spoonbills is in late summer when they congregate at traditional resting sites and sleep for most of the day. The adults are then usually accompanied by their young, which are still begging for food. In Western Europe, Spoonbill colonies are found only in the Netherlands, France and Spain. In autumn, they migrate along a narrow flyway to West Africa to winter in tidal wetlands between the Sahara and the Atlantic Ocean, although a handful of birds may arrive to spend the winter in the quieter estuaries of southwest England.

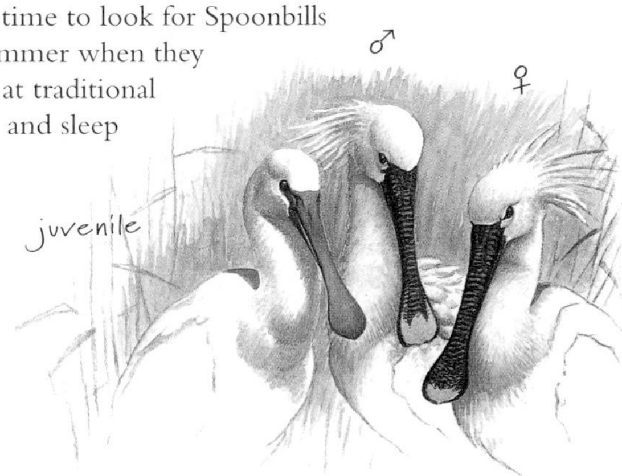

FIELD NOTES

- *31½–35½" (80–90 cm)*
- *Black, spoon-shaped bill with yellow tip*
- *Ivory plumage with crest and yellow breast patch in spring*
- *Black legs*
- *Flies with outstretched neck*
- *Small branches in trees or on the ground in reedbeds*

Greater Flamingo

Phoenicopterus ruber

Greater Flamingos are wading birds with extremely long legs and neck. They frequent shallow lagoons, usually saline, brackish or alkaline. Their flight silhouette is unmistakable: a long, stretched neck and equally long legs trailing behind.

The unique, crooked bill of the flamingo is perfectly adapted for filter-feeding. The birds consume minute aquatic invertebrates, such as brine shrimps, midge larvae and small worms, by pumping water in and out and filtering it with their lamellae.

Females are similar in plumage to the males, but are up to 20 per cent smaller in size. Juveniles are easy to pick by their grey-brown plumage and brown legs, as well as by their smaller size.

In Europe, Greater Flamingos are found in the Mediterranean, concentrating in a few large colonies in France, Sardinia and Spain. Breeding is often irregular and numbers fluctuate considerably from year to year as there are regular movements between Europe, Africa and Asia. Colonies usually consist of several thousands of pairs and are established in large wetlands, far from human disturbance and inaccessible to terrestrial predators such as foxes.

FIELD NOTES

- 47¼–57" (120–145 cm)
- Unmistakable, extremely long neck and legs
- Pinkish plumage
- Feeds with submerged head
- Nest: Mound of mud with shallow bowl on top
- ♪ A goose-like "gragg-agg" or "gegg-egg"

Greylag Goose

Anser anser

The Greylag Goose is the most southerly breeding and wintering of the grey-brown geese in Europe. The uniform greyish plumage and completely orange bill distinguishes them from all other geese. In winter, they are characteristic birds of lowland farmland, such as crop and stubble fields; in summer, they nest in undisturbed areas along seashores or lakes.

Greylags remain paired for life. Both male and female incubate and rear the brood. When the young can fly, the whole family will join large flocks and make the journey together to their winter quarters, where the families remain together until into the following spring. The juveniles will often fly back to the breeding grounds in the company of their parents.

The yearlings do not breed yet, but spend the summer in their parents' nesting territory and might contribute to its defence, perhaps even helping to defend their younger siblings.

Over much of their range, Greylag Geese are subject to human persecution. An increase in the number of European Greylag Geese is primarily due to reduced and regulated shooting in some countries. Greylags have been successfully reintroduced into many parts of Britain.

FIELD NOTES

- *30–35" (76–89 cm)*
- *Orange bill, pink legs*
- *Forewings pale grey*
- *V-formation in flight*
- *Platform of reed stems and grass lined with down*
- *When flying, a cackling, nasal "aahng-ahng-ung"*

Gadwall

Anas strepera

The Gadwall is a typical duck of lowland areas with shallow freshwater lakes and marshes fringed with extensive vegetation. Shallow water is preferred, because they feed on waterplants by dabbling with their heads submerged. In winter, they can also be found on larger lakes and in estuaries.

J F M A M J J A S O N D

The males are grey with a characteristic black rear end. Females are difficult to tell from female Mallards, but have yellow-orange bill sides.

Gadwalls usually occur in pairs or small parties, mixing freely with other dabbling ducks. Pair formation starts in late summer and continues through autumn and winter. Display flights can be frequently observed in spring, when several males may chase a single female. The white inner secondaries, forming a conspicuous white rectangle on the rear inner wing, are then distinctive features.

Gadwalls were introduced into much of Britain and can now be observed virtually all year. Winter numbers are boosted by birds from Iceland and Continental Europe.

FIELD NOTES

- *18–22¾" (46–58 cm)*
- *White rectangle on rear inner wing (speculum)*
- *Male: greyish with black stern*
- *Female: like female Mallard, smaller, orange-sided bill*
- *Cup of grass and dry leaves lined with down*
- ♪ *Male: grating "errp"; female: quacks*

Teal

Anas crecca

Teals are small dabbling ducks, common across Europe. They nest in tall grass and reeds around lakes and marshes, and in winter favour muddy channels in marshes and estuaries for feeding. Non-breeding Teals often occur in fairly large flocks that fly rapidly in a tightly grouped formation. They associate with other dabbling ducks while feeding, but although a single Teal may fly with Mallards or other ducks, the species tend to separate when in flight.

Teals are partially migratory: while the northernmost European breeding birds disperse to lower latitudes in winter, breeders of more temperate regions are resident.

With its pure white supercilium running from above the eye to the nape, and long, blue-grey scapulars, the male of the Garganey (*A. querquedula;* 14½–16" [37–41 cm]) is unmistakable. The female, however, is hard to distinguish from female Teal. In flight, both sexes of Garganey are readily distinguished from Teal by their light grey-blue forewings. The Garganey is highly migratory, and most European birds winter in sub-Saharan Africa.

FIELD NOTES

- 13½–15" (34–38 cm)
- Male: chestnut and bottle-green head
- Female: plain head, green speculum
- ▲ Garganey male: white supercilium, pale grey-blue upperwing; female: very similar to Teal
- Depression in ground lined with dry leaves and down
- ♪ Male: a high, far-carrying, whistle "preep"; female: nasal quacks

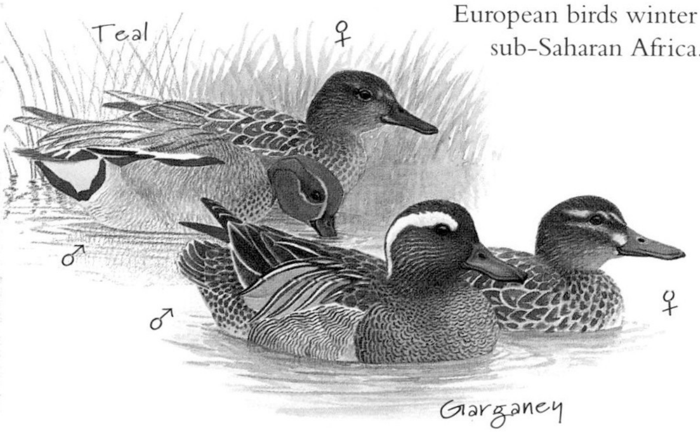

Pintail

Anas acuta

J F M A M J J A S O N D

The Pintail's long neck enables it to feed by up-ending in deeper water than other dabbling ducks. In general, it is a bird of open wetlands, avoiding wooded areas. It breeds in wet meadows, on marshy lakesides or near slow-moving rivers.

Large numbers migrate southwest in winter to estuarine flats, brackish marshes and coastal lagoons, feeding mainly on aquatic plants and seeds, but also on various invertebrates. Pintails forage chiefly in the evening and at night; most of the day is spent loafing on shores and mudflats.

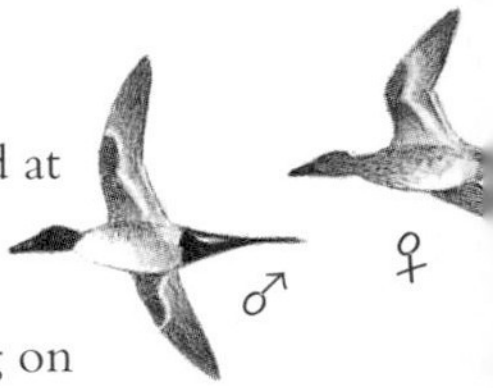

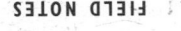

The male, when not in eclipse plumage, is unmistakable, with his attenuated, pin-like central tail feathers (making up almost a quarter of his total length) and his brown head and white foreneck. The female is generally paler and greyer than other dabbling ducks, and has something of the male's elegant, long-necked and long-tailed appearance. In flight, the female Pintail's best field mark is the white edge on the brown speculum of her upperwing.

FIELD NOTES

- *20–26" (51–66 cm)*
- *Slim and elegant*
- *Long and slender neck*
- *Male: brown head, white foreneck, long tail*
- *Female: plain head, pointed tail, grey legs*
- *Depression in ground lined with grass, leaves and down*
- ♪ *Male: a mellow "proop-proop"; female: repeated descending low quacks*

Shoveler

Anas clypeata

J F M A M J J A S O N D

In profile, the heavy, shovel-like bill, which is longer than its head, makes the Shoveler one of the most distinctive of the dabbling ducks. In flight, it appears top-heavy, with its large bill, relatively long neck and short tail combining to give the appearance of the wings having been placed towards the rear of its body.

When feeding, usually in shallow water, the Shoveler extends its neck forward and swings its bill from side to side just under the water's surface. The small comb-like teeth along the sides of the bill are used as a strainer, retaining mostly small-sized aquatic food items.

A male in eclipse plumage looks like a female, but the body plumage is darker and more rufous. From September to November, males attain a plumage stage somewhere between summer and eclipse plumages, known as the sub-eclipse or supplementary plumage. Immatures also acquire a supplementary plumage in autumn, and do not attain adult plumage until late winter. You may, therefore, see the distinctive immature male plumage, with a mottled whitish crescent forward of the eyes, right through until New Year.

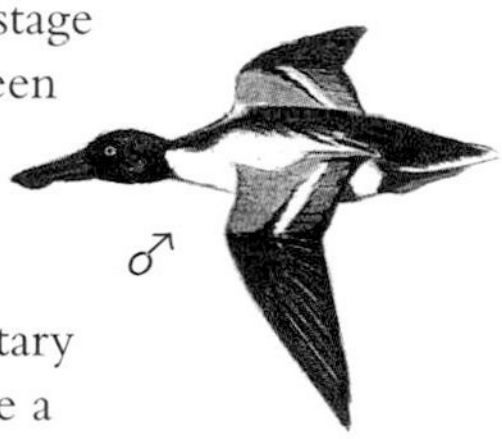

FIELD NOTES

- *17¼–20½" (44–52 cm)*
- *Huge, spatulate bill*
- *Male summer: dark green head, white breast, chestnut flanks*
- *Female: mottled brown*
- *Depression in grass lined with grass and some feathers*
- ♪ *Male: a repeated hollow "took-took"; female: low quacks*

Tufted Duck

Aythya fuligula

The increase in numbers of Tufted Ducks in Europe is remarkable. In Britain, breeding was first recorded in 1849, and it is now a common and widespread breeding bird. This outstanding success is mainly due to the bird's adaptability in colonising new human-created habitats, such as parks, lakes and reservoirs, as well as to the colonisation of Northwestern Europe by exotic molluscs, particularly the zebra mussel, on which Tufted Ducks at times rely almost entirely for food.

J F M A M J J A S O N D

Outside the breeding season, they concentrate in large flocks on open waters, and also—especially when these are frozen up—in sheltered sea bays and harbours.

In these flocks, Pochards (*A. ferina;* 16½–22¾" [42–58 cm]) may often be encountered as well. Numbers of this species have also increased in Europe, although not as much as the Tufted Duck; this is probably due to its more specialised demands for breeding habitat. Pochards prefer well-vegetated swamps, marshes and lakes with areas of open water, whereas Tufted Ducks breed in a greater variety of wetlands, including meadows.

FIELD NOTES

■ *15¾–18½" (40–47 cm)*

■ *Male: black with white sides*

■ *Female: dark brown*

■ *Drooping crest, much longer in male*

▲ *Pochard male: chestnut head, black breast, pale grey back and flanks; female: mostly grey-brown*

Platform of grass and sedges lined with down

♪ *Displaying male: a whistling "pee-yee-peep-peep"*

Goosander

Mergus merganser

J F M A M J J A S O N D

The Goosander is one of three species of "saw-bill" in Europe, all of which are specialised fish-eaters. The bill is sharply serrated along its cutting edges, giving a firm grip on slippery prey. Goosanders hunt for fish with their neck stretched forward, propelling themselves along with their feet.

Outside the breeding season, Goosanders occur on large freshwater bodies, gathering in flocks to hunt for fish. Most migration takes place when these lakes freeze up.

The slightly smaller Red-breasted Merganser (*M. serrator*; 20½–22¾" [52–58 cm]) has a more marine distribution, especially outside the breeding season. The male is easily distinguished by the black-marked rusty-brown breast. The Smew (*M. albellus*; 13¾–17¼" [35–44 cm]) is the smallest "saw-bill" in Europe, and a rare winter visitor to Britain. Adult males are white with elegant black marks; females and immature males, collectively known as "redheads", have a chestnut head and white cheeks.

FIELD NOTES

■ *22¾–26" (58–66 cm)*
■ *Large with "saw bill"*
■ *Male: breast and flanks creamy salmon-pink*
■ *Female: contrasting brown head and pale neck*
▲ *Red-breasted Merganser male: rusty-brown breast; female: no contrast between head and neck*
▲ *Smew male: white with black markings; female: chestnut head, white cheeks*
Cavity lined with pure down
♪ *Male: a faint, frog-like "kuorr-kuorr"*

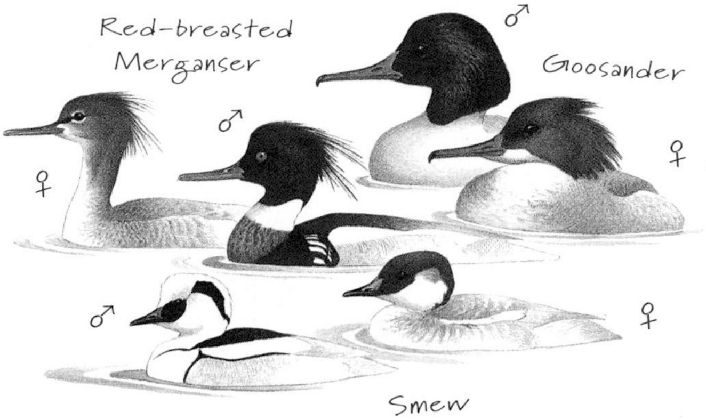

Marsh Harrier

Circus aeruginosus

The Marsh Harrier hunts over extensive areas of dense marshland vegetation, especially reeds, and other aquatic habitats such as lagoons and meadows. In flight, it is immediately recognisable as a harrier by its low, leisurely progress, with wings held in a shallow V, and its long tail. Harriers usually locate their prey by sound and vision, trying to surprise their quarry in a "pouncing" attack.

In spring, the male performs a slow-motion flight up and down above his territory while calling constantly. When he approaches his incubating partner with prey, the female hears his high-pitched, piping call and flies toward him. The female turns herself onto her back mid-flight, and the male drops or lowers the prey into her talons.

J F M A M J J A S O N D

Marsh Harriers are found commonly all over Europe, but they are a rare and localised breeding bird in Britain. The smaller Hen Harrier (*C. cyaneus;* 17–20½" [43–52 cm]) is more numerous in Britain, and breeds in drier habitats, such as the moorlands of Scotland and Ireland. The male is pale grey, the female brown with a white rump.

FIELD NOTES

- *18¾–22" (48–56 cm)*
- *Gliding and soaring with wings in shallow V*
- *Male: grey tail and wing patch, pale underwing*
- *Female: chocolate-brown, yellowish crown*
- ▲ *Hen Harrier male: grey, black wing tips; female: brown, white rump*
- *Platform of reeds and rushes*
- ♪ *Male utters a shrill "kee-oo"*

Adult

Osprey

Pandion haliaetus

The Osprey is a cosmopolitan bird of prey that occurs in shallow waters, inland and coastal, and feeds almost exclusively on fish. After a successful plunge into the water, it holds its legs one behind the other, so that it can carry its catch, sometimes weighing one kilogram or more, head facing forwards and thus be more streamlined for flying. When it reaches its feeding perch, it waits for its prey to die before eating it, in the meantime, drying and preening its soaked plumage.

FIELD NOTES

- *21½–26¾" (55–68 cm)*
- *Dark brown above, white below with dark "wrist" patches; clear brown breast band in female*
- *White head with brown line through eye*
- *Wings long and narrow, angled like large gull*
- *Huge platform of sticks and flotsam*
- *Slow series of whistled notes, falling in pitch*

Ospreys usually build their huge nests on trees or cliffs but on islands that are free from ground predators, they will even build nests on the ground.

With its long and rather narrow wings, the Osprey is not primarily a soaring migrant, but it nevertheless crosses water barriers and deserts—such as the Mediterranean Sea and the Sahara—to reach areas where fish are readily available in winter.

Ospreys are persecuted by shooters (often when migrating) and as pests by fish farmers, and populations have suffered from pesticide pollution, which affects their reproduction. But as well as this, habitat destruction and acidification of water bodies are still threats to this magnificent bird.

Adult

Water Rail

Rallus aquaticus

J F M A M J J A S O N D

Water Rails are usually only noticed when we hear their calls, which are among the most peculiar sounds birds can make, more like a squealing and grunting pig than a bird. If you wait patiently, keeping an eye on the edge of a reedbed, a Water Rail might appear briefly, walking slowly among the reed stems, especially around dusk.

A Water Rail is an opportunistic feeder: it will eat almost everything it finds while foraging. It will even catch birds, such as unwary young Wrens and Reed Warblers. The unfortunate victims are either killed instantly with one blow of the bill or drowned.

adult

Although Water Rails are typical ground-dwelling birds with short, rounded wings and strong legs, and walk around for most of their lives, they can also fly over surprisingly long distances. This is particularly so with birds from Northern Europe, the majority of which migrate toward Southwestern Europe, a fact we have learned from recoveries of ringed birds.

In winter, Water Rails occasionally have to leave dense reedbeds to find food, much increasing our chances of actually seeing one.

chicks

FIELD NOTES

- *8½–11½" (22–29 cm)*
- *Long, slightly curved bill, strong legs*
- *Short, rounded wings*
- *Whitish undertail*
- *Boldly barred flanks*
- *Cavity made in vegetation*
- *Peculiar grunting and groaning sounds*

Adults

Common Crane

Grus grus

A flock of migrating Common Cranes is often heralded by their far-carrying calls of nasally grating trumpet blasts. Although they can soar like raptors, they usually fly in V-formation like geese and also migrate during the night.

Adult Common Cranes are grey with a black-and-white head. The juveniles lack the head pattern of adults, and have shorter "tail plumes", formed out of elongated tertials.

Throughout the year, but especially in spring on or near their breeding grounds, they perform a dance in which the birds leap up with raised wings, their "tail plumes" erect, and trumpet loudly.

J F M A M J J A S O N D

In their wintering grounds, cranes feed primarily on plant material, such as cereals, potatoes and acorns. They breed in open bogs or marshland, where they also take insects—which are particularly important for chicks—and other animal food items including fish.

Cranes have traditional wintering sites in Southern Europe and North Africa, as well as migratory staging posts. The species is a rare passage migrant in Britain, particularly in periods with strong easterly winds.

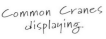

Common Cranes displaying

FIELD NOTES

- *45–51" (114–130 cm)*
- *Huge size, long neck and legs*
- *Black-and-white head; bare, red crown patch*
- *Elongated feathers drooping over tail*
- *Flies in V-formation*
- *Platform of dry grass*
- *A trumpeting, rolling "krroo" or "krruee-krro"; juveniles have high-pitched, piping calls*

Adult male (summer plumage)

Ruff

Philomachus pugnax

The Ruff is one of the most peculiar of waders in Europe. In May and early June, the males gather at special arenas, or leks, to display. Dark-coloured males defend particular spots, about 3 feet (1 m) apart, sometimes by kicking and pecking. Others, known as satellite males and usually with a white collar, move more freely in the arena and behave opportunistically. Females visit these leks to choose a mate, more often than not, a dark-coloured male, then make a nest at some distance from the lek and raise the brood single-handed.

J F M A M J J A S O N D

The males are much larger than the females and in summer plumage are instantly recognisable by their head tufts, long ruffs and other variegated feathers.

By June, males have lost their head tufts and ruffs, and moulted to a dull grey winter plumage. Most birds winter in Africa, including those from the easternmost range in Siberia. Ruffs return to the breeding grounds along a more easterly route than they took in autumn, a phenomenon also known as loop migration.

FIELD NOTES

- *Male: $10\frac{1}{4}$–$12\frac{1}{2}$" (26–32 cm), female: $7\frac{3}{4}$–$9\frac{3}{4}$" (20–25 cm)*
- *Winter adult: dull grey with orange legs*
- *Juvenile: buffish, greenish legs*
- *Summer male: variably coloured head tufts and ruffs; summer female: brown, variegated with black*
- *Hidden in long clump of grass, lined with grass*
- *Silent, sometimes a low "wek-wek-wek" or "kuk-uk"*

Common Snipe

Gallinago gallinago

The Common Snipe is a fairly widespread breeding bird of marshlands, bogs, moors and meadows. In spring, males make a curious sound during their aerial display flights. While diving fast at a steep angle, the outer tail feathers are spread out and vibrated to produce a mechanical bleating sound. When the bird gains height, it will give a monotonously repeated *chick-a, chick-a.*

J F M A M J J A S O N D

at song post

Common Snipes feed rather jerkily in soft muds, probing vertically with their long bills. During the day they rest in cover, but feed in more open sites, chiefly at night. When disturbed, they fly off in a characteristic zigzag pattern and call out, then they tower with rapid wing beats and tilt from side to side with the bill pointing down.

The British population is mainly resident, but some move to Southern Europe, and many birds from Northern Europe spend the winter in Britain. Common Snipes are still sought-after game for hunters, especially in Southern Europe and North Africa.

FIELD NOTES

- *9¾–10½" (25–27 cm)*
- *Short legs, long bill*
- *Medium size*
- *Pronounced markings on head and back*
- *In flight, white line along rear of wing*
- *Cup of grass well hidden in vegetation*
- ♪ *A harsh "etsch" when flushed*

Curlew

Numenius arquata

Curlews are large waders with long, decurved bills. They breed on moors and open marshland. Locally, the species has successfully colonised agricultural grasslands. When in the vicinity of a breeding pair, the singing male is soon noticed planing down on bowed wings above its territory. The song is a beautiful sequence of bubbling phrases, accelerating and rising in pitch.

On passage and in winter, Curlews are found in estuaries and tidal wetlands. It is one of the most vocal waders, and even in winter, its song can often be heard as it defends a feeding territory or perches in a roost.

Although Curlews have a varied diet, they often favour large polychaete worms, which they find by touch and skilfully extract from the mud with their long bills. Crabs are taken, too, usually located by sight and swallowed whole.

The smaller Whimbrel (*N. phaeopus;* 15¾–18" [40–46 cm]) breeds on low arctic moorland and tundra, not far from the treeline, such as in the northernmost parts of Scotland. European Whimbrels winter almost exclusively in the mangroves of West Africa, where they feed on fiddler crabs.

FIELD NOTES

- 19½–23½" (50–60 cm)
- Large size, decurved bill
- Plumage brown with pale markings, whitish rump
- Females are larger than males
- ▲ Whimbrel: smaller, striped crown; call: tittering whistle "bibibibibibibi"
- Shallow cup in the ground sparsely lined with grass
- ♪ A rising "coour-lee"

Redshank

Tringa totanus

Large flocks of Redshanks often gather in coastal wetlands to feed on tidal mudflats. They are very vocal and are often the first of a group of waders rising and calling a warning if a bird of prey approaches.

The Redshank is a medium-sized shorebird with a straight bill and long, orange-red legs. In summer plumage, Redshanks are spotted and streaked below, and streaked dark brown above. In autumn, they moult to a plain brown-grey above and unstreaked white below.

The male has a distinctive song, a repeated *tyoo* and yodelling *taludl*, performed while rising and falling in the air with rapid, shallow wing beats.

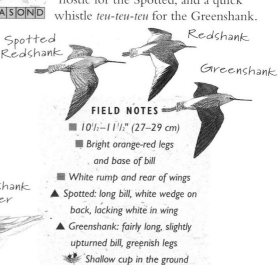

The closely related Spotted Redshank (*T. erythropus;* 11½–12½" [29–32 cm]) is very similar, but has a much longer bill and different wing pattern. The Greenshank (*T. nebularia*; 11¾–13¾" [30–35 cm]) has a fairly long, slightly upturned bill and long, greenish legs. In flight, they are easily distinguished by distinctive calls: a sharp whistle *tchuwit* is diagnostic for the Spotted, and a quick whistle *teu-teu-teu* for the Greenshank.

FIELD NOTES

- *10½–11½" (27–29 cm)*
- *Bright orange-red legs and base of bill*
- *White rump and rear of wings*
- ▲ *Spotted: long bill, white wedge on back, lacking white in wing*
- ▲ *Greenshank: fairly long, slightly upturned bill, greenish legs*
- *Shallow cup in the ground lined with grass*
- ♪ *Whistling "tyoo" or "taludl"*

Common Sandpiper

Actitis hypoleucos

Common Sandpipers are often noticed flying away low over water, alternating distinctive short glides on stiff, down-bowed wings with flickering wing beats. At rest, the Common Sandpiper is easily distinguished from other waders by its "bobbing" gait, wagging its rear end up and down. It has a slow and deliberate feeding action, and continues to teeter and bob as it feeds.

It tends not to occur in large flocks, and is often found alone rather than with shorebirds of other species.

The species occurs in virtually all types of wetland habitat, but prefers sandy or stony shores, especially along rivers where it nests in summer.

In courtship flight, the male circles rapidly around with shallow, vibrating wing beats. Its song consists of repeated shrill, sharp notes, and this is also heard in winter quarters and on migration.

Southward migration starts as early as late June. Although a few birds winter in the northern hemisphere, including in Britain, most migrate to the southern half of Africa.

FIELD NOTES

- *7½–8¼" (19–21 cm)*
- *Grey above, white below*
- *Short bill, short, greenish legs*
- *Teeters and bobs almost constantly*
- *Flies with rapid, shallow wing beats*
- *Hollow in ground hidden by grass*
- *♪ A thin, piping "dee-dee-dee"*

Black Tern

Chlidonias niger

Black Terns are one of Europe's three species of marsh tern. In summer, they are sooty black, with greyish wings and tail. They nest on floating vegetation in shallow freshwater lakes, using rosettes of water-soldier and leaves or floating roots of waterlilies, which protect against the wind and waves.

In the breeding season, Black Terns take insects and their larvae from the water's surface, either in flight like a Swallow, or after hovering like a Kestrel.

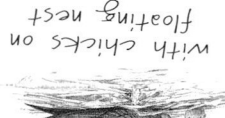

with chicks on floating nest

In August and September, large numbers gather in the Netherlands, virtually the whole European population, to undergo a complete moult before migrating to coastal areas in tropical Africa. The winter plumage of adult and juvenile birds is grey above and white below, with a characteristic black cap. Most first-summer birds remain in the winter quarters, returning to Europe only when they are at least two years old.

Black Tern numbers in Europe have declined in recent decades, due to loss of habitat and wetland deterioration by drainage, pollution and human recreational activities.

FIELD NOTES

- *8½–9½" (22–24 cm)*
- *Small size*
- *Summer: sooty black, grey wings and tail*
- *Winter: black cap, grey above, white below*
- *Shallowly forked tail*
- *Platform of reeds on floating vegetation*
- *A shrill "kyay" or "kyek" or a short "kik"*

moulting adult summer

adults in winter plumage

Kingfisher

Alcedo atthis

The Kingfisher is undoubtedly one of the most beautiful birds in Britain and Europe, a stunning combination of turquoise-blue and chestnut-red. Despite this, the Kingfisher is not always easily seen. Often, it is just a bright blue flash as it flies low over the water with whirring wing beats.

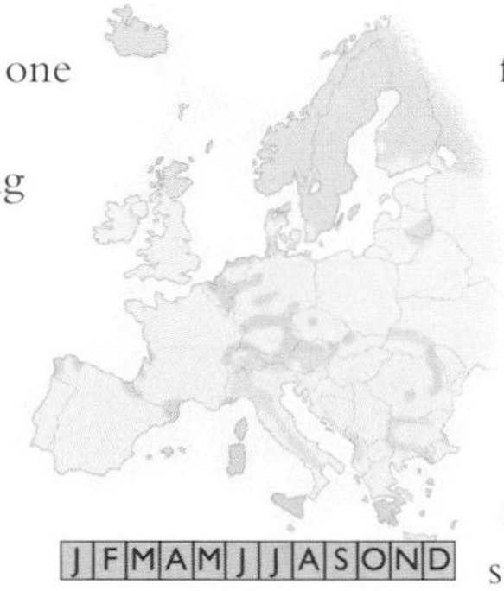

Care is needed when trying to approach a Kingfisher perched on a branch above the water. Bill pointed down, now and then it turns around, bobbing its head and body when food is detected. Suddenly, it plunges down to seize its prey. Under water, the wings open; the eyes are open with a protective third eyelid drawn over them. The bird rises beak-first from the water and flies back to its perch. This whole dive takes less than two seconds.

Numbers of Kingfishers are severely depleted by harsh winters. They require ice-free water for fishing and many try to move southward or to the coast in an effort to survive. An overall decline, however, is attributable to industrial and agricultural pollution and to canalisation of rivers.

FIELD NOTES

■ *6–6¾" (15–17 cm)*

■ *Bright green-blue upperparts and chestnut underparts*

■ *Short tail and big head with dagger-like bill*

■ *Flight fast, low over water, showing brilliant blue of mantle*

Natural hollows or shallow burrows dug in vertical bank of river

♪ *A short shrill whistle "chee", repeated two or three times*

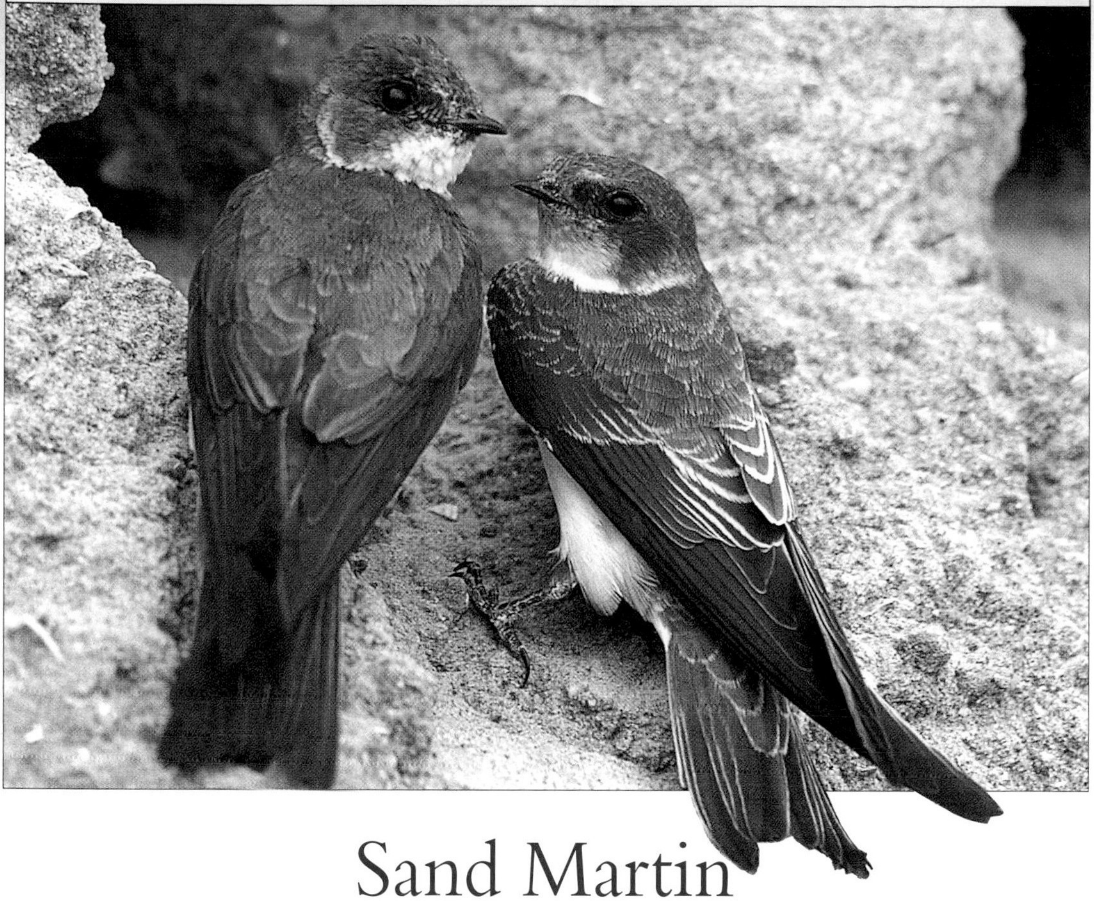

Adult (left) and juvenile

Sand Martin

Riparia riparia

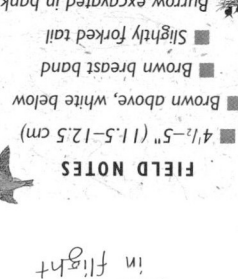

In summer, if suitable nesting sites are available, Sand Martins are a common sight above ponds and lakes. They are similar to House Martins (p. 110) in size and flight silhouette, but are easily distinguished by their dull brown plumage, brown breast band and lack of a white rump.

They often breed in huge colonies, where the nest burrows are dug out in a vertical sandbank by the males. From the entrances of the tunnels, the males perform advertising displays to attract females. The fledglings return to the burrow for a few days after their first flight, then gather in "creches" where the parents can recognise their own chicks by their particular calls.

Sand Martins arrive as early as March from their tropical winter haunts in Africa, often returning to the same site as in the previous year, especially if they have bred successfully. In their winter quarters, they depend heavily on Sahelian wetlands, and the severe declines in population in recent decades are thought to be caused by the prolonged drought in this region.

FIELD NOTES

- *4½–5" (11.5–12.5 cm)*
- *Brown above, white below*
- *Brown breast band*
- *Slightly forked tail*
- *Burrow excavated in bank, lined with feathers*
- ♪ *A harsh and dry "trchr"*

Adult male

Bluethroat

Luscinia svecica

J F M A M J J A S O N D

The Bluethroat is a small, unobtrusive bird, closely related to the Nightingale (p. 139) and occurring in swamps, on lakeshores and ditch banks with bushes. The male of the race *cyanecula*—known as the white-spotted Bluethroat and occurring in Western and Southern Europe—has a blue gorget with a white centre, edged below by bands of black and chestnut.

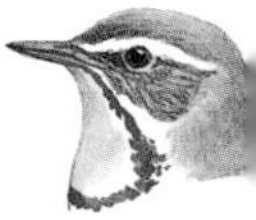

The female only has dark brown malar stripes continuing in an irregular breast band, although some older females may have traces of blue on the breast. In the Scandinavian mountains and in western Russia, another race occurs, the red-spotted Bluethroat (*L. s. svecica*) of which the male has a red throat patch.

Like the Nightingale, male Bluethroats are excellent songsters—giving a highly variable song with fine ringing notes, often accelerating it and including mimicry. Their song can easily be confused with that of the Marsh Warbler (p. 224), which often breeds in the same habitat and also has a lively song, full of mimicry.

In Britain, both races are occasionally seen and heard as they pass through on their autumn and spring migrations, but have been known to bred only a few times.

FIELD NOTES

- *5¼–5½" (13.5–14.5 cm)*
- *Greyish brown above, whitish supercilium*
- *Summer male: blue throat, fringed black and chestnut, with red or white spot, according to race*
- *Sides of tail rusty red*
- *Juvenile: dark brown, with pale yellow and light brown speckling*
- *Ground nest of moss, hair and down*
- *Call: "tchak" or "tsee-tchak-tchak"*

Sedge Warbler

Acrocephalus schoenobaenus

The Sedge Warbler is one of the most distinctive members of the difficult group of *Acrocephalus* warblers (p. 224). The buffish-white supercilium, dark eyestripe, pale brown streaked mantle and cinnamon rump are important field characteristics. The song is also distinctive, more lively and varied than the Reed Warbler's (p. 224), with rattling *trrrr* notes and sometimes Canary-like trills. It is often given during a fluttering display flight.

Most Sedge Warblers return in April from their African winter quarters to their breeding sites, which are usually swamps with reedbeds and bushes. Their food consists of small insects, such as aphids, which they find on young, growing reed stems. In August, Sedge Warblers prepare themselves for a southward-bound, long-distance migration by exploiting Aphid-rich reedbeds in Western Europe to build up large energy stores in the form of body fat. As with several other bird species dependent on Sahelian wetlands in winter, their survival rates have been found to depend on the amount of rainfall in West Africa.

FIELD NOTES

- *$4\frac{3}{4}$–5" (12–13 cm)*
- *Buffish-white supercilium*
- *Streaked pale brown mantle*
- *Dark eyestripe*
- *Cup of stalks, stems and moss lined with hair and feathers*
- *♪ A hard "chek" and a dry "trrr"*

Reed Warbler

Acrocephalus scirpaceus

Reed Warblers are small, brown warblers commonly found in marshes with reedbeds, often satisfied with surprisingly small areas of reed, provided the distance between the stems is not too large to weave the nest between. They usually remain well hidden among the reed stems and are best detected by song, a monotonous stream of short, grating notes, always with a rolling *r*, repeated two to four times, and performed during the day as well as at night.

The closely related Marsh Warbler (*A. palustris*; 4¾–5" [12–13 cm]) is best distinguished from its sibling by its rich and lively song, full of trills and warbles.

J F M A M J J A S O N D

The Great Reed Warbler (*A. arundinaceus*; 7–7¾" [18–20 cm]) looks about twice the size of a Reed Warbler, with a stout, long bill. It favours high, firm stands of old reed in deeper water, with thin vegetation in the lower layers. Marsh Warblers are rare and sporadic breeding birds in Britain; the Great Reed Warbler is only infrequently seen on passage.

FIELD NOTES

- 4¾–5" (12–13 cm)
- Unstreaked olive-brown above
- Plain head
- Rounded tail, grey-brown legs
- ▲ Marsh: almost identical to Reed; best distinguished by song
- ▲ Great Reed: large, stout bill, broad supercilium
- Cup of reed stalks woven between three stems
- ♪ Call: a low "kresh" or "krrrrr"

Adult male

Bearded Tit

Panurus biarmicus

Bearded Tits are usually first noticed by their characteristic calls, like a plucked guitar string. These are given while fluttering low over the reeds with a loose, twisting tail.

The life cycle of this beautiful bird depends completely on reedbeds. In summer, Bearded Tits take insects from the reed stems, while in winter they feed on the seeds. This change in diet involves a physiological adaptation of the stomach. If in spring, after a period of mild weather, a late period of frost sets in, Bearded Tits may get into serious trouble. If they have already switched internally to an insectivorous diet, many may die, unable to digest seeds that are still abundantly available. Losses can be quickly made up though, as one pair may have three or four broods each year and young birds from early broods may produce young in the same year.

Between 1965 and 1977, large numbers dispersed over Western and Central Europe from the Netherlands, where species numbers had increased tremendously in the huge reedbeds of reclaimed areas in the IJsselmeer. After the reedbeds disappeared under cultivation, Bearded Tit numbers declined again.

J F M A M J J A S O N D

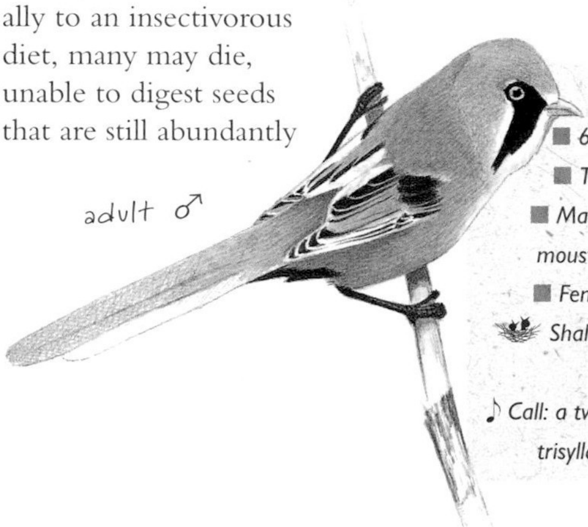

FIELD NOTES

- $6\frac{1}{4}$–$6\frac{3}{4}$" (16–17 cm)
- *Tawny above; long tail*
- *Male: grey head and black moustache sides, orange bill*
- *Female: plain, tawny head*
- *Shallow cup of reed leaves lined with feathers*
- *Call: a twanging "ping-ping"; song: a trisyllabic "tsjip tsjip tsjeerr"*

Reed Bunting

Emberiza schoeniclus

J F M A M J J A S O N D

Reed Buntings are common and widespread breeding birds of vegetated marshy areas in Britain and Europe. The male has a very simple song of two to five wheezy notes, then a faster *zizzizzizi,* but it may vary remarkably in construction.

A summer male Reed Bunting is unmistakable, with its black head and throat, white collar across the nape and white, drooping moustache. A female has no clear markings, but has a white supercilium, brown cheeks, dark malar stripes and buff underside with streaks. After a moult in autumn, both sexes look very similar, as the dark feathers of the males are "hidden" by brown fringes, which will wear off during winter, and the distinctive head pattern will gradually reappear in spring.

Northern European populations of Reed Buntings migrate southwards in September to December and return to their breeding grounds in February to April. In autumn, migrating Reed Buntings can often be seen during the day, usually singly or in small groups, flying jerkily and calling distinctively: a harsh *chup* or a shrill *tseeu.*

♂ winter

♀

singing ♂ summer

FIELD NOTES

- *5½–6¼" (14–16 cm)*
- *Streaked brown, reddish rump, white outer tail feathers*
- *Summer male: black head, white collar*
- *Female: brown, streaked on breast*
- *Cup of grass near the ground*
- ♪ *A shrill "tseeu"*

Seashores

SANDY BEACHES When not feeding offshore, terns are fond of loafing in large flocks on beaches. Sanderlings habitually forage along the shore, and gulls patrol tidelines for carrion. Another beach specialist is the Kentish Plover.

ESTUARIES and SALTMARSHES Many waders, such as Dunlins and Whimbrels, prefer open estuarine mudflats, exposed at low tide, on which they forage. At high tide, they may retire to saltmarshes or shingle beaches to roost in dense flocks.

CLIFFS and STACKS are prime nesting sites for colonies of Shags, Fulmars, Puffins and other auks, and some species of gull.

Seashores

Beaches, Sand Dunes, Coastal Cliffs, Estuaries, Saltmarshes

The seashore—where the land meets the sea—is a clearly defined but wonderfully varied environment. From the icy winter shores of Scandinavia to the tidal saltmarshes of eastern and southern Britain, Europe's varied coastline encompasses a vast array of places where birds can live.

The most obvious seashore habitats are cliffs, beaches, surf-washed rocks, muddy estuaries and saltmarshes. While there is considerable overlap, certain bird groups are associated with particular habitats: Cormorants and Shags with cliffs, terns with beaches, waders with estuaries, and so on.

Climate, of course, affects the habitat and the type of food available to birds, and thus influences the species found in different coastal surroundings. Auks and gulls, for example, tend to favour colder environments and are thus associated more with Northern European coasts; terns are common along warmer Southern shores.

The sea itself provides a variety of bird habitats, although as these are defined by factors such as depth, temperature, and salinity they are less easily recognised by humans. For example, the truly pelagic birds—especially the tubenoses, such as storm-petrels and shearwaters—seldom come close to land except in adverse weather conditions, and there is a noticeable difference between offshore and inshore bird communities. The sea off northern and western Britain is especially rich in birdlife, with large populations of breeding auks and Cormorants in summer and numerous sea ducks, such as scoters, in winter.

OFFSHORE Pelagic seabirds such as Manx Shearwaters and other tubenoses normally remain far offshore.

INSHORE Depending on location, inshore waters may host feeding Cormorants and Northern Gannets and, particularly in winter, rafts of divers, grebes, scoters and auks.

BIRDWATCHING *at* SEASHORES

Seashores are demanding birdwatching environments. You may study your garden or local patch for the sheer pleasure of watching birds going about their daily affairs, but sea coasts are where you go for the thrill of having your identification skills challenged and extended.

Birdwatching would not be the fun it is if all birds were easy to identify, and seashores are where you will come up against three of the most challenging groups of birds: gulls, migratory waders and seabirds.

GULLS

Everyone knows a seagull when they see one, but for the beginner, the sheer number of species makes positive identification difficult. In addition, each gull takes between two and four years to reach maturity, each year giving rise to a different plumage. And to compound the problem further, most species have distinct winter and summer plumages (and this sometimes applies to the immatures as well). Thus, a birdwatcher is faced with a quite bewildering array of alternatives.

Working through all these possibilities is the real problem; once you've done that, making a positive identification just takes time. At least gulls are (usually) fearless enough to let you look at them closely.

Critical points you should note when trying to identify a strange gull are:

- colour and shape of bill
- leg colour
- wing-tip pattern
- whether it has a dark tail band

WADERS

Migratory waders are less cooperative than gulls. They are generally extremely wary, and habitually congregate in large flocks, often of mixed

COASTAL HABITATS *are often dominated by Oystercatchers like this flock (above) and gulls, such as the Glaucous Gull (above right). Black Guillemots (right) and Cormorants (top) are good divers for fish.*

AT THE SEASHORE *the telescope (left) really comes into its own. Its greater power is particularly useful when it comes to identifying small shorebirds such as Sanderlings (below) as they scuttle in front of the surf.*

species, making them difficult to single out for study. Identification often has to be made at long distance. Like gulls, there are many species. In breeding plumage they are generally very distinctive, but juveniles and birds in winter plumage are often similar. In a few cases, the similarities are such that positive identification depends almost literally on a feather-by-feather analysis or a detailed examination of the extremely subtle variations in relative size and form. For the most part, however, you are half way there if you carefully note:

- leg colour
- length and shape of bill
- pattern (if any) of the upperwing
- whether it has a white rump

Seabirds

The third group that causes problems is the seabirds, especially the tubenoses. There are two difficulties with tubenoses. First, these are pelagic birds that generally remain far offshore. Viewing opportunities from land are therefore limited, and few of us get out to sea often enough to become familiar with them. Second, many species have rather similar plumage, differing in nuances of flight style and body proportions, which can be difficult to describe.

You really need on-the-spot, one-to-one help from an expert to master identification of these birds. Some birdwatching groups organise pelagic trips, chartering a boat to ferry birdwatchers far out to sea to look for shearwaters, stormpetrels and other species. In such a group, you are sure to find experts familiar with seabirds.

Tides

Birds living on either land or sea can, like us, run their lives according to the cycle of day and night, but birds living at the interface between the two must pay attention to the tides. Many feed at low tide and sleep while the tide is high; others do the opposite. If you live on the coast or often go birdwatching at the seashore, you'll be aware of the importance of tides.

Low tide is generally the best time for birdwatching, being when birds come together to feed on exposed beaches and mudflats. But in places with an extensive intertidal zone you may choose to go birdwatching when the tide is rising, as it will push birds in close enough for you to see them clearly. In some areas, waders gather at high-tide roosts where you can watch them before the tide recedes and they set off again to feed. Local knowledge will help you make the most of your trip.

Seashore Gear

Tidal flats, estuaries and similar localities are places where the spotting scope really comes into its own, giving you greater "reach" than most binoculars can deliver. Many coastal birds are wary and highly mobile, and it is often more difficult to follow a particular bird at the seashore than it is in, say, a park or garden. You will be called upon to exercise your identification skills at greater distances than in almost any other habitat.

Telescope magnifications somewhere between 20x and 40x are probably best for seashore conditions. If you go much above this you start to magnify atmospheric conditions rather than birds. A spotting scope is almost useless without a tripod, especially on seashores where it may be windy and wet. For more information on spotting scopes and tripods, see p. 64.

Great Northern Diver

Gavia immer

Great Northern Divers are usually observed only along the coast or, if you are lucky, on rivers or large freshwater lakes, slowly swimming and diving into the water for fish.

They differ from Cormorants (p. 236) by their white underparts and heavy, straight bill, held horizontally (usually held obliquely upwards by Cormorants).

Adults in summer plumage have a black bill, greenish-black head, black upperparts boldly blotched white, and a black breast band. They are much larger than other divers and, in winter plumage, have a dusky breast band. Juveniles look like adults, but lack the white spots and their upperparts look scaly.

Red-throated (*G. stellata*; 21½–25½" [55–65 cm]) and Black-throated (*G. arctica*; 23½–31½" [60–80 cm]) Divers are much smaller. Red-throated Divers have a narrow bill and, in winter, grey upperparts with tiny white spots. Black-throated Divers have a blacker cap, sharply demarcated from the white cheeks, with the white thigh patch in swimming birds being a good field mark.

FIELD NOTES

■ *27½–35½" (70–90 cm)*

■ *Heavy, straight bill*

■ *White on cheek vaguely demarcated from dark cap in winter*

▲ *Black-throated Diver in winter has a black cap, sharply demarcated from white cheeks, and a white thigh patch*

▲ *Red-throated Diver in winter has a finer, upturned bill and grey upperparts with small white spots*

Shallow depression in marsh or raft of aquatic plants

♪ *Silent; in flight a barking "kwuk"*

Fulmar

Fulmarus glacialis

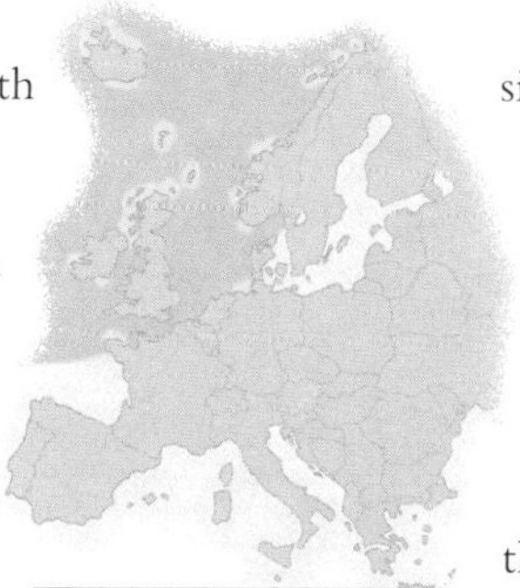

J F M A M J J A S O N D

Although similar to large gulls, with their grey-and white plumage Fulmars are, in fact, very different. They can be commonly seen along rocky shores in Britain, where thousands breed on steep cliffs. If a breeding bird is approached too closely, it will spit an oily substance from its stomach at the intruder.

At sea, Fulmars are among the most common birds around fishing vessels, where they feed on discarded fish and fish remains. Their flight is characteristic and similar to the shearwater: a series of fast wing beats interspersed by effortless low and fast skimming and shearing with some high arcs.

The peculiar-looking yellow-blue bill has several horn-plates, and tubes instead of "holes" as nostrils; these tubes are for excreting the surplus salt, which they take in during feeding and drinking.

In arctic waters, many birds are entirely pale grey or dark grey instead of white on the head and underparts. These dark-coloured birds can sometimes be seen in Northwestern Europe in winter.

FIELD NOTES

- 17¼–20" (44–51 cm)
- Gull-like in coloration, but with straight wings without black tips
- Stocky build with short neck
- Low shearing flight
- Only stones or some plant material on ledges
- ♪ Silent; grumbling and other guttural sounds at colony

Sooty Shearwater

Puffinus griseus

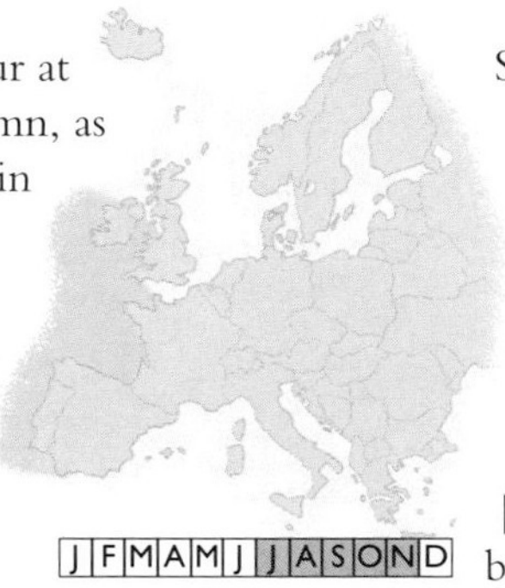

In Britain, Sooty Shearwaters occur at sea only in late summer and autumn, as they visit their breeding colonies in the southern hemisphere between October and April. When there are strong onshore winds, these birds can usually be observed from the coast, as black, long-winged birds with an angular silhouette, flying fast along the coast in high, bouncing arcs. If they are not too far away, a diagnostic whitish band across the underwing may be visible. The rather long and slender bill looks like that of the Fulmar, to which the Sooty Shearwater is related.

Sooty Shearwaters are most often seen in very small numbers but can occur in flocks of hundreds or even thousands, often together with Manx Shearwaters (*P. puffinus*; 13–15¾" [33–40 cm]). The latter commonly breeds in the British Isles. It is smaller than the Sooty Shearwater, black above and white below. In rough weather, the flight is similar, with quicker wing beats and usually with less regular and lower arcs; during calm weather, the flight is more relaxed with less shearing.

FIELD NOTES

- *16½–20½" (42–52 cm)*
- *Blackish brown with long narrow wings*
- *White flash on underwing*
- *High arcs during stormy conditions*
- ▲ *Manx Shearwater is smaller and boldly black and white*
- *In burrows in ground*
- ♪ *Silent at sea*

Male and female

Northern Gannet

Morus bassanus

J F M A M J J A S O N D

A group of Northern Gannets in a variety of plumages, wheeling around and diving—more like stones than birds—from heights of up to 100 feet (30 m) into the sea to catch fish, is an unforgettable sight.

Northern Gannets are among the largest seabirds and can be seen at long range from the coast. They breed on rocky islands in large colonies, numbering from a few hundred to tens of thousands.

The adults are white with a yellowish head and large, black wing tips. The juveniles are brown, with many small white spots. In the course of five years, the birds gain adult plumage, slowly getting whiter as the moult progresses. Large feeding flocks often comprise birds in all plumage stages, from almost entirely juvenile to fully adult.

Their flight is powerful and straight, but in strong headwinds the birds shear in high arcs, as do many other seabirds.

FIELD NOTES

- *34¼–39½" (87–100 cm)*
- *Adult: white with black wing tips*
- *Juvenile: brown with tiny white spots*
- *Many intermediate plumages*
- *Plunge-dive from great heights*
- *Large cup of seaweed, feathers and plastic debris*
- ♪ *Guttural sounds at colony*

Adults (Continental race)

Cormorant

Phalacrocorax carbo

J F M A M J J A S O N D

Cormorants are related to pelicans and gannets and, like them, have webs between four toes (only three toes are webbed in ducks). They can often be seen sitting on a pole or rock, wings outstretched, slowly moving them about to dry.

In Europe, two races occur, the British race (*P. c. carbo*) breeding along rocky shores, and the Continental race (*P. c. sinensis*) breeding in trees. Adults are black with a blue or green sheen, with some white feathers on the head and a white thigh patch—which is flashed at the partner from the nest during courtship. Juveniles are brown, often with white on the underparts. Adult plumage is acquired in the third calendar year. In summer, the Continental race has more white on the head on average.

The Shag (*P. aristotelis*; 27½–31½" [70–80 cm]), commonly found along Atlantic coasts of Europe, is black with an oily green sheen and lacks any white; during the breeding season, it has a short, up-curled crest. It also has a more slender bill and less bare skin at the base of the bill. Juveniles are brown.

FIELD NOTES

- 35½" (90 cm)
- Adult: black, with white on thigh and head in summer
- Juvenile: brown with white underparts
- Often seen with wings outstretched
- ▲ Shag is smaller and lacks white
- On rocks: large cup of seaweed; in trees: strong nest of sticks
- ♪ Guttural sounds at colony

Brent Goose

Branta bernicla

J F M A M J J A S O N D

Always found in flocks, usually in saltmarshes and other coastal fields, Brent Geese feed on grasses and marine algae. As with other geese, family groups stay together during winter. Juveniles are recognisable by two narrow wingbars and a small white spot on the neck. In some years (approximately one out of four), however, there are hardly any young accompanying the adults, as a result of predation of eggs or chicks by Arctic Foxes.

In Western Europe, two subspecies of the Brent Goose occur: the pale-bellied Brent (*B. b. hrota*) from Greenland and Spitzbergen, which winters mainly in Britain, Ireland and the US, and the dark-bellied Brent (*B. b. bernicla*) from Siberia, which winters mainly on coasts of the southern North Sea. The Black Brent (*B. b. nigricans*; 22–24¾" [56–63 cm]), breeding in northwestern Canada, Alaska and northeastern Russia, is extremely rare in Europe in winter.

Brent Geese nest on the high arctic tundra, and since they are one of the most northerly of breeding birds, they leave for their breeding grounds the latest of all geese in spring.

FIELD NOTES

- 22–24¾" (56–63 cm)
- *Dark grey; white patch on black neck; wide rear end*
- *Juveniles like adults, but with narrow, white wingbars*
- *Cup of herbs on tundra, lined with feathers*
- ♪ *A soft "rot rot"*

Adult male

Shelduck

Tadorna tadorna

Shelducks are among the easiest of coastal birds to identify. They are the size of a goose and look white and black from a distance, but appear surprisingly colourful close up. Males are larger than females and can be easily recognised by the large red knob on the forehead. The downy young are beautifully black and white. Several broods may gather together to form large "creches". The juveniles are greyish above and white below, and smaller than adults. After the moult in summer, sub-adults can be identified by the white trailing-edge on the wing.

Shelducks breed in holes, preferably rabbit burrows. If these are not available, other sheltered places are chosen, such as old barns, hollow trees, haystacks and piles of driftwood. Shelducks feed mainly on small molluscs, crustaceans and insects, but they also eat some vegetable matter.

In July and August, Shelducks from a large area of Europe migrate to a selected number of sites—such as Germany's Wadden Sea—to moult their feathers. After the wing feathers are fully regrown, the birds disperse again back to their original haunts.

FIELD NOTES

■ *Male 23½–27½" (60–70 cm); female 19½–23½" (50–60 cm)*

■ *Adult: black and white with brown breast band*

■ *Males: large red knob on bill*

■ *Juveniles: grey and white*

In sheltered places lined with much white down

♪ *Male: a high whistling trill; female: a gaggling "gagagaga"*

Common Eider

Somateria mollissima

J F M A M J J A S O N D

A line of large brown and black-and-white ducks flying low over the sea, or swimming and diving behind surf off a beach or headland, can only be a party of Common Eider.

The shape of the head, with the long sloping forehead, is characteristic of this species. Females are densely barred brown with pale underwings, without any obvious field marks, but males are mostly unmistakable. From late summer until early winter, however, they become more difficult to recognise as they moult their contrasting plumage into a duller, mainly dark-brown and black plumage. Young males are blackish brown, but the first white feathers start to appear from October onwards.

Their preferred food consists of shellfish, such as cockles and mussels, and seastars. After the brown chicks have hatched, the females accompany them to the sea where—as with the Shelduck (p. 238)—large creches of several broods can form. Unlike Shelducks, however, female Common Eiders can defend their chicks very well against fierce attacks by large gulls.

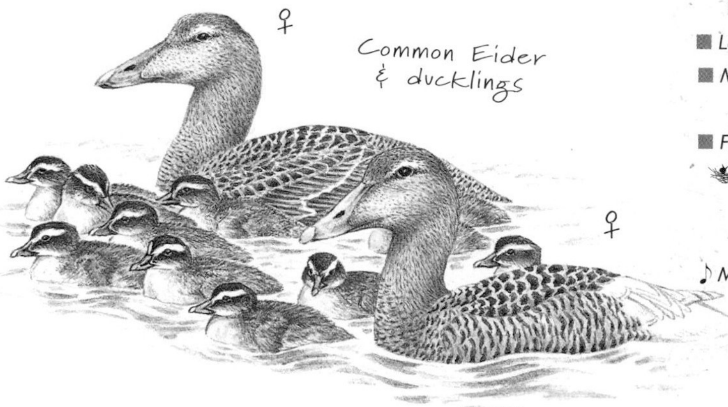

FIELD NOTES

- *21½–27½" (55–70 cm)*
- *Large; often fairly low over water*
- *Male: black and white with pink breast, sloping forehead*
- *Female: brown, sloping forehead*

Nest: Under bushes or in crevices lined with greyish-brown, pale speckled down

♪ Male during courtship: moaning "koo-roo-ooh"; female: low "kok-kok-kok"

Common Scoter

Melanitta nigra

Large flocks of ducks, flying fast and low over the sea in long lines or irregular, dense groups, far away from the coast, are almost invariably Common Scoters. Outside the breeding season, they occur in flocks of up to several thousand birds. Only on close view can the male's yellow-and-black bill with its large knob, or the pale cheeks of the female be seen.

J F M A M J J A S O N D

The superficially similar, slightly larger and always less numerous Velvet Scoters (*M. fusca*; 21¼–23½" [54–60 cm]) often accompany Common Scoters. Males have a different bill and a small white spot below the eye; females have two white spots on the side of the head. In flight, Velvet Scoters are immediately identifiable in mixed flocks by their white speculum.

Both species breed on the ground, along the coast or near freshwater lakes on the tundra or in wooded areas. In marine areas, their food consists mainly of molluscs, but in freshwater habitats, they also eat insects.

FIELD NOTES

■ *Male 17–22" (43–56 cm)*

■ *Male: entirely black; yellow-and-black bill; large knob on forehead*

■ *Female: brown with grey-white cheeks*

▲ *Velvet Scoter has white speculum*

On ground close to water, often in a sheltered place, lined with brown down

♪ *Male has a melodious whistling and giggling; female a sharp moaning*

Oystercatcher

Haematopus ostralegus

J F M A M J J A S O N D

Oystercatchers are easy to identify: they are usually extremely noisy and not very shy. Although part of the large order of waders, they differ in several respects from other waders. Parent birds, for example, bring food to their chicks, and after fledging, the young remain dependent on their parents for food for some time.

Individual Oystercatchers specialise in catching a specific kind of food: some feed mainly on worms, while others catch crabs, and again others mussels or cockles. By looking closely at the shape of its bill tip, it is possible to deduce what a bird's feeding preferences are.

In saltmarshes, Oystercatchers sometimes breed close together. Here they compete for the best partner and for the best breeding site, which will be close to the mudflats where they feed. When a high breeding density is reached, many birds may not be able to find a suitable place to breed and have to fight their way in, which can take many years.

FIELD NOTES

- *15¾–18" (40–46 cm)*
- *Black and white, with long orange bill and pink legs*
- *White rump and white wingbar*
- *Shallow cup on the ground in saltmarshes or meadows with or without vegetable matter, small stones and shells*
- ♪ *A loud "tepeet tepeet", "kleep" or higher-pitched trill*

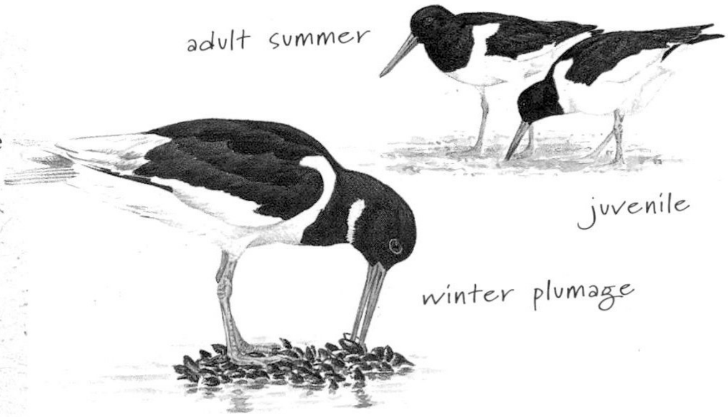

Avocet

Recurvirostra avosetta

J F M A M J J A S O N D

Because of their black-and-white plumage, distinctive call and especially their peculiar upturned bill, Avocets are easy to recognise. They can be found in places with soft mud, where they feed by making horizontal sweeps through the upper surface of the mud while walking slowly along. If they feel a small crustacean or worm, they immediately close their bill and swallow the prey. Because of their sensitive and flexible bill, they cannot probe in firm ground as, for instance, Oystercatchers (p. 241) do, and they are, therefore, rarely seen in sandy or rocky places.

Avocets usually breed in colonies. If an intruder (for instance, a Marsh Harrier) approaches the colony, it is so fiercely attacked by the parent Avocets—although they are incapable of actually wounding it—that the predator quickly backs off. The bills of the downy young are short, but even at such an early age already slightly upturned.

Most Avocets leave Northwestern Europe in winter, but small numbers stay, especially during mild winters.

FIELD NOTES

■ *16½–18½" (42–47 cm)*

■ *Black and white, with slender upturned bill*

Shallow cup on the ground in saltmarshes or meadows, with little vegetable matter

♪ *A clear ringing "kleep kleep"*

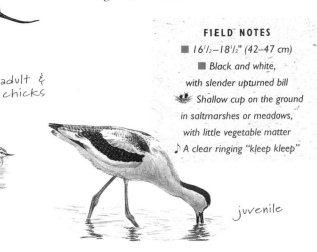

Adult (summer plumage)

Ringed Plover

Charadrius hiaticula

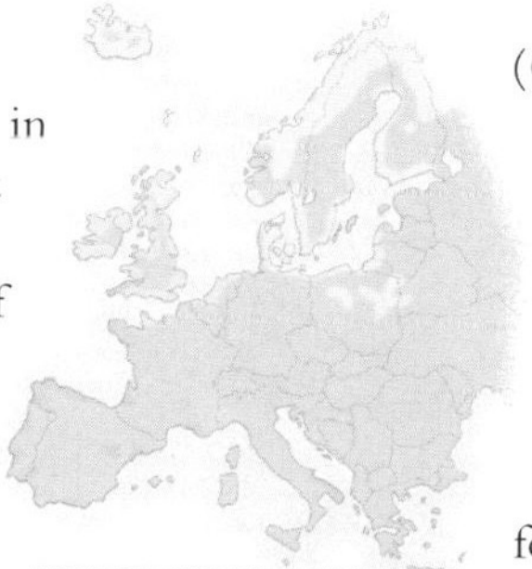

J F M A M J J A S O N D

Of the "difficult" small, brown waders, adult Ringed Plovers in summer are one of the easiest to identify. First, they differ from stints by having the typical plover method of feeding: they stand still, but suddenly run forward a few steps and peck. Second, they have bright orange legs and an orange bill with a black tip, which also distinguishes them from the superficially similar Kentish Plover (*C. alexandrinus*; 6" [15 cm]) and Little Ringed Plover (*C. dubius*; 6¼" [16 cm]).

The timid Little Ringed Plover prefers fresh water and is rarely seen in saline habitats. It is usually found alone or in pairs. Little Ringed Plovers have a yellow eye-ring and a hunched, horizontal stance. They lack a white wingbar, which makes identification in flight straightforward.

The Kentish Plover always lacks a complete breast band and males have a beautiful rusty cap. Juveniles are more difficult to identify, but even very young Ringed Plovers have yellowish-orange legs and base of bill, unlike the black, bare part in Kentish Plovers.

FIELD NOTES

■ *7–8" (18–20 cm)*

■ *Broad, black breast band and black mask*

■ *Orange legs and bill with black tip*

■ *White wingbar in flight*

▲ *Little Ringed Plover is smaller, lacks orange legs and bill; call a soft "peeuw"*

▲ *Kentish Plover lacks full breastband; call "prrrr" and shrill "pweet"*

Shallow cup on bare ground without lining or with some small stones and vegetable matter

♪ *A soft but far-carrying "poo-eep"*

Grey Plover

Pluvialis squatarola

J F M A M J J A S O N D

Grey Plovers breed on the high arctic tundra but can be seen in Northwest Europe most of the year. In the spring months at least, males in full summer plumage have entirely black underparts, except for the white vent and line on the side of the neck, and black upperparts boldly spangled with white. In winter plumage, Grey Plovers are truly grey, with few obvious field marks. They can then be identified by their fairly large size, short bill and typical plover-like way of feeding (see Ringed Plover, p. 243). In flight, they always show black axillaries (armpits), a feature not shared by other waders and visible over long distances. Juveniles are spangled golden on the upperparts and often misidentified as Golden Plovers (p. 173), which are, in fact, slightly smaller, less often found in coastal habitats and always lack the black axillaries.

Outside the breeding season, Grey Plovers occur almost exclusively along the coast, where they mainly feed on worms, but also on snails and crustaceans.

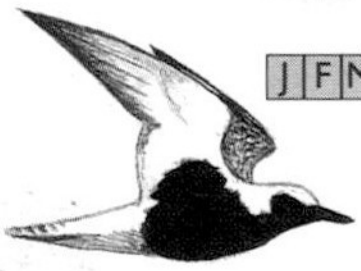

FIELD NOTES

- *11–12½" (28–32 cm)*
- *Summer: uniformly black underparts, black-and-white upperparts*
- *Winter: grey with narrow, white wingbar and greyish-white rump*
- *Juveniles: pale golden spots on upperparts*
- *Nest: Only in high arctic; shallow cup on bare ground lined with lichens and mosses*
- *♪ A plaintive "tlee-uu-ee"*

Adult (winter plumage)

Sanderling

Calidris alba

Sanderlings breed in high arctic areas and belong to the most northerly group of breeding waders. Outside the breeding season, they can be found on sandy beaches all over the world. They follow the edge of the tide with enormous energy, running restlessly back and forth and swallowing small worms and crustaceans.

In summer plumage, the reddest individuals resemble the much smaller Little Stint (*C. minuta;* (5½" [14 cm]) somewhat in coloration. In winter plumage, Sanderlings are the whitest sandpipers, with a broad white wingbar. Juveniles in early autumn are similar to adults, but the upperparts are brightly spotted black and buffish-white. Sanderlings are the only sandpipers with three toes.

Knots (*C. canutus*; 9½–24½" [24–62 cm]) are superficially similar to Sanderlings but much larger. They are grey in winter with a narrow wingbar, pale grey rump and greenish legs. They are occasionally found feeding on sandy beaches but prefer mudflats, where they gather in tight feeding flocks. In summer, they are bright rufous on the underparts.

FIELD NOTES

- *7½–8¼" (19–21 cm)*
- *In winter plumage very white*
- *Black legs and bill*
- *Constantly running and feeding on sandy beaches*

▲ *Knot is larger, darker grey with green legs; in summer bright rufous below*

Only in high arctic usually along the coast; shallow cup on bare ground lined with leaves and grasses

♪ *A soft "twik"*

Purple Sandpiper

Calidris maritima

Outside the breeding season Purple Sandpipers are found only on rocky coasts, breakwaters and piers. They are almost never seen on sandy beaches or mudflats and are commonly found with Turnstones (p. 248).

They are easy to identify: apart from the habitat—which is often a good clue—Purple Sandpipers are one of the most compact waders. They are a little bigger than Dunlins (p. 247), with very dark purplish-grey feathers, a medium-long, slightly curved bill with orange base, and orange legs. In flight, a narrow white wingbar is visible, but overall the impression is darker than that of any other small wader. Purple Sandpipers are among the most confident shorebirds, and are often quite approachable.

They search for small worms on rocks and for crustaceans among seaweed. If a wave sweeps over the rock they're feeding on, they often stay put, letting the water lift them up and put them down again, after which they continue as if nothing had happened.

FIELD NOTES

- *$8^1/_4$–9" (21–23 cm)*
- *Very dark purple-grey winter plumage*
- *Rusty upperparts in summer, but still very dark*
- *Outside breeding season, feeds only along rocky coasts*
- *Rather deep cup on open tundra, lined with dead leaves*
- *♪ A low, soft but sharp "wit wit"*

Adult (summer plumage)

Dunlin

Calidris alpina

J F M A M J J A S O N D

Marine wetlands and estuaries in Europe are seldom without Dunlins. These small waders congregate in huge flocks at roosting sites during high tide. At low tide, Dunlins search the mud for small worms and mud snails, making fast "stitching" movements with their bills.

The Dunlin can be confused with the slightly larger Curlew Sandpiper (*C. ferruginea;* 7–9" [18–23 cm]). This closely related species is distinctive in its summer plumage, being brownish red from top to bottom, but is very similar to Dunlins in winter and in juvenile plumage. It is rare in spring but can be observed in small numbers in marine and inland wetlands during autumn migration between July and September.

Dunlins are typical breeding birds of the arctic tundra from Norway to eastern Siberia, but small numbers also breed on the high moorlands of Britain. While Curlew Sandpipers spend the winter in Africa, many Dunlins risk an occasional harsh winter and stay in Europe. Bleak days in winter can be brightened by the spectacular sight of Dunlin flocks of hundreds or thousands flashing grey and white in their synchronous aerial movements.

FIELD NOTES

- *6¼–8¼" (16–21 cm)*
- *Long, black bill*
- *Summer: black belly, reddish-brown upperparts*
- *Winter: white belly, grey upperparts*
- *Small depression in wet tundra*
- *A high-pitched "trriep"*

Adult male (summer plumage)

Turnstone

Arenaria interpres

A small, pied wader purposefully walking around, turning over pieces of seaweed, small rocks or pieces of wood with its short, pointed, slightly upturned bill, and squabbling with its congeners, can only be a Turnstone.

Turnstones are most common on intertidal mudflats and rocky shores, usually alone or in small flocks, often in company with Purple Sandpipers (p. 246). Although the two species apparently choose to flock together, they are constantly quarrelling. Turnstones' preferred food consists of small worms and crustaceans, which they find under the small items they turn over, but they will also feed on dead fish or other carrion.

J F M A M J J A S O N D

In summer plumage, males are most beautifully coloured, with a white head and bright orange and black upperparts. Females look like males but their colours are somewhat duller. Juveniles and adults in winter have scaly, brown upperparts, but can still be recognised by the black bands on the head and neck and their short, orange legs.

FIELD NOTES

- *8½–9½" (22–24 cm)*
- *Pied plumage, with short orange legs*
- *Shallow cup on stony ground, often close to coastline, with or without lining*
- *A metallic toneless trill or "kuttuk"*

Adults

Herring Gull

Larus argentatus

J F M A M J J A S O N D

Together with Black-headed Gulls (p. 105), Herring Gulls are the most abundant gulls in Europe and can commonly be seen in coastal areas. They belong to the group known as large gulls, also called "four-year gulls" because the moult from brown juvenile plumage to grey-and-white adult plumage takes four years.

Herring Gulls have black wing tips with two round white "mirrors". They have a stout, yellow bill with a red spot, and pale yellow eyes, which give them a fierce look. An important identification marker is the pink leg colour, which separates them from Lesser Black-backed Gulls (p. 250); the similar but slightly darker Yellow-legged Gulls (*L. cachinnans*; 21½–27½" [55–70 cm]) of the Mediterranean and Atlantic coasts of Spain and France, and the smaller Common Gull (*L. canus*; 16½" [42 cm]). The latter—a "three-year gull"—has slightly darker upperparts, green legs and bill, and dark eyes, which give it a "friendly" look.

FIELD NOTES

- *21½–27½" (55–70 cm)*
- *Pink legs, yellow eyes*
- ▲ *Yellow-legged Gull has darker upperparts, yellow legs and red orbital ring*
- ▲ *Common Gull is smaller and has dark eyes, green legs and bill*
- *Deep cup on ground in dunes or on grassy plateaus along coast, built up with vegetable matter*
- ♪ *Calls "kleeeuw", "ak ak ak", "aauw"*

Adult (summer plumage)

Great Black-backed Gull

Larus marinus

J F M A M J J A S O N D

Adult Great Black-backed Gulls are the largest gulls in Northwestern Europe—together with the scarce arctic Glaucous Gull (*L. hyperboreus;* 25½–31½" [65–80 cm]). With their broad wings and relaxed wing beats, their flight is almost as heavy as that of the Grey Heron (p. 200).

Adults are deep black above, with white distal tips to the wings. The similarly patterned but paler Lesser Black-backed Gull (*L. fuscus;* 19½–25½" [50–65 cm]) is of Herring Gull size and has, like that species, white "mirrors" in its black wing tips. The flight is more elegant than that of Herring Gulls. The leg colour provides an easy field marker for standing birds: pink in Great Black-backed, bright yellow in Lesser Black-backed. Juveniles, which have flesh-coloured legs, are superficially similar, but can be distinguished by size, the much heavier bill and the whiter appearance of the Great Black-backed. The juvenile Lesser Black-backed is darker brown than the juvenile Herring Gull.

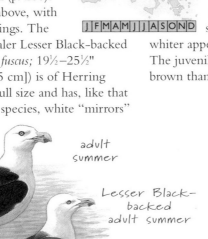

FIELD NOTES

- *25½–31½" (65–80 cm)*
- *Very large, deep-black back, wing tips white*
- *Pink legs*
- ▲ *Lesser Black-backed Gull is greyer, smaller, and has yellow legs and narrower wings with white "mirrors"*
- *Large cup on the ground, usually on rocks, made of vegetable matter and branches*
- ♪ *A deep "ooow"*

Kittiwake

Rissa tridactyla

Kittiwakes are the most pelagic of the Northwestern European gulls; they come ashore only to breed, spending the remainder of the year at sea, often far away from land. They are often said to resemble Common Gulls, being the same size, but they are, in fact, very different. The upperparts are paler grey, the wing tips are black without white "mirrors", the black tips have a different shape, and the rear wing is translucent. The flight is also different, with shallower, stiffer wing beats. In rough weather, they fly in fast, bouncing arcs. The juvenile is similar to, but larger than, the juvenile Little Gull (*Larus minutus;* 10½–11¾" [27–30 cm]), with a black W pattern on the upperwing, a black collar and a black band on the tail.

Kittiwakes breed on ledges of steep cliffs, usually in company with Guillemots (p. 255) and Razorbills (p. 256). The young don't fall off the ledges because, unlike other gull chicks, they instinctively face away from steep drops.

FIELD NOTES

- $15\frac{3}{4}$–$17\frac{1}{4}$" (40–44 cm)
- *Pale grey with short black legs and uniformly black wing tips*
- *Stiffer flight than Common Gull*
- *Firm nest of mud and seaweed on steep cliff*
- ♪ *A nasal "kitti-wake"*

Adult (summer plumage)

Caspian Tern

Sterna caspia

The largest tern in the world, the Caspian Tern, breeds on all continents except South America and Antarctica. Although a typical tern, with its black cap, short legs and forked tail, it is about the size of a Herring Gull and very unlike the more slenderly built Common or Arctic Tern (p. 254). It is usually seen either resting on a sandbank together with other terns and gulls—often among Black-headed Gulls (p. 105)—or flying several feet above the water. It gives a raw call while looking down in search of fish.

Birds from the Baltic breeding population migrate south over land or along the coast to their wintering areas in West Africa or the Mediterranean. Juveniles follow their parents on this journey, and even in their winter haunts, the young can be seen—and heard—begging for food.

The large size, huge red bill and black underside of the primaries distinguish this bird from all other tern species.

FIELD NOTES

- ■ $19^1/_2$–$23^1/_2$" (50–60 cm)
- ■ Size of Herring Gull
- ■ Large red bill, black underside of primaries
- Shallow scrape on ground along sandy or rocky coasts, with or without a little vegetable matter
- ♪ Adult has a raucous "aaaah", juvenile a high whistling "whi whi"

Adult (summer plumage)

Sandwich Tern

Sterna sandvicensis

Sandwich Terns often first reveal their presence by their characteristic call, and even when they have been heard several times they can still be difficult to see because of their slender appearance and white plumage.

Sandwich Terns can be distinguished from Common Terns by their larger size, whiter plumage, relatively short tail, black crest and long, black, yellow-tipped bill. In late summer and autumn, many birds have a less conspicuous yellow tip to the bill; young birds have a shorter, entirely black bill.

Sandwich Terns winter off West Africa, and return to Northwest European waters from the end of March onward. They breed in large colonies on islands, where ground predators, such as foxes and Brown Rats, cannot reach them. The chicks are fed mainly with sandeels, which are caught by means of spectacular dives into the sea. Even after the young are fledged, they stay with the parents and keep on begging for food, in the same manner as young Caspian Terns (p. 252).

male & female displaying

FIELD NOTES

- 15¼–17¼" (40–45 cm)
- Pale grey and white, black cap with short crest
- Slender black bill with yellow tip
- Shallow scrape on ground with or without vegetable matter
- ♪ A rasping "kirrick"

Adult and juvenile

Common Tern

Sterna hirundo

J F M A M J J A S O N D

In Western Europe, the Common Tern occurs most commonly from central Britain and the Low Countries southward, while its "twin species", the Arctic Tern (*S. paradisaea*; 15–17¾" [38–45 cm]), is more common in Northern areas. Both can be seen along the coast, but the Common Tern is also often seen inland, even in built-up areas, if there are suitable water bodies.

The two species are extremely similar. In the Common Tern, the bill is orange with a black tip. The Arctic Tern has a slightly shorter, coral-red bill, slightly shorter legs, longer outer tail feathers and slightly longer wings, giving a different flight silhouette. The black line along the underside of the primary tips is narrower and longer than in the Common Tern. In Arctic Tern, all flight feathers are translucent when viewed from below, while in Common Tern only the inner primaries are translucent. Common Tern may show a dark grey wedge shape, formed by the outer primaries, on the upperwing.

FIELD NOTES

■ *15–17¼" (38–45 cm)*

■ *Orange bill with black tip*

■ *Grey wedge on upperwing, broad, short, black line on underwing*

▲ *Arctic Tern has shorter, red bill, longer, narrower black line on underwing, translucent flight feathers*

Shallow scrape on ground with little or no lining; the two species often breed together along the coast

♪ *A high "krieeerrr" or short "kik"*

Adult (summer plumage)

Guillemot

Uria aalge

J F M A M J J A S O N D

Like all auks, Guillemots are plump seabirds with relatively short, narrow wings. Their flight is, therefore, very fast with whirring wing beats, but usually low. They breed on steep cliffs along the coast, often together with Razorbills (p. 256), Kittiwakes (p. 251) and Fulmars (p. 233). Outside the breeding season they stay at sea, far away from the coast. In summer plumage, the head is dark grey-brown, like the upperparts, but in winter, it is white with a dark cap and dark grey line behind the eye.

The similar but much smaller Black Guillemot (*Cepphus grylle;* 12½–15" [32–38 cm]) is also found along rocky coasts. This species doesn't breed on ledges but among boulders and in crevices. In summer, the whole plumage is deep black, except for white upperwing patches. In autumn, the black plumage moults into grey and white, but the species can still be recognised by its bright white upperwing patches. Black Guillemots always stay closer to the coast than Guillemots.

Guillemot winter

Black Guillemot juvenile/ first-winter

Guillemot summer

Black Guillemot summer

FIELD NOTES

- ■ *15¾–18" (40–46 cm)*
- ■ *Brown and white, pointed bill*
- ■ *In winter, sides of head whiter with black line behind eye*
- ▲ *Black Guillemot is much smaller, in winter much whiter but still with white upperwing patches*
- *On steep cliffs without lining*
- ♪ *In colonies, a low raucous "arrr"*

Adult (summer plumage)

Puffin

Fratercula arctica

J F M A M J J A S O N D

Puffins are the most colourful auks in the North Atlantic. They are plain black and white, but in summer, they have a deep orange, blue and yellow bill. Unlike other auks, they breed in burrows they dig for themselves on vegetated parts of rocky islands and on top of cliffs.

The single chick is fed until it is heavier than its parents. At the end of the breeding season, it is left to fend for itself. The chick leaves the nest only at night, when it cannot be preyed upon by Great Black-backed Gulls.

Another auk breeding on cliffs, often among Guillemots, is the Razorbill (*Alca torda*; 15¾–17¾" [40–45 cm]). Razorbills also have peculiar bills, which, together with their black, not brown, plumage and long pointed tails, differentiate them from the otherwise similar Guillemots. As with the Guillemot, both parents help raise the offspring, but only one accompanies the single chick to sea when it is half-grown.

Razorbill juvenile

Razorbill summer

Puffin summer

Razorbill winter

Puffin winter

FIELD NOTES

■ *11¾–15¾" (30–40 cm)*

■ *Black and white, in summer deeply colourful bill, orange legs*

▲ *Razorbill much bigger, very similar to Guillemot, but black and white with different bill*

In burrows

♪ *At sea and near colonies, grumbling "orr" or "oww"*

Mountains

OVERHEAD Vultures, eagles and Ravens spend much of the day soaring, especially where high hills and sheer cliffs provide strong thermals.
STUNTED PINES at the treeline offer the right habitat for Coal Tits and Citril Finches, while birds like Black Woodpeckers nd Common Crossbills are mmon in mature beech and forests at lower levels.
ALPINE MEADOWS offer food for ground-feeding birds, such as Water Pipits, Mistle Thru and Choughs.
CLIFFS and BOULDERS are good places to look for birds such as Alpine Accentors, Black Redstarts, Rock Thrushes and the elusive Wallcreeper.

MOUNTAINS

Pine and Beech Forests, Alpine Meadows, Crags and Plateaus

Most of us probably think of mountains as areas where a large proportion of the land is above the level where trees can survive. Since the average annual temperature gets lower toward the north, it is obvious that the treeline is at a much higher altitude in southern France than, for instance, in Scotland. This explains why some so-called mountain birds actually breed at low elevations near the Arctic Circle in Scandinavia.

In this chapter, we confine ourselves to the highest mountains, where large areas are above an altitude of 1300 to 1850 feet (1500-2000 m). In Western Europe, such high mountain ranges can be found in central Norway, northern Slovakia, Austria, Switzerland, Italy, France and Spain. Most of these are situated in a west-to-east chain. As a consequence, massive and extensive chains of mountain ranges, such as the Alps and the Pyrenees, form a formidable barrier for birds on migration.

Depending on the prevailing winds, some high mountain slopes are wet while others are arid. For instance, the northern, French sides of the Pyrenees are usually much greener than the southern, Spanish sides. Both in the Alps and in the Pyrenees, the first snowfall above the treeline may be as early as September, and snow cover may last into June or, around high peaks, be permanent.

Clearly, vegetation varies greatly according to the altitude and provides, in turn, a wide range of bird habitats. The highest forests consist mainly of beeches and pines. Near the treeline, above stunted pines, flowering alpine meadows emerge as soon as the snow has melted. Around rocky streams and upland valleys, you often find large tracts of rocks and huge boulders underneath high, precipitous cliffs.

...NTAIN STREAMS are ...me breeding habitats for ...rey Wagtails and Dippers, and attract different kinds ...of autumn migrants.

BIRDWATCHING *in* MOUNTAINS

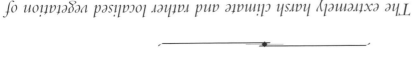

The extremely harsh climate and rather localised vegetation of high mountains support a specialised and distinctive community of bird species, many of which seldom occur in any other type of habitat.

Woodland and wetland birds move around enough for you to have some hope of seeing many of them, at least as vagrants or casual visitors, in your local marsh or park. But to see certain bird species you have to go to the high mountains. Most birdwatchers who don't live in Central Europe will, therefore, sooner or later want to travel to the Alps or the Pyrenees to see this particular avifauna for themselves.

High mountains can be impenetrable during winter when snow and ice prevail, pushing most birds down into low valleys. During summer, birds and birdwatchers follow the snowline, to ever-higher altitudes. Being out and about early is important in spring and early summer. By mid-morning, birds that have been active early on seem to melt into their surroundings and can be difficult to locate. As in woodlands and grasslands, finding birds by song is therefore important. Because vegetation above the treeline is sparse, territories can be large and many birds, including Wallcreepers, have songs that carry long distances.

Around chalets and mountain huts, characteristic high-mountain species, such as Alpine Accentors, Snow Finches and Citril Finches, can be quite approachable, especially when crumbs of bread are provided.

THE PYRENEES *offer visiting birdwatchers a combination of spectacular scenery (below) and sightings of birds of prey, such as the Golden Eagle (below right)—a truly memorable experience.*

WHERE TO LOOK

Keep scanning the skies—a Lammergeier, Griffon Vulture, Golden Eagle or Raven soaring high in the sky may be looking for lunch. During migration periods, especially in the Pyrenees in September, you may see large numbers of migrant raptors, such as Honey Buzzards, Short-toed Eagles or kites, spiralling high using thermals at foothills and continuing, often in a broad front, across the peaks.

When passing a bridge, look to see whether boulders in or alongside the stream have white droppings on top. If so, watch carefully for the highly specialised Dipper, which may sit motionless for long periods showing its dazzling white bib. At the same stream you may find the long-tailed Grey Wagtail, while other passerines are often also attracted by the water.

MOUNTAIN GEAR

Temperatures in high mountains may vary greatly. When the sun is shining, it can become hot. However, low clouds may cross the sky quite quickly, causing a sharp temperature drop. So whatever season, always take some warm clothing, and protection from rain. Good walking shoes with firm soles are essential. In mid-summer, a wide-brimmed hat or cap not only protects you from the strong high-elevation sunlight, but

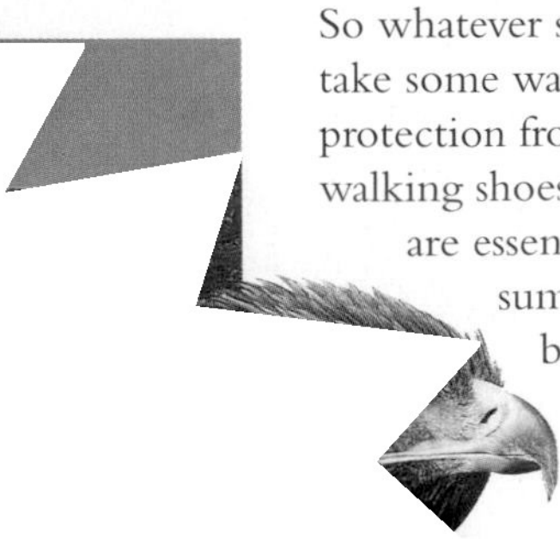

also makes spotting birds in harsh glare just that little bit easier. Some food, soft drinks and a thermos flask slung into a small rucksack are by no means a bad idea, either.

Mountain birds have a way of leading you on, and you may well find yourself much farther away and on more precarious slopes than you originally intended to be.

If you happen to live in, or do most of your birdwatching in, a high mountain area, this may influence your choice of binoculars (p. 62). In the deep shade of woodland or forest, wide angles and big, bright images are important, both for locating the bird in the field of view and enjoying the image when you have it. But wide angles and large images come at the cost of sizcable chunks of glass inside the binoculars, and glass is very heavy. This might be cumbersome when you have to walk long distances on steep mountain trails. You may find that binoculars with a narrower field of view and less magnification will deliver the kind of image you are comfortable with, and they will be easier to carry.

HIGH SPOTS *When birdwatching in high mountains (above), make sure you wear sturdy shoes, and have extra clothing to be prepared for sudden weather changes. When the trail is not too difficult, a 'scope can be very useful.*

If you travel by car, however, it is highly recommended that you take a telescope to watch distant birds on sheer cliffs and other unreachable sites.

HIGH MOUNTAIN BIRDS *include two huge carrion feeders, the Lammergeier (far right) and Griffon Vulture (above). They search for the carcasses of chamois or sheep on high-altitude slopes.*

Griffon Vulture

Gyps fulvus

Griffon Vultures are the largest raptors in Europe. Although Lammergeiers (*Gypaetus barbatus;* 39¼–47¼" [100–120 cm]) have a slightly larger wing span, the wings of Griffons are broader, which make them look more massive.

Griffon Vultures are usually seen soaring in flocks, high over mountains or plains, looking for dead animals, such as goats or sheep. They have broad wings, very short tails and sandy-brown plumage. The Lammergeier is black with an orange belly, long wings and a long, broad, wedge-shaped tail. They are superb fliers and are often seen gliding alone or in pairs, from one side of a valley to the other, or searching along a mountain ridge. Their food consists mainly of bone marrow, which they reach by dropping large bones from considerable heights onto rocks until the bones split. Sometimes they will swallow whole bones.

J F M A M J J A S O N D

FIELD NOTES

■ 37½–43¼" (95–110 cm); wing span 98½" (250 cm)

■ Pale brown with very short tail

▲ Lammergeier is dark grey or black with orange belly; juvenile dark

Large nest made of branches, on a ridge

♪ Silent; in colony, moaning and croaking sounds

Adult

Golden Eagle

Aquila chrysaetos

Although a well-known bird, the Golden Eagle occurs in small numbers in high mountains. The English name was inspired by the golden-yellow neck patch worn by adults and juveniles. Juveniles differ from adults in having conspicuous white patches on upper- and underwings and a white tail base.

Adults are uniformly dark brown, but some, especially Northern European birds, are paler brown and grey. Golden Eagles differ from Griffon Vultures (p. 262) in that their plumage is dark brown and, especially, by having longer tails.

Golden Eagles are typically seen soaring very high above mountain peaks, alone or in pairs, with wings held in a shallow V. They are looking for prey, which consists mainly of medium-sized mammals, such as hares, or large birds, such as pheasants and partridges. Adults stay in their large territory year round, but juveniles may wander away and be seen in lower-lying areas during winter.

FIELD NOTES

- $27^{1}/_{2}$–$35^{1}/_{2}$" (70–90 cm)
- *Dark brown with yellowish patch on neck; long tail*
- *Juvenile with white tail base and white wing patches*
- *Large nest on cliff or in trees, made of branches*
- ♪ *A barking, fairly high "keeak keeak"*

Adult (winter plumage)

Water Pipit

Anthus spinoletta

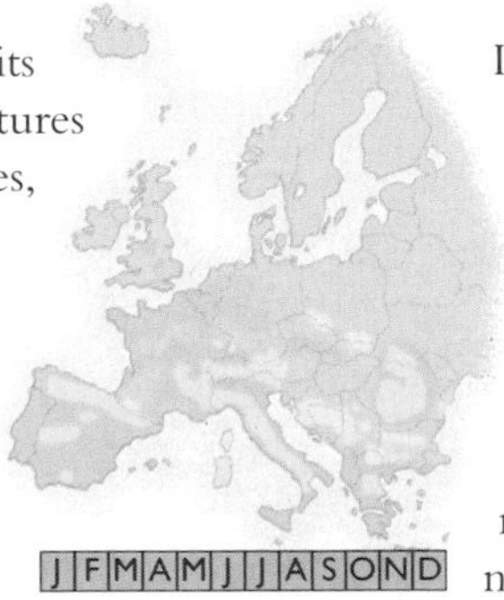

Water Pipits are the only pipits found as high as Alpine pastures in summer. At lower altitudes, they are replaced by Meadow Pipits (p. 182). Water Pipits differ from Meadow Pipits in having a greyish back with a few ill-defined dark marks, and in summer plumage, a deep-pink underside with only a few vague blackish streaks on the flanks. Their legs are black or deep brownish, like the legs of the Rock Pipit (p. 182).

In winter, Water Pipits lack the pink underparts and look much like Rock Pipits, but differ in having a brighter, whitish supercilium and white on the outer tail feathers (dark grey in Rock Pipit).

Unlike any other songbird in Europe, some of the Water Pipits migrate from Central Europe in a northwesterly direction in autumn, probably following large rivers, to winter in the Low Countries and southern England. In winter, they can be found along freshwater lakes and near rivers, while Rock Pipits are usually encountered along the coast.

FIELD NOTES

- 6¼" (16 cm)
- *Pink underparts, blackish legs*
- *In winter grey, with whitish supercilium; outer tail feathers also white*
- *Fairly large cup of grasses, moss and other plants lined with hairs, feathers and so on, on the ground*
- *Song rather similar to song of Meadow Pipit; call: a "dzeet", like the Rock Pipit.*

adult summer

Adult female (summer plumage)

Grey Wagtail

Motacilla cinerea

Grey Wagtails are found near water more often than the other wagtails occurring in Europe. In summer, they are usually seen along streams with pebbles and rocks. Males in summer plumage differ from females in having a black throat, although some females have blackish mottling. In winter, they frequent flowing water such as rivers or brooks, but also lakes and even ornamental waters in city parks.

J F M A M J J A S O N D

♀ summer

In winter plumage, adults and young birds look alike: the underparts are mainly white and only the undertail coverts are rich yellow. Throughout the year they differ from Yellow Wagtails (p. 183) in having grey, not green, upperparts and a much longer tail. Their flight is even more undulating than that of White Wagtails. The call sounds more like the White Wagtail (p. 111) and is very different from that of the Yellow Wagtail. Like other wagtails, Grey Wagtails have a habit of wagging their tail, and even their whole rear parts.

FIELD NOTES

- 7" (18 cm)
- Grey back, in summer underparts mainly yellow
- In winter underparts whitish, but undertail coverts still yellow
- Small or large cup of sticks, roots, grass and moss lined with hairs, feathers and so on, usually in crevices or between tree roots along streams
- ♪ Song is a warbling twitter of calls; call: a sharp "tittit" or "zit"

♂ summer

Adult

Dipper

Cinclus cinclus

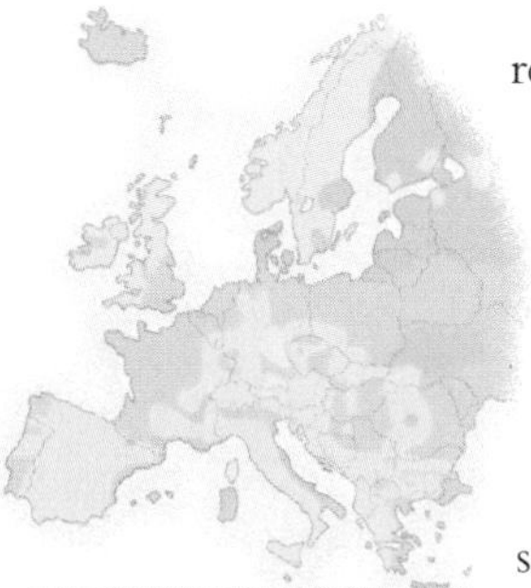

J F M A M J J A S O N D

One of the most peculiar songbirds is the Dipper. It is the only bird that will freely swim and dive in rapid rivers and brooks, and even walk under water on a stream bed.

Dippers are usually seen sitting on rocks in fast-flowing water, bobbing their bodies and blinking their white eyelids, but because of the moving background they can be surprisingly difficult to detect. Their flight is low above the water with whirring wing beats. In winter, the birds often remain along mountain streams and can be seen sitting on snow-covered rocks or diving into the ice-cold water.

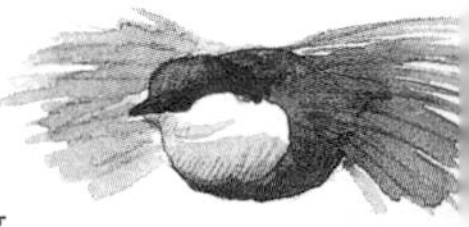

whirring wing beats

With its round appearance, short square tail, dark brown plumage, black or reddish-brown underparts and large white bib, it is impossible to confuse a Dipper with any other bird. The shape of the bird recalls the much smaller Wren (p. 137), to which it is distantly related.

FIELD NOTES

■ *7" (18 cm)*

■ *Brown; short tail, black or reddish-brown belly, white bib*

Large round "ball" of moss with entrance directed downwards; nest hidden in river banks or under bridges.

♪ *Song is a soft warbling chitter, interspersed with liquid tones; call: a metallic "trits" or "zit"*

■ First-winter

Alpine Accentor

Prunella collaris

The Alpine Accentor is the high-altitude counterpart of the smaller Dunnock (p. 138), of which it is a close relative. Like the Dunnock, it has a grey head and brown upperparts with black streaks. The pale tips to the tail feathers are obvious only when it flies away. Better field markers are the dark greater coverts, flanked by two white wingbars, the rufous streaks on the flanks, and the black-and-white spotted throat. It feeds on the ground with short jerky movements, like a Dunnock, in low vegetation or on bare gravel. The species is not shy but behaves inconspicuously and is often heard without being seen. Males, however, sing from elevated song posts, such as rocks or low bushes.

Like many birds of the high mountains, Alpine Accentors are found above the treeline in summer; they don't migrate southward in winter, but move to snow-free areas at lower altitudes, where they move around in small flocks.

J F M A M J J A S O N D

FIELD NOTES

■ *7" (18 cm)*

■ *Grey head, brown back with black streaks, rufous flank streaks*

■ *Dark wing panel, two white wingbars*

Deep round cup of stems and roots lined with moss, lichens and feathers, in crevices or between rocks

♪ *Song is a rather monotonous warble, reminiscent of that of Skylarks and Dunnocks; call: a Skylark-like "chirrip"*

Adult male (summer plumage)

Rock Thrush

Monticola saxatilis

The beautiful male Rock Thrush is orange below, slate-blue above and has a white rump. The female is less colourful, rather like a short-tailed juvenile Blackbird; the upperparts are brown with yellowish spots, the underparts are barred whitish and black, with orange on the lower belly and tail. The slightly larger Blue Rock Thrush (*M. solitarius*; 8¼" [21 cm]) is much darker. Although the male is dark slate-blue, it looks blackish from a distance. The female is much darker brown than the female Rock Thrush, without any orange, yellow or white, and looks even more like a short-tailed female Blackbird.

Both species are shy and often disappear from view when discovered. The Rock Thrush is usually found at higher altitudes than the Blue Rock Thrush, but both species can be seen in dry, rocky, low-lying habitat. The Blue Rock Thrush is also seen on steep, well-vegetated sea cliffs.

FIELD NOTES

■ *7½" (19 cm)*

■ *Male: blue with orange underparts and white rump*

■ *Female: brown, underparts barred whitish and black, orange (under)tail*

▲ *Blue Rock Thrush: male uniformly dark blue; female dark brown with barred brown underparts*

Sloppy cup of vegetable matter lined with roots and small herbs; nest in shallow crevice, under rocks or in walls

♪ *Song soft, with thrush-like repetitive whistling; call: "chak"*

■ Adult male (summer plumage)

Wallcreeper

Tichodroma muraria

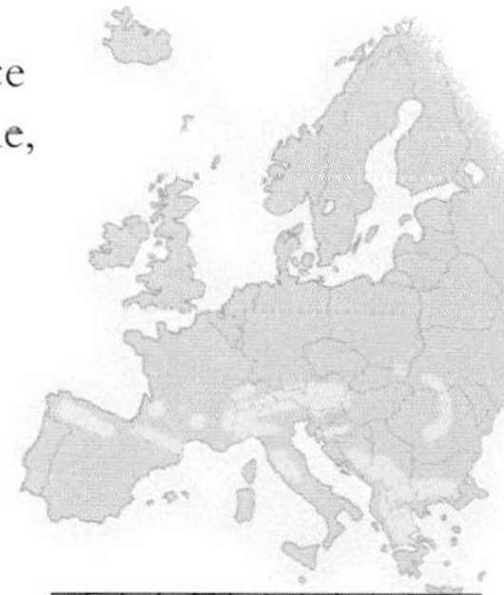

J F M A M J J A S O N D

A Wallcreeper is unmistakable once it has been located. To find one, however, is a challenge: Wallcreepers are not shy but behave inconspicuously. They are normally either seen flying overhead—looking like a large butterfly or a small Hoopoe—or creeping sideways up rocks. When searching for food, which consists of insects and spiders, they constantly flick their wings, showing carmine red, with large white spots on the primaries.

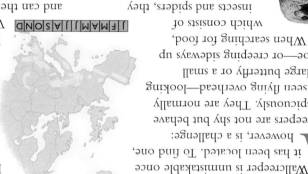

In summer plumage, the underparts are dark grey and black, usually more extensive in the male than the female, but in winter, the underparts are pale grey.

A pair will occupy a large territory, which in summer will be above the treeline. In winter, Wallcreepers move to lower regions and can then sometimes be encountered on rocky walls in mountain villages or on ruins.

adult ♂ summer

FIELD NOTES

■ *6¼" (16 cm)*

■ *Grey; broad, rounded wings with red; large white spots on primaries; short tail*

■ *Climbs up steep rocks, flicking wings*

Cup of vegetable matter and hair, lined with hair and feathers; nest in crevice, under rocks or in caves

♪ *Song is short and rising, with bright whistling tones; call: "trui" or "toeet"*

adult ♀ summer

■ Adult

Alpine Chough

Pyrrhocorax graculus

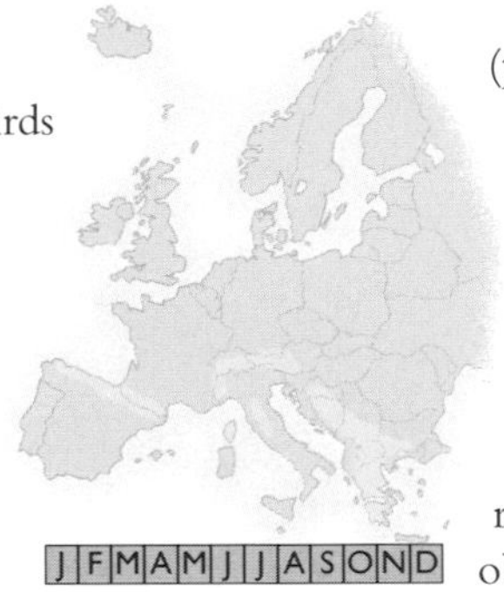

Alpine Choughs are always found in flocks, varying from a few birds up to a hundred or more. Like many corvids, they are entirely black, but they have a slender, bright yellow bill (like a Blackbird) and pinkish or red legs.

The Chough (*P. pyrrhocorax*; 15–16½" [38–42 cm]) is similar in size and colour, except for the longer coral-red bill. Juvenile Choughs have a shorter yellow-orange bill, and the flight silhouette is a little different, with a slightly shorter tail and slightly broader wings. Choughs are seen in high mountains as well as on lowland ridges and sea cliffs. Keep a lookout for Jackdaws (p. 115), which are sometimes seen at great heights in mountains, always near human settlement.

Alpine Choughs can be very tame and are sometimes easily approachable around refuse at alpine camps or ski centres. Choughs apparently do not visit refuse tips and are therefore less easily observed at close range. Distant flocks can be difficult to identify and the calls may then be of great help.

FIELD NOTES

■ *14¼–15¾" (36–40 cm)*

■ *Bright yellow bill; entirely black plumage*

▲ *Chough similar, but has longer coral-red bill; calls: Jackdaw-like "kaa", "tschrrrr" and characteristic puffing "tschuff"*

Large nest, often well-hidden in deep crevices or caves, of roots and branches, lined with small branches and grass

♪ *A high and sometimes metallic "chuiiir", "kruuu" or "seee"*

First-winter

Citril Finch

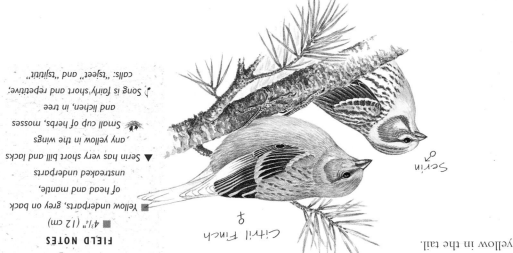

Serinus citrinella

Citril Finches are rather scarce and widespread in mountains close to the treeline. They live in pairs, but outside the breeding season they gather in small flocks. In summer, their food consists of insects and seeds; in winter, they feed on the ground on seeds of pine trees and herbs. Although the species is resident, it moves to areas at lower altitudes in winter. Both sexes look quite dull because of the dusky yellow below and the greenish and grey upperparts. They have two dusky-yellow wingbars, but lack yellow in the tail.

The related Serin (*S. serinus;* 4¼" [11 cm]) is similar in size, but otherwise very different. The male has a bright yellow head, and is streaked on the head, back and flanks. The female is similar to the male, but has little yellow on the head and is more heavily streaked. Serins lack any yellow in the wings and tail and have a very short bill. They can be very common in Central and Southern European villages.

FIELD NOTES

■ 4¾" (12 cm)

■ Yellow underparts, grey on back of head and mantle, unstreaked underparts

▲ Serin has very short bill and lacks any yellow in the wings

Small cup of herbs, mosses and lichen, in tree

♪ Song is fairly short and repetitive; calls: "tsjeet" and "tsjititit"

■ Adult

Rock Bunting

Emberiza cia

The male Rock Bunting is easily recognisable by its grey head with black stripes and rufous underparts. The supercilium sometimes appears almost white. The female is less vividly coloured but resembles the male and should not be difficult to identify. Both sexes have a thin white wingbar and a rufous rump.

The Cirl Bunting (p. 187) has an olive rump, while the adult Yellowhammer (p. 187), which also has a rufous rump, always has a lot of yellow on its feathers. Young female Cirl Buntings have yellow at least on the undertail coverts and lack black stripes on the head.

Rock Buntings are rather common on fairly low, stony hillsides with scattered bushes. They feed on the ground and constantly flick their tail, which makes the white on the outer tail feathers visible. In winter, they move to areas at lower altitudes, where they are often seen with Cirl Buntings and finches.

FIELD NOTES

■ *6¼" (16 cm)*

■ *Grey head with black stripes, rufous rump and underparts, white on outer tail feathers*

■ *Inhabits low, stony hillsides*

Cup of grass, moss and bark lined with hair and fine herbs, between rocks or in low bushes

♪ *Song is a high, fairly long "see see see sir"; calls include a thin "see", "tuup" and "chit"*

Resources Directory

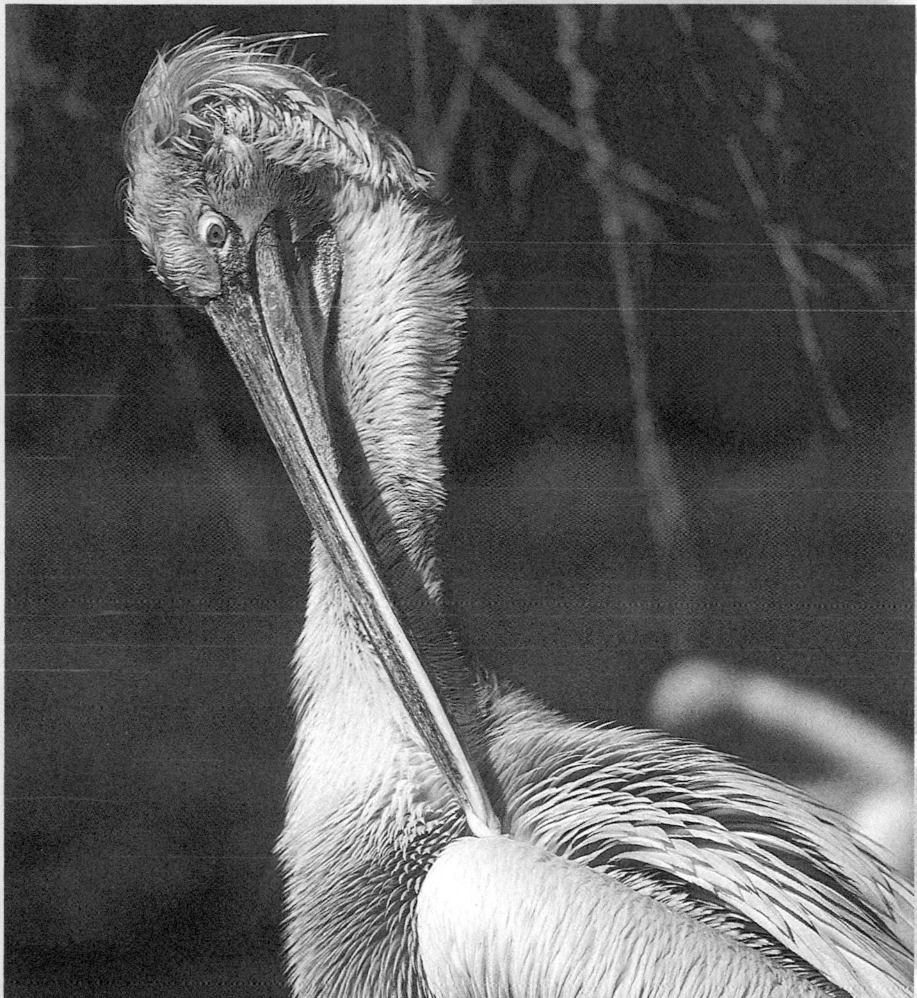

Further Reading

This is by no means a complete list of books and periodicals but it should provide a solid foundation of references on which a newcomer to birdwatching can build. The following abbreviations have been used: BTO (British Trust for Ornithology), SOF (Sveriges Ornitologiska Förening), LPO (Ligue Française pour la Protection des Oiseaux).

Understanding Birds

A Dictionary of Birds edited by B Campbell and E Lack (T & A D Poyser, 1985). A comprehensive A–Z digest of facts about birds.

Birds and Weather by S Moss (Hamlyn, 1995). The weather and its effect on birds and migration explained in clear and informative language.

Cambridge Encyclopaedia of Ornithology edited by M Brooks and T Birkhead (Cambridge University Press, 1992). A wealth of information on every aspect of ornithology.

Garden Birds

Birdfeeder Handbook by R Burton (Dorling Kindersley, 1990). Highly accessible guide to attracting and observing birds in the garden.

The Complete Garden Bird Book by M Golley and S Moss (New Holland, 1996). Beautifully illustrated guide to feeding and watching garden birds.

Identification

Bird Identification: a Reference Guide by K Adolfsson and S Cherrug (SOF, 1995). Offers all relevant references for identification papers and rare photographs in different European (and some American) journals.

Birds by Character by R Hume (Papermac, 1990). Small but useful guide to identification by general appearance.

Birds of Britain and Europe by H Heinzel, R Fitter and J Parslow (HarperCollins, new edition, 1995). Excellent and affordable fully revised pocket field guide with more than 3,000 illustrations.

Birds of Europe by L Jonsson (Helm, 1992). Classic work from an acclaimed artist.

Buntings and Sparrows: an Identification Guide by C Byers, U Olsson and J Curson (Pica Press, 1995). A guide to 110 species of buntings and American sparrows.

The Complete British List (Birdwatch, second edition, 1994). An up-to-date checklist of 550 species recorded in Britain and Ireland in practical "tick-list" format.

A Field Guide to the Rare Birds of Britain and Europe by I Lewington, P Alström and P Colston (HarperCollins, 1991). Specialised identification guidance and comprehensive illustrations covering rare and vagrant species in Europe.

Finches and Sparrows: an Identification Guide by P Clement, A Harris and J Davis (Helm 1993). The standard reference for this group of birds.

Flight Identification of European Raptors by R F Porter, I Willis, S Christensen and B P Nielsen (Calton, 1981). Specialised identification guidance.

Gulls: a Guide to Identification by P J Grant (T & A D Poyser, second edition, 1986). Succinct but thorough gull guide, illustrated with line drawings and photographs.

Identification Guide to European Non-Passerines by K Baker. (BTO Guide 24, 1993) and *Identification Guide to European Passerines* by L Svensson (BTO, fourth edition, 1992). More ringers' manuals than field guides, but packed full of useful and detailed information.

The Macmillan Birder's Guide to European and Middle Eastern Birds by A Harris, H. Shirihai and D Christie (Macmillan, 1996) and *The Macmillan Field Guide to Bird Identification* by A Harris, K Vinicombe and L Tucker

(Macmillan, 1990). Highly rated pocket guides to the field separation of confusing species.

Photographic Guide to the Birds of Britain and Europe by H Delin and L Svensson (Hamlyn, 1993). The most comprehensive photographic reference to European birds.

Seabirds: an Identification Guide by P Harrison (Helm, 1985). Authoritative manual on the seabirds of the world.

Shorebirds: an Identification Guide by P J Hayman and A J Prater (Helm, 1987). Authoritative manual on the waders of the world.

Stimmen der Vögel Europas by H H Bergmann and H W Helb (BLV, 1982). Useful guide to the identification of European birds by their song or call.

Terns of Europe and North America by K M Olsen and H Larsson (Helm, 1994). Compact but thorough identification guide.

Tits, Nuthatches and Treecreepers by S Harrap and D Quinn (Helm, 1996). A guide to identification and many other ornithological aspects of 110 species.

Wildfowl: an Identification Guide by S Madge and H Burn (Helm, 1987). All the world's wildfowl are brought together in this comprehensive volume.

Reference

Atlas der Verbreitung und Häutigkeit der Brutvögel Deutschlands by G Rheinwald (Dachverband Deutscher Avifaunisten, 1993) and *Atlas der Brutvögel Deutschlands* by B Nicolai (Gustav Fischer Verlag, 1993). The breeding bird atlases of Germany.

Atlas des Oiseaux de France en Hiver by D Yeatman-Berthelot (Société Ornithologique de France, 1991). Distribution maps for birds in the winter in France.

The Atlas of Wintering Birds in Britain and Ireland by P Lack (T & A D Poyser, 1986). Accounts and distribution maps of winter visitors.

Atlas van de Nederlandse vogels by Samenwerkende Organisaties Vogelonderzoek Nederland (SOVON, 1987). Distribution maps for birds in every season in the Netherlands.

Birds in Europe: their Conservation Status by G Tucker and M Heath (BirdLife International, 1995). Award-winning reference book on threatened birds in Europe.

Danmarks Fugle—en Oversigt by K M Olsen. (Dansk Ornitologisk Forening, 1992). Survey of the birds of Denmark.

Handbook of the Birds of Europe, the Middle East and North Africa: the Birds of the Western Palearctic edited by S Cramp *et al.* (Oxford University Press, 1977–1995). Landmark nine-volume series detailing every aspect of every bird recorded in Europe and its environs. Perhaps the most exhaustive bird reference in the world.

Handbuch der Vögel Mitteleuropas 1–13 by U N Glutz von Blotzheim and K M Bauer (Aula Verlag 1966–1993). This is the German language counterpart of Cramp's Handbook series. The Handbuch series is confined to birds recorded in Central Europe (including the Netherlands, Belgium, Luxemburg, Germany, Poland, Czech Republic, Slovakia, Hungary, Austria and Switzerland) and gives, in some respects, even more detailed information than Cramp. One more volume is to be published shortly.

The New Atlas of Breeding Birds in Britain and Ireland 1988–91 by D W Gibbons, J B Reid and R A Chapman (Academic Press, 1993). The results of the most extensive field survey of birds in Western Europe mapped and discussed.

Les Oiseaux Rares en France by P J Dubois, P Yésou and LPO (Chabaud, 1992). Analysis of officially accepted rare birds in France.

Palearctic Birds: a Checklist of the Birds of Europe, North Africa and Asia by M Beaman (Harrier Publications, 1995). Covers a large geographical area, but lists all species with proposed new standard English names and taxonomic notes.

Rare Birds in Britain and Ireland by J N Dymond, P A Fraser and S Gantlett (T & A D Poyser, 1989). No longer up-to-date, but still the most recent analysis of officially accepted rare birds in Britain and Ireland.

Sällsynta Fåglar i Sverige by B Briefe, E Hirschfield, N Kjellén and M Ullman. (Skånes Ornithologiska Förening, 1990). Analysis of officially accepted rare birds in Sweden.

Sveriges Fåglar by Sveriges Ornithologiska Förening (SOF, 1990). Distribution maps of the birds of Sweden.

Vogels in Vlaanderen: Voorkomen en Verspreiding by Vlaamse Avifaunacommissie (Bornem, 1989). Guide to the occurrence of birds in Flanders.

Site Guides

The Most Important Bird Areas in Europe by R F Grimmett and T Jones (Cambridge, 1989). Landmark work.

Vogelparadiese 1–3 by M Lohmann *et al.* (Paul Parey Verlag, 1989–91). The best birdwatching sites in Germany.

Where to Watch Birds in Britain and Europe by J Gooders (Hamlyn, 1994). More than 200 of the best birdwatching sites in Europe and North Africa.

Where to Watch Birds in Eastern Europe by G Gorman (Hamlyn/Reed, 1994) About 140 of the best sites in the Czech Republic, Slovakia, Hungary, Romania and Bulgaria.

Where to Watch Birds in France by LPO (Helm, 1989). Best French birdwatching sites.

Where to Watch Birds in Holland, Belgium and Northern France by A B van den Berg and D Lafontaine (Hamlyn/Reed, 1996). More than 200 of the best birdwatching sites.

Where to Watch Birds in Ireland by C Hutchinson (Helm, 1994). The best 143 birdwatching sites.

Where to Watch Birds in Italy by Lega Italiana Protezione Uccelli (Helm, 1994). The best 103 birdwatching sites.

Where to Watch Birds in Scandinavia by G Aulén (Hamlyn/Reed, 1996). The best 180 birdwatching sites in Denmark, Finland, Iceland, Norway and Sweden.

Where to Watch Birds in Scotland by M Madders and J Welstead (Helm, 1993) New edition of Scotland's premier birdwatching site guide.

Where to Watch Birds in Southern Spain by E Garcia and A Paterson (Helm, 1994). The best 92 birdwatching sites in Andalucía, Extremadura and Gibraltar.

Where to Watch Birds in Spain and Portugal by L Rose (Hamlyn/Reed, 1995) About 190 of the best birdwatching sites.

Where to Watch Birds in Spain by la Sociedad Española de Ornithologia (Lynx, 1994). The best 309 birdwatching sites in Spain.

Journals and Magazines

In addition to the journals of the organisations mentioned on p. 277, the following birdwatching periodicals are recommended.

Alula. Finnish periodical for keen birdwatchers. Bilingual. Alula, PO Box 85, SF–02271, Espoo, Finland.

Birding World. The leading British monthly journal for world birders and twitchers. Bird Information Services, Stonerunner, Coast Road, Cley next the Sea, Holt, Norfolk NR25 7RZ, England.

Birdwatch. The leading British monthly magazine for keen birdwatchers. Solo Publishing, 310 Bow House, 153–159 Bow Road, London E3 2SE, England.

Bird Watching. A monthly magazine with information about birdwatching. Bretton Court, Bretton, Peterborough PE3 8DZ, England.

Bliki. Iceland's leading periodical. Icelandic Institute of Natural History, PO Box 5320, IS–125 Reykjavík, Iceland.

British Birds. The long-standing (since 1907) British monthly journal for ornithology. British Birds Ltd., Fountains, Park Lane, Blunham, Bedford MK44 3NJ, England.

Butlletí del Grup Català d'Annellament. Catalan magazine. Grup Català d'Anellament, Musea de Zoologia, Ap. 593, E–08080 Barcelona, Spain.

Irish Birdwatching. Ireland's periodical for birdwatchers. 46 Claremount Court, Glasnevin Dublin 11, Ireland.

Limicola. German periodical for bird identification. Limicola, Über dem Salzgraben 11, D–37574 Einbeck-Drüber, Germany.

Rivista Italiana di Birdwatching. Italian periodical for keen birdwatchers. Arex Spix Ed, via Chiesa 10, I–25058 Sulzano (BS), Italy

CDs & CD-Roms

Birdwatching. Photo-CD with a collection of 100 photographs (Opera Multimedia, 1995).

Birds of Europe. Interactive CD-ROM with drawings, photographs, text and sound records (Springer-Verlag, 1994).

Tous les oiseaux d'Europe. 4 CDs with sound records and a booklet by J C Roché, *et al.* (La Mure, 1990).

Virtual Reality Bird. An educational multimedia guide to the world of birds (Dorling Kindersley, 1995).

European Organisations *and* Birdlines

The following national organisations publish newsletters (in the respective language unless indicated otherwise) and organise field trips. Most of them also have a network of local or regional branches or representatives who will be able to tell you about their work and activities and who may also be able to put you in touch with other birdwatchers and bird clubs.

Some European countries have birdlines and hotlines. Birdlines allow you to listen to reports on interesting or rare sightings in a country. These lines are generally in the respective languages. Hotlines allow you to report interesting or rare birds you have discovered in a certain country. These messages can be made in English. These lines are not accessible from abroad unless otherwise indicated.

Organisations

Austria

BirdLife Austria
Naturhistorisches Museum
Burgring 7, A–1014 Wien
Tel: (43 1) 523 4651
Fax: (43 1) 523 5254
Journal: *Egretta*

Belgium

De Wielewaal
Graatakker 11, B–2300,
Turnhout
Tel: (32 14) 412252
Fax: (32 14) 439651
Flemish bird and nature study society
Journal: *Oriolus*

Koninklijk Belgisch Verbond voor de Bescherming van Vogels (KBVBV)
Veeweidestraat 43,
B–1070 Brussel
Tel: (32 2) 5212850
Fax: (32 2) 5270989
Society for the protection of birds
Journal: *Mens en Vogel/ l'Homme et l'Oiseau*

Société d'Etudes Ornithologiques (SEO)
Maison Liégeoise de l'Environnement
Rue de la Régence 36,
B–4000 Liège
Tel: (32 41) 222025
Fax: (32 41) 221689
Wallonian society for the study of birds
Journal: *Aves*

Britain

British Trust for Ornithology (BTO)
National Centre for Ornithology,
The Nunnery, Thetford,
Norfolk IP24 2PU,
England
Tel: (44 1842) 750050
Fax: (44 1842) 750030
Journal: *Ringing and Migration*

Royal Society for the Protection of Birds (RSPB)
The Lodge, Sandy,
Bedfordshire SG19 2DL,
England
Tel: (44 1767) 680551
Fax: (44 1767) 692365
Journal: *Birds*

BirdLife International
Wellbrook Court, Girton
Road, Cambridge CB3 0NA,
England
Tel: (44 1223) 277318
Fax: (44 1223) 277200
Journals: *World Birdwatch, Bird Conservation International*

Scottish Ornithologists' Club
21 Regent Terrace,
Edinburgh EH7 5BT,
Scotland
Tel: (44 131) 556 6042
Bird study society
Journal: *Scottish Birds*

Denmark

Dansk Ornitologisk Forening (DOF) BirdLife Denmark
Vesterbrogade 140A,
DK–1620 København V
Tel: (45) 31 314404
Fax: (45) 31 312435
Bird study society and society for the protection of birds
Journals: *Dansk Ornitologisk Forenings Tidsskrift, Fugle og Natur*

Finland

BirdLife Suomi Finland
PL 17, SF–18101 Heinola
Tel: (358 06) 6854700
Fax: (358 06) 6854722
Society for the protection of birds
Journal: *Linnut*

France

Ligue Française pour la Protection des Oiseaux (LPO)
La Corderie Royale, BP 263,
F–17035 Rochefort Cedex
Tel: (33) 46821234
Fax: (33) 46839586
Society for the protection of birds
Journals: *Ornithos, l'Oiseau Magazine*

Société d'Etudes Ornithologiques de France (SEO)
Museum National d'Histoire Naturelle, 55 Rue Buffon,
F–75005 Paris
Tel: (33) 40793834
Fax: (33) 40793063
Bird study society
Journal: *Alauda*

Germany

Naturschutzbund Deutschland (DBV) BirdLife Germany
PO Box 200413 D–5300 Bonn 2
Tel: (49 228) 975610
Fax: (49 228) 9756190
Society for the protection of birds
Journal: *Naturschutz Heute*

Gesellschaft Rheinischer Ornithologen und Westfälische Ornithologen-Gesellschaft
Im Rauland 37,
D–50127 Bergheim
Tel: (49 228) 482648
Regional bird study society
Journal: *Charadrius*

Ireland

Irish Wildbird Conservancy (IWC)
Ruttledge House,
8 Longford Place,
Monkstown, Co Dublin
Tel: (353 1) 2804322
Fax: (353 1) 2844 407
Journal: *Irish Birds*

Italy

Lega Italiana Protezione Uccelli (LIPU) BirdLife Italy
Vicolo San Tiburzio 5,
I–43100 Parma
Tel: (39 521) 230380
Fax: (39 521) 287116
Society for the protection of birds
Journal: *Ali Notizi*

Luxemburg

Lëtzebuerger Natur-a Vulleschutsliga
Rue de Bettembourg, L–1899 Kokelscheuer, Luxembourg
Tel: (352) 290404
Fax: (352) 290504
Society for the protection of birds and nature
Journal: *Regulus*

Netherlands

Dutch Birding Association (DBA)
PO Box 75611,
NL–1070 AP Amsterdam
Fax: (31 23) 5376749
e-mail: http://www.hol.nl/-mebweb/dba.haml
Journal: *Dutch Birding* (bilingual)

BirdLife/Vogelbescherming Nederland
Driebergseweg 16C,
NL–3708 JB Zeist
Tel: (31 30) 6937700
Fax: (31 30) 6918844
Society for the protection of birds
Journal: *Vogels*

Norway

Norsk Ornitologisk Forening (NOF) BirdLife Norway
Seminarplassen 5,
N–7060 Klæbu
Tel: (47) 72831166
Fax: (47) 72831255
Bird study society and society for the protection of birds
Journal: *Vår Fuglefauna*

Portugal

Centro de Estudos de Migrações e Protecção de Aves (CEMPA)
Rua Filipe Folque, 46-3°,
P–1000 Lisboa
Tel: (351 1) 3523018
Society for the protection of birds
Journal: *Airo*

Spain

La Sociedad Española de Ornitología (SEO) BirdLife Spain
Carretera de Húmera, 63–1,
E–28224 Pozuelo de Alarcón, Madrid
Tel: (34 1) 3511045
Fax: (34 1) 3511386
Bird study society and society for the protection of birds
Journals: *Ardeola, La Garcilla*

Sweden

Sveriges Ornitologiska Förening (SOF) BirdLife Sweden
PO Box 14219,
S–10440 Stockholm
Tel: (46 8) 6626434
Fax: (46 8) 6626988
Bird study society and society for the protection of birds
Journals: *Vår Fågelvärld, Ornis Svecica*

Skånes Ornitologiska Förening (SkOF)
Ekologihuset, S–223 62 Lund
Tel. & fax: (46 46) 146608
e-mail: Skof@algonet.se
Regional bird study society
Journal: *Anser*

Switzerland

Schweizer Vogelschutz (SVS) BirdLife Switzerland
PO Box CH–8036, Zürich
Tel: (41 41) 1 4637271
Fax: (41 41) 1 4614778
Society for the protection of birds
Journal: *Ornis*

Schweizerische Vogelwarte
PO Box CH–6024, Sempach
Tel: (41 41) 4629700
Fax: (41 41) 4629710
Bird study society
Journal: *Ornithologische Beobachter*

Rarities Committees

Details on rare birds can be sent to the following committees of the respective countries (most committees accept incoming reports in English). Annual reports are published in the indicated magazines.

Austria
Avifaunistische Kommission (AFK)
c/o Naturhistorisches Museum Wien, Burgring 7, A–1014 Wien
Journal: *Egretta*

Belgium
Flanders
Belgische Avifaunistische Homologatiecommissie (BAHC)
Erfgoedlaan 8, B–9800 Deinze
Journal: *Oriolus*

Wallonia
Commission d'Homologation (CH)
Rue A. Markelbach 68, B–1030 Bruxelles
Journal: *Aves*

Britain
British Birds Rarities Committee (BBRC)
2 Churchtown Cottages, Towednack, St Ives, Cornwall TR26 3AZ
Journal: *British Birds*

Denmark
Sjaldenhedsudvalget (SU)
Vesterbrogade 140, DK–1620 København V
Journal: *Dansk Ornitologisk Förening Tidsskrift*

Finland
Suomen Lintutietellisen Yhdistyksen Rartiteettikomitea (SLY RK)
Mannerheimintie 64 A2, SF–00260 Helsinki 10
Journal: *Linnut*

France
Comité d'Homologation National (CHN)
c/o LPO, La Corderie Royale, BP263, F–17305 Rochefort Cedex
Journal: *Ornithos* and *Alauda*

Germany
Deutsche Seltenheitenkommission
c/o Limicola, Über dem Salzgraben 11, D–37574 Einbeck-Drüber
Journal: *Limicola*

Ireland
Irish Rare Birds Committee (IRBC)
Ballykennealy, Ballymacoda, Co Cork
Journal: *Irish Birds* and *British Birds*

Italy
Comitatio di Ornologazione Italiano (COI)
Via Venato 30, I–25020 Verolavecchia (BS)
Journal: *Rivista Italiana di Ornitologia*

Netherlands
Commissie Dwaalgasten Nederlandse Avifauna (CDNA)
PO Box 45, NL–2080 AA Santpoort-Zuid
Journal: *Dutch Birding*

Norway
Norsk Sjeldenhetskomite for Fugle (NSKF)
Rød, Asmaløy, N–1684 Vesterøy
Journal: *Vår Fuglefauna*

Spain
Comite Iberico de Rareras
CIR de SEO
Facultad de Biologia, Planta 9, E–28040 Madrid
Journal: *Ardeola*

Sweden
Sveriges Ornithologiska Förenings Raritetskommitte (SOFRK)
Segerstad Fyr, S–38065 Degerhamn
Journal: *Vår Fågelvärld*

Switzerland
Schweizerische Avifaunistische Kommission (SAK)
Schweizerische Vogelwarte Sempach, CH–6204 Sempach
Journal: *Ornithologische Beobachter*

Birdlines and Hotlines

Belgium
Birdline: 32 (0)3 4880194
Hotline: 32 (0)3 4880194
(accessible from abroad)

Britain
Birdline: 0891 700222
Hotline: 0263 741140

Denmark
Birdline: (45) 90 232400
Hotline: (45) 33 255300
(accessible from abroad)

France
Birdline: 33 (0)44 201897
Hotline: 33 (0)44 201897
(accessible from abroad)

Ireland
Birdline: 1550 111700
Hotline: 01 348917

Netherlands
Birdline: 06 32032128
Hotline: 078 6180935

Norway
Birdline: 8205050
Hotline: 8205050

Sweden
Birdline: 071 268300
Hotline: 020 768030

Switzerland
Birdline: 41 (0)31 8093324
Hotline: 41 (0)31 8093324
(accessible from abroad)

INDEX *and* GLOSSARY

In this combined index and glossary, bold page numbers indicate the main reference, while italics indicate illustrations and photographs.

CAPTIONS

Page 1: The Spotted Flycatcher can often be seen catching flying insects from an exposed perch.
Page 2: Greylag Geese typically remain paired for life. When agitated or in display, the feathers of the neck are furrowed.
Page 4–5: "Dancing" of Common Cranes.
Page 6–7: Nightingales are famous for their splendid vocal abilities.
Page 8–9: The Sanderling is more easily identified by behaviour, such as chasing waves on beaches, than by appearance.
Page 10–11: Puffins breed in excavated shallow burrows, usually on grassy slopes of rocky islands at sea.
Page 12–13: A flock of Avocets taking off.
Page 44–45: Like many other species, Hawfinches can be attracted to a birdfeeder in winter.
Page 58–59: White Storks are typical birds of Continental river meadows and wet grasslands.
Page 84–85: Whooper Swans are breeding birds of the arctic tundra and can be found in Britain and Europe in winter.
Page 95: A group of Starlings (top inset) perched on powerlines. House Sparrows (bottom inset) rival the Starlings in abundance.
Page 119: Although common in all kinds of wooded areas, including suburbs, Dunnocks (top inset) are easily overlooked. The Willow Warbler (bottom inset) is a numerous long-distance migrant, wintering in tropical Africa.
Page 159: A Skylark (top inset) not only sings in flight but also on the ground. A flock of Wigeons (bottom inset) foraging.
Page 189: A male Reed Bunting (top inset) is unmistakable, with its black head and white collar. The northernmost breeding colonies of Spoonbills (bottom inset) are found on the Dutch Wadden islands.
Page 227: A lone Avocet (bottom inset) feeds at water's edge as the sun sets.
Page 257: Like other vultures, the Lammergeier (top inset) searches for food by scanning in flight. A Rock Thrush (bottom inset) on a favourite perch.
Page 273: A Dalmatian Pelican preening.

PICTURE AND ILLUSTRATION CREDITS
(t = top, b = bottom, l = left, r = right, c = center, bkgr = background. A = Auscape International Pty Ltd; AA/ES = Animals Animals/Earth Scenes; BAL = Bridgeman Art Library, London; BC = Bruce Coleman Limited; BPL = Boltin Picture Library; BW = Birdwatch; Cornell = Cornell Laboratory of Ornithology; Culver = Culver Pictures, Inc.; DJC = DJC & Associates; DRK = DRK Photo; FN = Foto Natura; IB = The Image Bank; J = Jacana; MEPL = Mary Evans Picture Library; MP = Minden Pictures; NHPA = Natural History Photographic Agency; NS = Natural Selection; NW = North Wind Picture Archives; OSF = Oxford Scientific Films Ltd; PA = Peter Arnold, Inc.; PE = Planet Earth Pictures; PI = Positive Images; PN = Photo/Nats, Inc.; PR = Photo Researchers, Inc.; S = Scala; SB = Stock Boston; TPL = The Photographic Library of Australia; TS = Tom Stack & Associates; V = Vireo; VU = Visuals Unlimited; WC = Woodfin Camp & Associates.)

1 Ben van den Brink/FN. **2** Wim Weenink/FN. **3** Thomas Buchholz/BCL. **4-5** Flip de Nooyer/FN. **6-7** F Houtkamp/FN. **8-9** William M Smithey Jr/PEP. **10-11** Frans Lanting/MP. **11** Fred Hazelhoff/FN. **12-13** Piet Munsterman/FN. **14-15** Robert Morton & David Wood. **16**t NW; bl Jean Vertut; bkgr NW. **17**tl C M Dixon; tr David Woo/SB; c by permission of the Linnean Society of London; b Lawrence Migdale. **18**t Louvre, Paris/BAL; cr David Kirshner; b William E Ferguson. **19**t & cr David Kirshner; b Gunter Ziesler/BCL. **20**tl Giraudon/BAL; tr B. Henry/V; bl John Gerlach/AA/ES; bc Wayne Lankinen/DRK; bkgr NW. **21**t MEPL; c Danny Ellinger/FN, b Will & Deni McIntyre/PR. **22**t Frans Lanting/BCL; c & b David Kirshner. **23**t Frank Knight; cl Jim Zipp/PR; cr Thomas Kitchin/TS; bl Frank Knight; br Lee Boltin/BPL. **24**tl Art Resource, NY/S; c Geoff Avern/Australian Museum; bl C Decout/FN; br Frank Knight. **25** David Kirshner. **26**tl Flip de Nooyer/FN; cr A. Morris/V; bl Stephen J. Krasemann/DRK. **27**tl Stephen J. Krasemann/DRK; tr Wayne Lankinen/DRK; b Herman Berkhoudt/FN. **28**tl H. Brandl/FN; tr R J Erwin/NHPA; cl Jordan Coonrad; b Andrew J. Purcell/BC. **29**t Frank Knight; cr Palazzo Vecchio, Firenze/S; b NW; bkgr MEPL. **30**t J. White/ET Archive; c J. Wegner/FN; b Frits van Daalen/FN. **31**tl NW; tr Danny Ellinger/FN; c1 Fred Hazelhoff/FN; c2 Gary Milburn/TS; b Fred Hazelhoff/FN. **32**tr BW; bl BW; br Gerald Driessens **33**tr BW; cr BW; b Gerald Driessens. **34**t C M Dixon; b Jaap Hoogeboom/FN. **35**tl Danny Ellinger/FN; tr F. Ribbers/FN; cl W Wisniewski/FN; br Thomas Kitchin/TS. **36**t Wim Weenink/FN; b Erich Hartmann/Magnum. **37**tl F Houtkamp/FN; tr Fred Hazelhoff/FN; cl Cornell. **38**tl C M Dixon; bl Anne Bowman; br Steve Kaufman/DRK. **39**tl Danny Ellinger/FN; tr Roger Tidman/NHPA; b Wide World Photos/AP. **40**tl J P Delobelle/FN; c1, 2 & 3 Breck P Kent/AA/ES; bl O Faulhaber/FN; bkgr Stephen J Krasemann/DRK. **41**t Life Magazine ©Time Warner/Nina Leen; c Tom J Ulrich; b Wayne Lankinen/DRK. **42**t Jonathan Blair/WC; c D Robert Franz/PE; b Piet Munsterman/FN. **44-45** F Cahez/FN. **46**tl Danny Ellinger/FN; tr J J Etienne/FN; cr P Garguil/FN; bl Culver. **47**t Casa del Bracciale d'Oro, Pompeii/S; b J Korenromp/FN. **48** Colin McRae Photography; tl J Korenromp/FN. **49**br J J Etienne/FN. **50** Colin McRae Photography; tl Arnoud van den Berg; c BW. **51** Colin McRae Photography; cl George H Harrison/Grant Heilman Photography; tr Jaap Hoogeboom/FN; cr Arnoud van den Berg; br Jaap Hoogeboom/FN. **52**tr Phillips, The International Fine Art Auction/BAL; bl J L Ziegler/FN; br Mary Clay/PE. **53**tr Jane Burton/BC; cl C M Dixon; br Arnoud van den Berg; bkgr FN. **54** Colin McRae Photography; tl Jerry Howard/PI; bl J van Arkel/FN. **55**tr Piet Munsterman; cr Blondeau/FN; bl Hirondelle/FN. **56**tr Casa del Bracciale d'Oro, Pompeii/S; bkgr NW; br Grace Davies/Envision. **57**t Philip Friskorn/FN; c Patti Murray/AA/ES; b Gerard Driessens. **58-59** Danny Ellinger/FN. **60**tl & tr Colin McRae Photography; cr Jiri Lochman; bl Susan Day. **61**t Hellio-Van Ingen/J/A; b Colin McRae Photography. **62**tl Paul Resendez/PI; tr Colin McRae Photography; b Dennis Frates/PI; inset Flip de Nooyer/FN. **63**t & c Stephen J Krasemann/DRK; b David Wood. **64**tl Tom Bean/DRK; cr William H Mullins/PR; cc Colin McRae Photography; b Jim Brandenburg/MP. **65**tl Frits van Dalen/FN; tr Jack Wilburn/AA/ES; bl Richard Day; br K. Beylevelt/FN. **66**t Culver; c Fred Hazelhoff/FN b Stephen J Krasemann/PR. **67**tl Eric Wanders/FN; tr H Polin/FN; cl Fred Hazelhoff/FN; bl Danny Ellinger/FN. **68**t Frits van Daalen/FN; c Fred Hazelhoff/FN; b Frans Lanting/MP. **69**tr, l & c Gerald Driessens; b George Holton/PR. **70**tl T Schenk/FN; cl H Brandl/FN; bl Henk Tromp/FN. **70-71** illust Danker Jan Oreel; **71**tr Arnoud van den Berg; cr Jean-Paul Ferrero/A; illust c Frank Knight; br Arnoud van den Berg. **72**t Colin McRae Photography; cr O Faulhaber/FN; br Cynthia Berger/Cornell; bkgr NW. **73**tl Haroldo Castro; bl Colin McRae Photography; tr Frits van Daalen/FN; br Steve Pantle. **74**tl Art Resource, NY/S; bl Gerald Driessens. **75**tl Candice Cochrane/PI; tr Colin McRae Photography; cr Mark Catesby/BPL; bl Cornell; bc Culver; br NW. **76**tl & r Colin McRae Photography; bl & r Joe McDonald/AA/ES. **77**t Courtesy R Gunz & Co Pty Ltd & Cannon Australia; bl Alan Briere; br Daniel J Cox/DJC. **78**tl Julie O'Neil/PN; cl Ron Austing; bl Alan Briere. **79**tr NW; tl Richard Day; bl Jim Kahnweiler/PI; bc William H Mullins/PR; br P Bulsing/FN. **80**tl Flip de Nooyer/FN; bl Culver; br NW. **81**tr Arnoud van den Berg; bl C Kalser/FN; br P Wegner/FN. **82**tr W Wisniewski/FN; cl & cc Flip de Nooyer/FN; cr Franz Kovacs/FN; br Brigitta Witte/FN. **83**tl Hans Hut/FN; tc W van Dijck/FN; tr H Heerink/FN; cr Wim Klomp/FN; b Wim Klomp/FN. **84-85** Rino Burgio/FN. **86**tl Wim Weenink/FN; br Henk Tromp/FN. **87**tl Danny Ellinger/FN; tr J C Malausa/FN; **88**tl J C Malausa/FN. **89**t R de Kam/FN; c1 R de Lange/FN; c2 Fred Hazelhoff/FN; b Flip de Nooyer/FN. **90**tl Gordon Langsbury/BC; tr Jaap Hoogeboom/FN; bl Francois Gohier/A. **91**tl H Wester/FN; tr Flip de Nooyer/FN; bl Danny Ellinger/FN; br Ad van Lokven/FN. **92**bl Fred Hazelhoff/FN; bc Flip de Nooyer; br H Wester/FN. **93**tl Fred Hazelhoff/FN; tr F Cahet/FN. **94** Philip Friskorn/FN. **95**bkgr Jerry Howard/PI; t Frans Lanting/MP; b Wim Weenink/FN. **96-97** Erik van Ommen **98**t Daniel J Cox/OSF; cl Wil Meinderts/FN; br Philip Friskorn/FN; bl Jan Baks/FN. **99**tl Inge Yspeert/FN; tr Wim Weenink/FN; cr Ben van den Brink/FN; b Julie O'Neil/PN. **100** Frits van Daalen/FN. **101** Tom Walker/A. **102** Do van Dijck/FN. **103** Hans Menop/FN. **104** Wim Klomp/FN. **105** Wil Meinderts/FN. **106** Manfred Danegger/A. **107** Ben van den Brink/FN. **108** Peter Bulsing/FN. **109** Hans Reinhard/BC. **110** Otto Faulhaber/FN. **111** Guy Robbrecht/FN. **112** Henk Tromp/FN. **113** Piet Munsterman/FN. **114** Wim Weenink/FN. **115** Wil Meinderts/FN. **116** A Morris/V. **117** R Villani/V. **118** Franz Kovacs/FN. **119** bkgr Catherine Ursillo/PR; t Do van Dijck/FN; b Ad van Lokven/FN. **120-121** Erik van Ommen. **122**t J Krasemann/DRK; cr Frits van Daalen/FN; bl Roger Tidman/NHPA; br Flip de Nooyer/FN. **123**t Do van Dijck/FN; c1 Ben van den Brink/FN; c2 Frits van Daalen/FN; b Francis Lepine/AA/ES. **126** Otto Faulhaber/FN. **127** Fred Hazelhoff/FN. **128** Frits van Daalen/FN. **129** Wim Weenink/FN. **130** Frits van Daalen/FN. **131** Eric Wanders/FN. **132** Flip de Nooyer/FN. **133** Harry Fiolet/FN. **134** Jaap Hoogeboom/FN. **135** Piet Munsterman/FN. **136** Wim Weenink/FN. **137** Frits Houtekamp/FN. **138** Otto Faulhaber/FN. **139** Frits van Daalen/FN. **140** Flip de Nooyer/FN. **141** Frits van Daalen/FN. **142** Frits van Daalen/FN. **143** Piet Munsterman/FN. **144** Gerard de Hoog/FN. **145** Flip de Nooyer/FN. **146** Ben van den Brink/FN. **147** Hans Schouten/FN. **148** Jos Korenromp/FN. **149** Rino Burgio/FN. **150** Otto Faulhaber/FN. **151** Frits van Daalen/FN. **152** C Decout/FN. **153** Hans Schouten/FN. **154** Piet Munsterman/FN. **155** Frits van Daalen/FN **156** Frits van Daalen/FN. **157** Flip de Nooyer/FN. **158** Leo Vogelenzang/FN. **159** bkgr R J Erwin/DKR; t Arnoud van den Berg; b Ad van Lokven/FN. **160-161** Erik van Ommen. **162**t Wim Weenink/FN; c Danny Ellinger/FN; bl Paul Rezendes/PI; br Joe McDonald/TS. **163**t Lone E Lauber/OSF; bl Michael Sacca/AA/ES; br Hans Gebuis/FN. **164** Jean-Louis le Moigne/A. **165** Eric Wanders/FN. **166** Oene Moedt/FN. **167** Hans Dekkers/FN. **168** Wim Weenink/FN. **169** Hans Dekkers/FN. **170** Gerard de Hoog/FN. **171** Flip de Nooyer/FN. **172** Jos Korenromp/FN. **173** Flip de Nooyer/FN. **174** Danny Ellinger/FN. **175** Oene Moedt/FN. **176** George McGarthy/BC. **177** Wim Weenink/FN. **178** Ad van Lokven/FN. **179** Jaap Hoogeboom/FN. **180** Franz Kovacs/FN. **181** Wim Weenink/FN. **182** Philip Friskorn/FN. **183** Piet Munsterman/FN. **184** Frits van Daalen/FN. **185** Frits van Daalen/FN. **186** Frits van Daalen/FN. **187** Jan Sleurink/FN. **188** Arnoud van den Berg. **189** bkgr Helen Cruickshank/V; t Piet Munsterman/FN; b Fred Hazelhoff/FN. **190-191** Erik van Ommen. **192**t Fred Hazelhoff/FN; bl R Glover/BC; br Piet Munsterman/FN. **193**tl Arnoud van den Berg; tr Fred Hazelhoff/FN; bl Stephen J Krasemann/PA; br Bert Muller/FN. **194** Do van Dijck/FN. **195** Danny Ellinger/FN. **196** Guy Robbrecht/FN. **197** Wim Klomp/FN. **198** Rinie van Meurs/BC. **199** Arnoud van den Berg. **200** Danny Ellinger/FN. **201** Philip Friskorn/FN. **202** Arnoud van den Berg. **203** Wil Meinderts/FN. **204** Oene Moedt/FN. **205** Herman Berkhoudt/FN. **206** Erwin & Peggy Bauer/A. **207** J R Woodward/V. **208** Danny Ellinger/FN. **209** Wim Weenink/FN. **210** Ben van den Brink/FN. **211** Fritz Polking/A. **212** Oene Moedt/FN. **213** Flip de Nooyer/FN. **214** Danny Ellinger/FN. **215** Frits van Daalen/FN. **216** Oene Moedt/FN. **217** Danny Ellinger/FN. **218** Philip Friskorn/FN. **219** Oene Moedt/FN. **220** Rob Reijnen/FN. **221** Otto Faulhaber/FN. **222** Ben van den Brink/FN. **223** Henk Tromp/FN. **224** Arnoud van den Berg. **225** Ben van den Brink/FN. **226** Flip de Nooyer/FN. **227** bkgr Brett Froomer/IB; t Gerard de Hoog/FN; b Hermann Brehm/BC. **228-229** Erik van Ommen. **230**t Arnoud van den Berg; bl Flip de Nooyer/FN; cr Flip de Nooyer/FN; br Leo Vogelenzang/FN. **231**tl Frans Lanting/MP; tr Stephen J Krasemann/DRK. **232** Erwin & Peggy Bauer/A. **233** Wil Meinderts/FN. **234** T H Davis/V. **235** Flip de Nooyer/FN. **236** Fred Hazelhoff/FN. **237** Arnoud van den Berg. **238** Wil Meinderts/FN. **239** Fred Hazelhoff/FN. **240** A Pons/FN. **241** Flip de Nooyer/FN. **242** Hans Schouten/FN. **243** Ad van Lokven/FN. **244** A & E Morris/V. **245** A & E Morris/V. **246** Jaap Hoogeboom/FN **247** Philip Friskorn/FN. **248** Doug Wechsler/V. **249** Wim Klomp/FN. **250** Philippe Prigent/A. **251** Eric Wanders/FN. **252** Helen Cruickshank/V. **253** FN. **254** Piet Munsterman/FN. **255** M & A Boet/A. **256** Jan van Arkel/FN. **257** bkgr Arnoud van den Berg; t Martin Harvey/FN; b Arnoud van den Berg. **258-259** Erik van Ommen. **260**t W Wisniewski/FN; bl W Wisniewski/FN; br Martin van Lokven/FN. **261** t Arnoud van den Berg; cr Nigel Dennis/FN; bl Martin Harvey/FN; br Brigitta Witte/FN. **262** Martijn de Jonge/FN. **263** J C Malausa/Bios/FN. **264** Gerard de Hoog/FN. **265** Frits van Daalen/FN. **266** Oene Moedt/FN. **267** Arnoud van den Berg. **268** G Bortolato/Bios/FN. **269** G Bortolato/FN. **270** Ben van den Brink/FN. **271** Arnoud van den Berg. **272** G Bortolato/FN. **273** Martin Harvey/FN. **281** Erik Sok **274-287** Steven Bray.

Illustrations in the Field Guide section are by **Helen Halliday** page trim, except Mountains; **Gerald Driessen** 112, 113, 114, 115, 116, 117, 118, 136, 137, 138, 139, 140, 141, 154, 155, 156, 157, 158, 170, 171, 172, 173, 174, 175, 206, 207, 208, 209, 210, 211, 223, 224, 225, 226, 244, 245, 246, 247, 248, 249; **Frits Jan Maas** 106, 107, 108, 109, 110, 111, 142, 143, 144, 145, 146, 164, 165, 166, 167, 168, 169, 182, 183, 184, 185, 186, 187, 188, 200, 201, 202, 203, 204, 205, 232, 233, 234, 235, 236, 237, 250, 251, 252, 253, 254, 255, 256; **Karel Mauer** 124, 125, 126, 127, 128, 129, 147, 148, 149, 150, 151, 152, 153, 176, 177, 178, 179, 180, 181, 212, 213, 214, 215, 216, 238, 239, 240, 241, 242, 243, 268, 269, 270, 271, 272; **Erik van Ommen** 96, 97, 100, 101, 102, 103, 104, 105, 120, 121, 130, 131, 132, 133, 134, 135, 160, 161, 190, 191, 194, 195, 196, 197, 198, 199, 217, 218, 219, 220, 221, 222, 228, 229, 258,259 (page trim for Mountains), 262, 263, 264, 265, 266, 267.

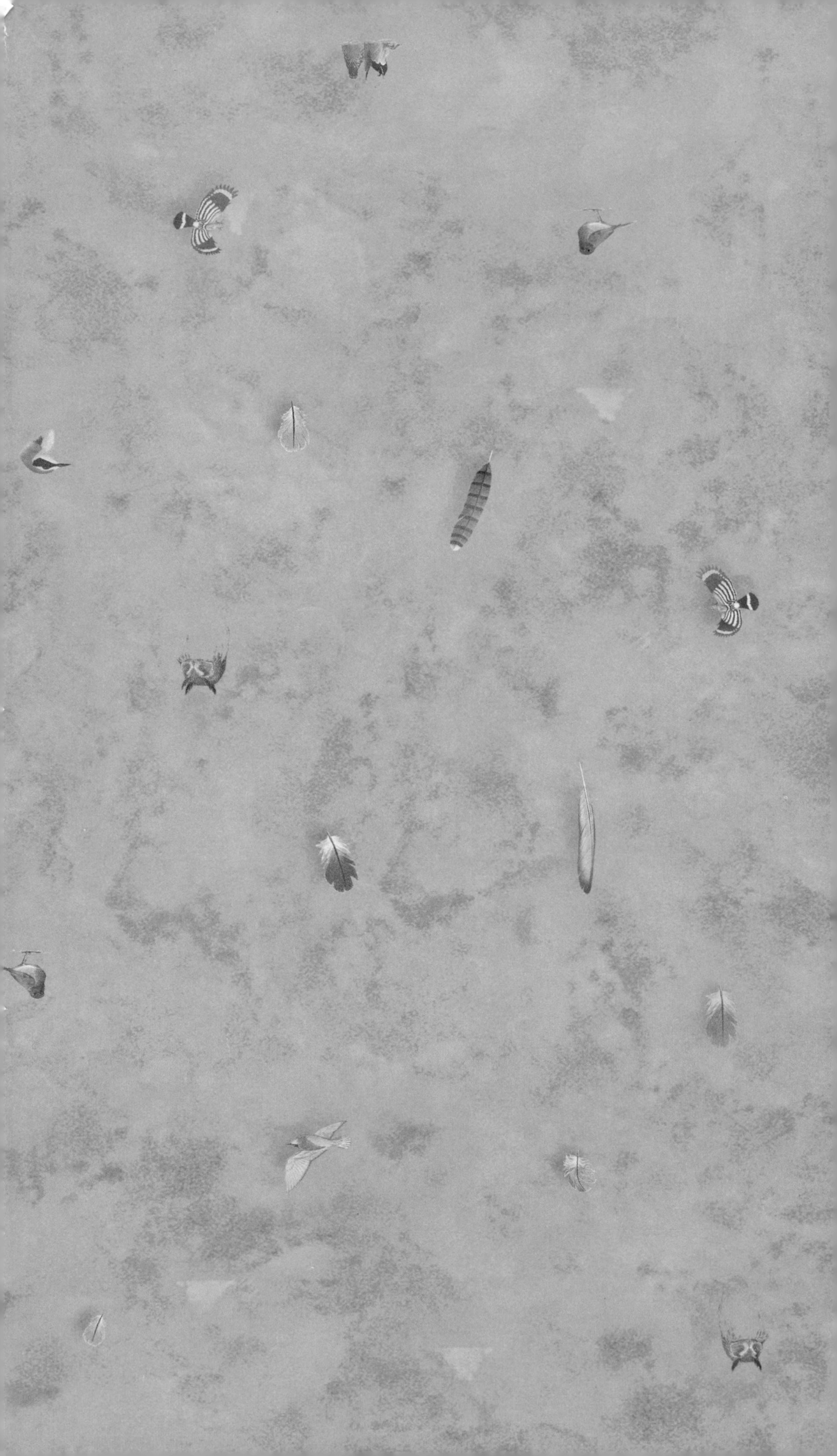